THE CHINABERRY TREE

The
CHINABERRY TREE

A NOVEL OF AMERICAN LIFE

By JESSIE FAUSET

NEGRO UNIVERSITIES PRESS
NEW YORK

PS
3511
.A864
C54
1969

Originally published in 1931
by the Frederick A. Stokes Company, New York

Reprinted 1969 by
Negro Universities Press
A DIVISION OF GREENWOOD PUBLISHING CORP.
NEW YORK

SBN 8371-1919-7

PRINTED IN UNITED STATES OF AMERICA

TO
ELLEN WINSOR
My Friend

INTRODUCTION

FOR a long time American readers have wondered why so little attention has been given to one particular class of Americans. Group after group has entered fiction—the New Englander, educated and uneducated, the Southerner, the Middle Westerner, the far-Westerner, the Canadian, developed or primitive; yet wherever the American Negro has appeared in fiction, only the uneducated Negro has been pictured.

It seems strange to affirm,—as news for many,—that there is in America a great group of Negroes of education and substance who are living lives of quiet interests and pursuits, quite unconnected with white folk save as these are casually met. That these men and women carry on their lives, educate their children, and fill their times with interests social, domestic, and philanthropic as if there were no white people in America, save those who serve them in shops and in traffic.

It is about these among the American population that Jessie Fauset has chosen to write. She foregoes the color, the richness, the possibility of travesty and comedy and the popular appeal of the uneducated Negro with his dialect and idiom, his limited outlook. And she has turned to this other field, less spectacular and, to "the General Public" less convincing because so little standardized. She has shown in her novels, men and women of the class to which she herself belongs, with her wide interests and her American and European experiences.

It seems an impertinence to say that such people are to be met, not only in New York and Chicago, but in the smaller towns of the East, the Middle West and the South. It seems an impertinence to stress their knowledge by the progress of art and music, science and social life in their own country, or to stress their study of that country's social conditions and inter-national relationships. Above all it seems an intrusion to observe that they are leading their own lives, even as do Nordics, without more consideration of those about them than is utilizable in their routine. From the homes of the thousands of the members of the National Federation of Colored Women to the homes of college professors at Hampton or Tuskegee, Howard or Wilberforce, these Americans are trying for a life of reason and culture.

And they merit the awareness of their fellow-countrymen.

ZONA GALE

FOREWORD

NOTHING,—and the Muses themselves would bear witness to this,—has ever been farther from my thought than writing to establish a thesis. Colored people have been the subjects which I have chosen for my novels partly because they are the ones I know best, partly because of all the other separate groups which constitute the American cosmogony none of them, to me, seems so naturally endowed with the stuff of which chronicles may be made. To be a Negro in America posits a dramatic situation. The elements of the play fall together involuntarily; they are just waiting for Fate the Producer to quicken them into movement,—for Chance the Prompter to interpret them with fidelity.

The mere juxtaposition of the races brings into existence this fateful quality. But of course there are breathing-spells, in-between spaces where colored men and women work and love and go their ways with no thought of the "problem." What are they like then? . . . So few of the other Americans know.

In the story of Aunt Sal, Laurentine, Melissa and the Chinaberry Tree I have depicted something of the homelife of the colored American who is not being pressed too hard by the Furies of Prejudice, Ignorance, and Economic Injustice. And behold he is not so vastly different from any other American, just distinctive. He is not rich but he moves in a society which has its spheres and alignments as

definitely as any other society the world over. He
is simple as befits one whose not too remote ancestors were connected with the soil, yet his sons and
daughters respond as completely as do the sons and
daughters of European settlers to modern American
sophistication. He has seen, he has been the victim
of many phases of immorality but he has his own
ideas about certain "Thou shalt nots." And acts
on them.

Finally he started out as a slave but he rarely
thinks of that. To himself he is a citizen of the
United States whose ancestors came over not along
with the emigrants in the Mayflower, it is true, but
merely a little earlier in the good year, 1619. His
forebears are to him quite simply the early settlers
who played a pretty large part in making the land
grow. He boasts no Association of the Sons and
Daughters of the Revolution, but he knows that as
a matter of fact and quite inevitably his sons and
daughters date their ancestry as far back as any.
So quite as naturally as his white compatriots he
speaks of his "old" Boston families, "old Philadelphians," "old Charlestonians." And he has a wholesome respect for family and education and labor
and the fruits of labor. He is still sufficiently con-
servative to lay a slightly greater stress on the first
two of these four.

Briefly he is a dark American who wears his joy
and rue very much as does the white American. He
may wear it with some differences but it is the same
joy and the same rue.

So in spite of other intentions I seem to have
pointed a moral.

JESSIE FAUSET

THE CHINABERRY TREE

CHAPTER I

AUNT SAL, Laurentine, and even Melissa loved
the house. It was trim and white with green
shutters, a green roof, and a porch which ran around
the front and one side. It stood at the end of a
street which terminated gracefully in a meadow.
But immediately about the trim dwelling lay miniature grounds extending for perhaps a tenth of an
acre, beautifully laid out and beautifully kept. It
was a lovely place sweet with velvet grass and three
or four varieties of trees. In the spring there were
crocuses and, later on, lilacs and peonies. In summer the place was lush with roses. Gladiolas flamed
in the fall and prim, hard, self-reliant asters. There
was a grape arbor and a vine with giant roots. And
some one had placed a swing on the back lawn. But
what the three women loved most in that most lovely
of places was the Chinaberry Tree.

Colonel Halloway had had it fetched years ago
for Aunt Sal's sake from Alabama. She was a girl
then; she who was slender, comely and upstanding
even now was in those days a slip of a brown girl,
slim and swaying like a birch tree—like a white lady
birch young Halloway had thought when he had
seen her first on his return from his junior year in
college. A white lady birch he thought and found
nothing incongruous in its application to this Negro
maid who waited on his mother.

1

She was an intelligent girl, a lady, decent, loyal and amazingly clear of vision. It was only her color that kept her, the daughter of a poor Alabama farmer, in menial service. In another day and another time she must have gone far. Halloway a lad of serious bent but of tearing tyrannical passion loved her . . . he could not marry her. The affair lasted all his life, it persisted (rooted at first in his father's connivance) in spite of that parent's eventual displeasure, his mother's dismay, his wife's disgust. And presently as the years slipped by there was Laurentine. And then the white house and the beautiful grounds and the Chinaberry Tree. The affair was the town's one and great scandal. It condemned it and was proud of it. It could not take too open a stand against the Halloways for the family for generations had afforded the township its existence. But it never forgot it.

But Aunt Sal cared nothing about all this. She loved Halloway with a selfless devotion and after his death lived only in that past which he and she had found so sweet. And every day she sat under the Chinaberry Tree's foliage on the circular hexagonal seat which ran around it and remembered. Laurentine too used to sit under the Tree and thought that she could not remember any time in her life when it had not cast its shadow on the side lawn. She had played under it as a child with two exquisite dolls, wondering rather wistfully why the few children in the neighborhood didn't play with her.

She remembered the tall, serious white man who came to see her mother daily—he used sometime to place his hand on her head and his eyes, she knew later, mutely implored her forgiveness. She remembered his death too, its mystery and solemnity, the worry on her mother's face and in her voice as she sent the colonel home to what was to be his last illness. And later the terrible knocking on the side door in the dead of night, and a voice at once measured but violent which said: "You are to come at once . . . at once, do you hear? He wants you ———" the voice trailed off into a sort of bitter emptiness.

She remembered her mother's soft startled rejoinder: "You don't mean you want me to go— there———"

A cold voice had replied in a sort of icy passion— "Of course I don't want you—but he does—are you coming?" And they had slipped into a waiting carriage and driven off into the shadowy night.

After Halloway's death Aunt Sal's sister Judy had come from Alabama to live with them for a while. She was a pretty, rather raw-boned girl, bold and tactless. Laurentine used to hear her quarreling with her mother. "God, Sarah, you don't have to shut yourself up like this just because you had a white man do you! You ain't the first and you won't be the last to do that little thing. Lawdy no! And ef you wants me to stay yere with you all you certainly will have to have some comp'ny around yere. I can't stand this kind of life I tell you, you hear me."

.   .   .   .   .

Laurentine hated her, hated her looks, her ways and her soft drawling nasal voice with its thick

Southern accent.   But in spite of that she felt a
sneaking gratitude toward her aunt.   Judy took her
to church, they met people; children came and played
tea party in the shade of the Chinaberry Tree. Judy
was a fine seamstress and taught Laurentine to use
her needle—the girl owed her present means of
earning a livelihood to those early instructions.

Adults were still a little chary of coming to the
house and meeting Aunt Sal with her cool proud indifference, so Judy struck up an acquaintance with
Mrs. Forten, a colored woman whose forebears had
been in Red Brook as long as the Halloways themselves.   She was a vapid, fading woman whose one
passion in life was to hold her handsome, selfish
husband.   Her daughters, thin suppressed little girls
knew that their mother would cheerfully have sent
them away anywhere, anyhow to please her Sylvester.   They were miserable and unhappy, worse
off than Laurentine who even as a child was re-
markably pretty, even beautiful, and who possessed
both a natural and acquired pride.

Sylvester Forten sneered at his wife, despised his
two plain little girls, liked rather deeply his infant
son Malory, and pursued his daily course of unhampered selfishness.   He worked from eleven to
two as caterer for the officials of the biggest bank
in Red Brook.   The rest of his time he spent fishing
in summer, and playing poker at all seasons of the
year, of the day and of the night in the rear of
George Hackett's pool room—Hackett maintained
this place for white patrons only and the scions of
the finest families of the town foregathered there.
But everybody knew that the basement of Hackett's

establishment was run for the benefit of the town's colored sports. They came in the back way.

.   .   .   .   .

Sylvester Forten spent most of his time at Hackett's, but one evening as he rose from supper—for like many caterers he insisted on his wife's cooking for him—he encountered Judy Strange entering his wife's door. He found her bold air and her coarse manner immensely engaging, sauntered on and forgot her. Afterwards he ran across her again talking to young Phil Hackett whose father ran the billiard parlor. Judy smiled at him, walked up the street with him to his wife's door and inaugurated the most gracious performance of her otherwise ungracious and ungainly life. She really liked Mrs. Forten and in some mysterious way she brought the despairing wife and her recreant Sylvester into a closer affinity. Forten frequently stayed home evenings now. The boarder next door washed and dressed after his long day at the mill and the four played whist.

Sometimes they danced, Mrs. Forten fluttering and complacent in her husband's arms, while Judy laughed up at Mr. Gathers, the boarder. Sylvester and Judy would dance too, with real beauty and a restrained abandon. They spent many pleasant evenings thus. At half-past ten Mr. Gathers arose and said with dignity—"I bid you all good-evening," and marched out doors. But Mrs. Forten and Sylvester used to take Judy home under the smiling stars. Sometimes Sylvester alone accompanied her. But Judy did not like this. She preferred for Mrs.

Forten to come along so that the husband and wife might have the stroll back together across the quiet town.

CHAPTER II

LAURENTINE'S meditations under the Chinaberry Tree, always lapsed, if they reached back this far, into a temporary confusion. She seemed to see her life in three divisions, a period of loneliness, relieved however by her mother's tenderness and care and Colonel Halloway's somewhat brooding kindness; a period of normal friendships engendered by her Aunt Judy's presence and then with Judy's departure a sudden dispersal of the friendships quite as though her aunt had shut them up and borne them off in her little horsehair trunk which Mr. Gathers morosely carried away one day on his truck.

For Judy did depart much more suddenly and with far less heralding than she came. Laurentine had seen her one evening laughing and talking with her sister Sarah and later mounting still laughing to her room. The evening had remained memorable because for once she had failed to go over to her friend Mrs. Forten and that in the light of further happenings seemed strange. In the morning it was discovered she had gone—gone without a word and without sleeping in her bed. Mr. Gathers came by in the afternoon and took her trunk. And suddenly it was as though Judy and everything connected with her had been swept into a void. Mrs. Forten whom Laurentine saw after a long interval at church had become so thin and shadowy that it seemed as if she were shrinking into herself—the young child thought vaguely that she might keep on shrinking and shrinking until she went out altogether as shadows do sometimes.

Reba and Harriett Forten went about more remote and owlish looking than ever. Neither in school nor in church did they ever utter an unnecessary word; but for Laurentine they preserved still further negation. They said to her no word at all neither necessary, nor unnecessary—yet this was not surprising inasmuch as no matter how closely thrown in contact they might be with Laurentine they appeared never to see her. And one certainly did not speak to the unseen.

Mr. Forten whom Laurentine had seen only twice, suddenly and with no preliminary illness died and was buried very quietly.

Aunt Sal proffered no explanations and Laurentine who inherited her mother's reticence asked for none. All these strange matters, even her aunt's disappearance would have been swallowed up in some cavern of oblivion in her mind had not one passing strange incident occurred. All of a sudden, the feeling which she somehow guessed the town had possessed for that unusual union of her father and mother, recrudesced, shot up and spattered over her anew like the lava from a miniature Vesuvius. She was always proud but she was also lonely, she craved companionship and understanding. For a brief season she had had both.

And suddenly all these things began to fall away from her. The children at school whether white or colored never included her in their play—she was no longer urged as she had once been for a too brief season to take part in the Sunday School pageant. With a sick heart and dry lips she asked herself at night on her bed—"What is the matter with me? What do I do?"

On a Saturday afternoon she came along Minor Street, past pleasant front yards—not one of them as large and pleasant as her own. In one of them little Lucy Stone was having a tea party with five other little girls. Only last fall she and Lucy had walked arm and arm to the pond and skated—she had lent Lucy her other pair of skates.

She swallowed her pride, she braced her courage, she walked straight up to the fence and looked through the palings. "Lucy," she called. The little Stone girl came to her slowly—not reluctantly,— more as though she were unwillingly checked by an invisible hand. "Lucy," said Laurentine, every nerve aquiver, "why don't you come around any more?" She choked. "Why, why didn't you ask me here this afternoon?"

Lucy stared at her, her eyes large and strangely gray in her dark face. "I wanted to Laurentine," she answered, "but my mumma say I dasn't. She say you got bad blood in your veins." Abruptly she left her former friend, ran to the table and came back with a tiny useless knife in her hand. "Don't you want me to cut yo' arm and let it out?" Laurentine had run home then quickly to her mother determined to have this matter explained. Sal was sitting on the back porch a letter in her hand. "It's from your Aunt Judy," she told Laurentine. "When she left here, she went to Philadelphia and married.

Now she has a little baby, Melissa. Aren't you glad
to know you have a little cousin, Laurentine?"
But she didn't herself seem glad. Perhaps Aunt
Judy had written her for help. That would be like
her the child thought, silent all these months and
then calling on her sister in her time of need. Her
mother looked tired, beaten and discouraged. Laurentine put her own grievances and bewilderment
resolutely behind her. She was young, anything
could happen, but she would never ask any one for
friendship again. She went down the porch steps,
and crossed the grass and sat down under the Chinaberry Tree. Some day, somehow she would get
away from Red Brook. There must be other people,
other places. The Chinaberry Tree and the future
were inextricably blended.

CHAPTER III

NOW suddenly and terrifyingly Laurentine was
twenty-four and nothing had happened. Nothing that is, that was permanent.

When she graduated from High School her
mother explained to her Colonel Halloway's legacy.
The house was hers by deed of gift, he had made a
present of it outright during his lifetime to one
Sarah Strange and no one could take it from her.
"I shall leave it to you," Sal said, "you may sell it
and do anything you choose with the proceeds, but I
don't want to sell it now," she finished and looked
at her daughter wistfully.

"I know you can't understand my view, daughter," she said, "but I was happy here and happiness no matter what its source is not to despised." Laurentine privately was of the same opinion but she said nothing. The habit of reticence had grown on her.

Her mother went on to explain that while the house was secure, Colonel Halloway's legacy was not. He had had the foresight to see that methods and modes of living would probably change bringing with them greater need for outlay and expense. He could not think of his dear girl, who had brought him so much joy, in want or need, so he had left her a percentage of the net income accruing from his factories. He should have added a proviso that this amount should never fall below a certain fixed sum.

Instead he had placed in his wife's relentless hands a weapon which she was quick to employ. Even Sal with a mind totally unfitted for business was able to realize that Mrs. Halloway at the risk of losing her own fortune was undoubtedly allowing her estate to be mishandled so as to minimize the share of this woman who had so grossly usurped her place.

Mr. Gathers who did trucking for the Halloway concern told weird tales of sabotage of machinery and implements, of wholesale thefts and breakage, of accidents which were never investigated but for which replacement was always forthcoming.

Mr. Gathers and Mr. Stede were both deacons in the Baptist Church. Mr. Stede took care of Aunt Sal's grounds and kept the place in the meticulous order which Colonel Halloway had long ago inaugurated. With a delicacy and lack of personalities which one would never have suspected he retailed to

Aunt Sal what Mr. Gathers had already retailed to him.

Aunt Sal thought Laurentine had better learn dressmaking.

A surprising thing happened. Laurentine could still recall that autumn day. There was a touch of the year's dying on everything; the air, the sky, the trees, the grass were full of the austere grandeur of October. Laurentine was stitching, her mother was getting supper when the bell rang. The girl went to the door to admit two young women of beautiful mien and dress. Laurentine, herself the essence of self-control, gaped, surprised. It was as though she were suddenly seeing herself in a mirror, a self curiously bleached and lightened.

For her black hair the two ladies had substituted ash blond, for her apricot skin, white and rose, but feature for feature the colored girl and the two white ones were exact replicas.

The oldest girl spoke. "I think you know we are Phebe and Diane Halloway and you are Laurentine—" she tried to say it but something that she had whipped into a semblance of resignation suddenly failed her.

"Laurentine Strange," said Aunt Sal proudly. "Sit down ladies."

It was a strange interview.

Neither side mentioned the Colonel's name, neither side spoke of that strange past which had brought at once such rapture and such pain.

"We have thought of you often," Diane told Laurentine smiling. "We knew your mother was probably taken care of but we couldn't tell about you. Phebe has always been interested in the factories—she means to run them some day. But we have nothing to do with them now. But we each have a little money to be paid to us on coming of age. Phebe was twenty-one two years ago and my birthday was last week. What do you want us to do Laurentine?"

They were three well-bred women facing a problem for which not one of them was responsible. Laurentine met generosity with generosity. She would not take money outright. But she would and could take training. She liked dressmaking and designing and if the girls would like to help her in her training she would be grateful.

Her sisters looked at her. They had lived abroad at intervals for ten years, they had some wealth, education and a name known and respected within the radius of Red Brook and its environment. But the shadow of their father's responsibilities had clouded their lives. Half dreading they knew not what they decided to proffer what help they could as soon as it was within their power. It was heartening to find Laurentine as she was.

Laurentine in turn gazed back at these two. She could not say to them, "Give me life, give me contacts, give me the good times which are every young girl's due. Don't leave me here to perish, to dry, to wither." But even as the thoughts went through her head, she sensed in those two fine faces a melancholy of the same stuff and substance and, perhaps, quality as her own.

"I don't believe they are happy either," she told herself that night lying face downward on her pillows. "And I believe in their way unhappiness comes from the same source as mine. Perhaps there is something in this 'sins of the fathers.' "

It was arranged that she should go to Newark for instruction, her sisters would be responsible for all costs.

Her mother came to her: "Laurentine, did you think? You might have gone anywhere, away from here—to New York, to Paris, perhaps you might have met people. You should meet them. I know you're lonely."

Laurentine said simply: "I couldn't go away and leave you here mother. And I knew you wouldn't leave."

Her mother's face quivered, its habitual calm broke, vanished. For the only time Laurentine saw her cry. "Oh, my daughter don't leave me—if you could stay with me a little while longer. He was God to me you know and you are his child, you are still Frank—I used to call him Frank you know— his wife called him Francis." Some dam in her broke. She babbled of Halloway, his youth, his wife's coldness, her own love. She talked about Judy and their childhood days in Alabama.

Laurentine went out in the chilly night and sat for hours under the Chinaberry Tree. When would that future, which she so clearly envisaged, come? It must be something very clean and sweet and bracing to rescue her soul from this welter, this tangle of human relations and passions and life and duty.

CHAPTER IV

MELISSA came strolling up the neat brick walk. She had had no trouble finding the house. Her mother Judy had described both it and its approach so accurately. Just as her mother had suggested she had left her little trunk and the small suitcase in the station. "Best do that," said Judy, "until you're sure whether or not they'll take you in. Sal will be all right but I don't know nothin' about your cousin Laurentine. She used to be kinda sulky—beautiful thing. Let's see now, I guess she's about twenty-four,—twenty-six. Wonder what she's like livin' in that little town all her life. Now 'Lissa don't you go puttin' on none of your airs with her."

"What would she do, if I did?" asked Melissa curiously. She was overbearing, inclined to be triumphant—no one knew why. She was poor, her father was dead, her mother a seamstress, not even a dressmaker. Yet somehow Melissa had always the sensation of living on top of the world. Perhaps she had inherited her conquering attitude toward life from her mother whom nothing seemed to down.

Melissa admired her mother—save for one thing. She did not like the constant succession of suitors who were ever at her door. Their presence made the household alive and merry and yet, somehow unseemly, thought Melissa. She herself was a gay and lively creature but with an unexpectedly strong feeling for the conventional. Also she meant to marry as soon as possible after eighteen, a man as unlike as he could be to these men who clustered about her mother's tiny house in one of those awful little side-streets in Philadelphia. She would marry a professional man, a lawyer or a doctor. These fellows were laboring men for the most part, truck drivers, road-menders from the South, big, hard, sweaty, black fellows, masons and bricklayers.

A few of them were recruited from the upper ranks of menials, a house-man, a waiter, an occasional chauffeur. It was with one of these last that Judy was now going to Chicago—to Melissa's dismay—but she made no protest. She had long since learned that eventually she and her giddy mother must part company. She even offered to stand up with her.

"You ought to have a bridesmaid, mother."

But Judy had protested, hurriedly averting a suddenly flushed face. "Nonsense baby. Stanton wouldn't like that foolishment. We'll stand up before a Justice of the Peace down in City Hall just before train time. You go on to your Aunt Sal. She'll take care of you. And anyways she'll let you stay with her for a few days until I can write you from Chicago. Just don't you go to stirrin' up Laurentine, that's all. She was awful high and mighty when she was a girl—she's got that bad white blood in her, you never kin tell."

. . . . .

Even before she rang the bell Melissa stopped to admire the garden. Her mother she decided, had not done the place justice. She had not dreamed of this exquisiteness, this beauty and cleanliness, this peace. A country town to her had meant up to this point bad, rutty roads, straggling farm lands, cows,

scattered poultry. Only rich people, she had supposed, lived in this beauty and serenity. There were,
she knew, rich colored people, there were some well-
to-do ones in the church which she attended on Lom-
bard Street in Philadelphia but she had never been
in their homes. Their affluence to her had meant
only lack of necessity for hard labor, plenty of
clothes, plenty of food. She had never thought of
their possible cultivation of taste, the development
of loveliness.

She was about to mount the steps of the front
porch and ring the bell when around the house in the
side yard just beyond the side porch she spied the
thick foliage and the circular shadow cast by the
Chinaberry Tree. She was a stranger, she had
never seen her aunt or her cousin, she did not know
whether or not they would take her in, but for all
that she ran down the side path, crossed the lawn
and sat down on the circular hexagonal seat. Here
she would stay, here in this house, in the shade of
this Tree she must and would live. Here under this
Tree she would talk with nice, quiet, country girls
and flirt with adoring, awkward, ambitious, country
boys, far away from her mother's friends, and the
hateful little house, and their disorderly, ragged
precarious life.

    ·   ·   ·   ·   ·

Laurentine, from her sewing-room had seen the
slight figure crossing. She came to the screen-door
and looked out as her cousin mounted the steps and
crossed the side-porch. Melissa caught sight of a
beautiful deep gold face, suspended apparently without body in the upper half of the screen-door, so

completely did the dark green dress which Laurentine was wearing blend and melt into the soft gloom within.

"Proud Laurentine," said Melissa to herself and henceforth always gave her that dramatic title in her meditations. In another moment another face, dark and tragic and likewise momentarily bodiless appeared over Laurentine's shoulder.

Melissa addressed herself to it, "Aunt Sal," she said, speaking with her mother's directness and with a personal sincerity and trust which Sal suddenly found very charming. "I am Melissa Paul, Judy's girl you know. Mumma sent me to you, she's going to be married again, she said you would take me. Aunt Sal, Laurentine, you won't turn me away will you? You're going to let me in?"

Her voice, her assured gaze wavered. She could not, she felt suddenly, leave this again, this beauty, this calm, the promise of the Chinaberry Tree.

Aunt Sal pushed the door backwards. "Come in my dear," she said slowly. "Come in. You c'n have the room across from Laurentine's."

    .   .   .   .   .

"Where are your things?" Laurentine asked her. "I'll telephone Mr. Gathers to go get them. You'll find us very, very quiet, Melissa, but I'm sure you'll be comfortable." She went out and closed the door, leaving Melissa to gaze dumbfounded about the pleasant room. The walls were tinted a delicate orchid, there was a fresh lavender and white cotton coverlet on the old-fashioned broad bed, two oval rag rugs in tones of purple and lavender lay at the side of the bed, before a plain vanity-table, with its

long, revealing mirror. A couple of fantastic creations by Maxfield Parrish adorned one wall. On
another hung a chastely mounted print of the head
and slender shoulders of a young girl, her eyes full
of dreams and beneath, the line——

"She dwelt among th' untrodden ways."

Melissa, the inherited mantle of her mother's
hardness slipping away from her own slender shoulders, stood before the little print entranced, the
tears pricking her eyelids. That girl in the slightly
yellowed print was Melissa. She had been inhabit-
ing this room for these sixteen years until its right-
ful owner should appear. Her mother, her mother's
friends, Alder Street in Philadelphia faded, disappeared into a fleeting, dissolving mist. She, Melissa
had come—no, she had returned—home.

    .   .   .   .   .

Laurentine had gone down stairs to her sewing-
room. She had a dress to finish by morning but
she dropped her work and in a sudden and unusual
fit of irresolution she sat for a few moments under
the Chinaberry Tree.

She did not want her cousin to live with them.
How like her Aunt Judy and her selfishness to send
the girl there at a moment's notice! Of course they
could take care of her. Laurentine's earnings alone
could do that and with no stint or effort. Besides,
Melissa would be useful, she could help Sal with
the housework and undoubtedly she had inherited
something of her mother's natural aptitude for the
needle. Of course, too, in the autumn she would
have to go to school. It wasn't as though she would

be useless or a source of expense, an incubus constantly clogging one's freedom.

But she didn't want her about, recalling Judy's sudden and mysterious disappearance and all the upheaval of Red Brook colored society connected vaguely and loosely with that phenomenon. To this day people spoke of the gloom which had settled on the Forten family soon after those far-off happenings.

"Seems like Mrs. Forten lost both her husband and her best friend at the same time, and they ain't none of them never got over it," people said. Reba and Harriett and their mother lived like wraiths remote and insubstantial. Only Malory, the boy who had been sent to Philadelphia to school almost immediately after his father's death, had remained, it was supposed, normal and unchanged. But most people had forgotten all about him; Laurentine had never consciously heard of him.

"I'm right keen to see that boy Malory again," Mr. Gathers used to remark to Mr. Stede.

Laurentine wanted nothing of any sort to be recalled which re-emphasized the apartness of her family. She had in her pride and sensitiveness withdrawn to herself and missed the fun and excitement and love-making due young people in their teens. But lately, it seemed to her that a special niche was being created for her in the little quiet, closely-knit Jersey town. Her work, her constantly increasing clientèle, her dignity, her remarkable beauty, her distinguished clothes were bringing her a half-begrudged, half-admiring recognition. She was still a creature apart, but no longer a pariah, rather some one choice, unique, different.

In the last two years she had been asked more than once to community bridge parties—she had been the most beautiful figure imaginable at the open air pageant held by the Baptist Church on the open Fair Grounds.

It was then that Phil Hackett, son of the wealthiest colored man in the town, George Hackett, ash-contractor, had recalled to her the fact that he had been in High School with her. He had taken her driving many times since then and they had gone a few times to the movies.

She knew her beauty stirred him; he liked and yet dreaded the effect of her distinguished appearance. Incomprehensibly, he liked that into which her strange life had transformed her and yet it seemed as though he could never reconcile himself to its sources.

Conscious that she did not yet love him and yet still more conscious that marriage with him meant turning the key forever in the door of the wall surrounding her past, she felt she must not lose him.

And now here was Melissa.

. . . . .

The glaring July sun slid down the sky, the heat began to drain out of the atmosphere, very much as color might be drained from a cloth, leaving the air cool and faded. Laurentine still sat pondering in the soft glow of the late midsummer afternoon.

After all, Melissa was young, she was alone.

With Judy's blood in her veins, Laurentine and her mother could not turn her out to fend for herself. "Perhaps if I am very good, Lord," she compromised . . . praying, "perhaps if I am very generous, I'll meet with generosity,—Lord, Thou knowest. Give me peace and security, a home life like other women, a name, protection. And Lord, don't make me wait too long. I feel," said Laurentine, at twenty-four, "I feel, Lord, so old."

CHAPTER V

CERTAINLY Melissa had no idea but that she was wanted, even needed in her aunt's little establishment. She could not conceal her amazement at the seclusion in which the two lived. All that abounding fellowship, the rich if homely possibilities of enjoying life all about them and Laurentine and Aunt Sal so completely out of it!

"My goodness me," she communed with herself many times during that first summer, "what if Aunt Sal and that old Colonel weren't married! What's Laurentine got to do with that? She needn't act as though she were under a curse—that sort of stuff is all out nowadays." She remembered then that her mother had explained to her something of the outside pressure which the Colonel's wife had brought to bear on this woman, this lowly, dark woman who had so ensnared her husband. She had, through her husband it is true, been the possessor of powerful weapons which she had not hesitated to use. Few people would have been willing to encounter the social or economic ostracism which she was able to exercise against them. Gradually, like the old definition of a simile, the case of Sal Strange and her daughter, Laurentine, became confused, the sign was accepted for the thing signified and a coldness and despite toward this unfortunate mother and child became a fetish without any real feeling or indignation on the part of the executioners for the offenses committed. Neglect of the two women became crystallized. On the other hand a reversion was already beginning to appear, the legend, although still extant and occasionally revived was beginning to be something quite apart and remote from the Mrs. Strange and her daughter whom colored Red Brook observed occasionally at church or community entertainment.

Melissa of course was too young to understand the philosophy of this. She had the modern young person's scorn for unnecessary formulæ, yet her own innate regard for convention made her slightly smug. "Still and all it is nice to be decent. I'm glad my father and mother were married," she thought, unconscious that such an idea had never crossed her mind before.

   .   .   .   .   .

Serene in her utter respectability, bolstered by a strong sense of rectitude springing from conformity to the merest conventionalities she sallied forth to make life full and joyous for herself and to lay some of its largess in the laps of her aunt and cousin, particularly in the lap of the latter.

For in spite of the eight years between them, she

was able to penetrate Laurentine's armor of pride
and to resolve it into its component parts of timidity and loneliness.

CHAPTER VI

LIFE in Red Brook was pleasanter in winter even
than in summer, Melissa found. But then all
her days were delightful. The peace and orderliness of her aunt's household acted like both a seda-
tive and a tonic on her young spirit which hitherto
had known only confusion and uncertainty. She
became not only gayer and more lively than she
had ever been before but, if possible, more assured
and triumphant.

Her place in the community was a strange one.
It was patent even to her non-introspective mind
that she was both of and yet not of this closely
knit society of the small town. She had never
known anything like this in her life in Philadelphia
with its distinct cliques. Some of the people there
based their social superiority merely on the fact
that they were "old Philadelphians." Others belonged
to professional groups; the families of doctors, law-
yers and school-teachers hobnobbed together. The
caterers possessed a distinct standing made possible
not only by their very real wealth, but by their
connection with outstanding white Philadelphians.
Poor people, like Judy and Melissa, were absolutely
beyond the pale of these groups. One read of their
doings in the *Tribune* and *Courier* and Judy sewed

sometimes for their families but there were no social connections.

But in Red Brook every colored person knew every one else; all were to be reckoned with, at least all who possessed any economic status. Thus the richest colored man and consequently the most influential character in the colored group was George Hackett, who held the contract for gathering ashes. His son, Phil, had had two years at Howard but had preferred his assured position in Red Brook to the uncertainties of life in the large centers. He had returned therefore to his father and was now running his billiard parlor. The Traceys, Cliftons and Greens were in the Taxi business, they were all comfortably situated, living each family in its own private cottage with pleasant yards on wide, tree-shaded streets. Mr. Epps owned a fine barber shop for white patrons only. He possessed a large, airy ten-room house which sheltered his sister, daughter, son-in-law, grand-daughter, and niece. He kept a handy-man who ran his car and kept his shop and house clean. This latter was lodged under the same roof as his employer and had visions of his own which included marriage with Mr. Epps' niece and a share in his business.

Into this life came Melissa, advancing with firm, assured stride. On the first Sabbath after her arrival, she had gone to church—gone alone. "That's all right," she told the somewhat hesitant Laurentine, "I don't mind introducing myself." After the service she went straight up to Reverend Simmons.

"I'm Melissa Paul, Mis' Sarah Strange's niece,"

she told him. "I'm going to live with her for a while. I was in Reverend Caldwell's church in Philadelphia, do you know him? I'd like to work in your Young Folks' Auxiliary."

Reverend Simmons called his wife. "This is Mis' Strange's niece, Annie. Le's see, your mother, now, was Judy Strange, wasn't she?"

"Judy Paul," said Melissa firmly. "My father's name was John Paul, but he's dead now. I can't even remember him myself. But my mother's told me all about him, many's the time. So you knew my mother?"

"Land yes!" Mrs. Simmons replied. "I c'n see Judy still just as plain. It seems only yesterday since she used to come walkin' into meetin'. Her and Mis' Forten used to come together, they was that thick. One couldn't step without the other. She must have spoke to you about Mis' Forten, I'm shore." Her rather beady eyes fastened themselves on the girl intently.

"No," said Melissa carelessly, "she never did. She said she liked Red Brook though and that she had a good time here. I'd like to meet some of the other girls, Mis' Simmons."

"She's a cool one," Mrs. Simmons told her husband later, "but she's full of pep and life. She'll be a good worker. After all, she can't help havin' that Strange blood."

In two months it seemed to Laurentine she was in everything that went on in colored Red Brook. Best of all she brought new life into the quiet household, compensating Laurentine vicariously for her own lost youth. Early in the morning before school girls stopped for Melissa; girls left her at her door when the session was over. They came over at night ostensibly to do Latin or algebra but spent most of their time in giggling, teaching each other new dance steps, displaying finery. The telephone, which up to this time had brought only messages delivered in the cool brittle tones of white patrons asking for "fittings," vibrated with the deep male notes of boys' voices inquiring everlastingly: "Is Melissa there? How are you, Mis' Strange? Ask her to come to the telephone, won't you?"

Laurentine loved all this. Once she would have resented it with a bitter jealousy, but now there was always Phil Hackett, still somewhat remóte and wary, it is true, but there. Her reasonable mind told her that she was doing as well as could be expected—her girlhood days would be lying behind her in any event. She could not begrudge her cousin the purely fortuitous results of a combination of youth and a changing public opinion. So she smiled on Melissa's little triumphs, made her the simple, distinguished dresses which best suited her reddish brown skin, her strange green eyes and her dark red hair. Melissa just missed that dreaded combination of skin and hair which colored people laughingly dub "rhiny," but Laurentine with her practiced eye and skilful hand knew how to turn these liabilities to the girl's advantage by dressing her in cool violets, greens, browns, creams and even occasionally black. Melissa was Laurentine's best advertisement. The girl lacked her older cousin's distinction and beauty, but she had as compensation grace, and youth and maidenly prettiness which enhanced by Laurentine's taste and her own happiness made her a notable figure.

Melissa was happy. She forgot Philadelphia, forgot even her mother and lived, it seemed to her, dreaming, in some unusual moment of leisure under the Chinaberry Tree, just as a young girl should. It was at times like these that she tasted most deeply her good fortune. The Chinaberry Tree brought back the past to Aunt Sal; to Laurentine it represented the future; but to fortunate Melissa, it meant now, the happy, happy present.

.   .   .   .   .

Still there were moments when she felt a vague disquietude. When older people said with a slight hint of meaning in their tone: "This is Sal Strange's niece, you know; you remember Judy Strange? Well, it's her daughter," she felt an odd resentment toward her aunt and her beautiful remote cousin, a half-shamed desire to separate herself completely from those two distinct peculiar entities with their too well-known past.

"But I am Melissa Paul," she would invariably counter. "My father was John Paul of Philadelphia. My mother married after she left here. And now she's married again and living in Chicago."

More than ever the double marriage seemed to bolster her conventional superiority to Aunt Sal and Laurentine. Even so, her statement hardly banished the slight gleam of malice in the eyes of her audience. Afterwards at home, in her dainty room, her better nature would assert itself. What did she care for these stupid people and their innuendoes? After all, folks were only folks whether their par-

ents had known wedlock or not. "And remember,
Miss," she would adjure herself reproachfully, "all
the good times you're having now you owe to Aunt
Sal and Laurentine just because their position is
what it is. But what a place! Imagine my coming
in for this sort of thing just because I'm a cousin.
Poor Laurentine, she's certainly got a bad break.
It's different with Aunt Sal," she told herself with
the hard clarity of modern youth, "she's had her
fun, but Laurentine sure is out of luck."

CHAPTER VII

HARRY ROBBINS drove his father's car up to
Melissa's gate and dismounted, crunching over
the hard walk just as Asshur Lane opened the gate.
The two of them crossed the front porch together,
eyeing each other with absolutely unconcealed male
disdain.

"Say, don't you have to do anything at all?"
Harry queried plaintively. "Bet Mis' Strange is
sick of seeing your ugly mug around these parts."

Asshur, tall and strong and confident, pushed him
back, his hard elbow planted squarely in his chest.

"Get back boy, get back," he said, his teeth
shining in his sudden infectious smile. "Melissa told
me to be here at five and here I am. Now I know
she didn't tell you to come too, did you Melissa?"

"No," said Melissa smiling, "but he can come in
just the same, Asshur. You wouldn't turn a poor
boy like that out in the cold, would you?"

Secretly she was glad to have the two together.

She did not like Robbins; for some obscure, inexplicable reason she even feared him. Now with
Asshur she was safe.

Robbins slouched in a little sulkily, perturbed by
Asshur's presence, his assured manner. In his hateful, selfish way he was wild about Melissa and was
ready to do anything to possess her—even to the
extent of offering her marriage, more than he had
offered any other girl. Moreover he had been born
and bred in Red Brook and so was more than ever
resentful of Asshur who had lived in Red Brook
only a year.

Aunt Sal came in and asked them to stay to
supper, but they couldn't accept her invitation, since
each of them worked at night and had to be at his
station by six-thirty. She sent them in then thick
slices of bread and butter, a pot of raspberry jam
and large cups of cocoa.

Beyond in the next room Laurentine's lovely fingers were flashing in and out of lengths of gorgeous
shades of silk, georgette and velvet while she directed Mattie Gathers and Johnasteen Stede, her
assistants. A warm sense of coziness pervaded the
household. Laurentine was happy in the matter of
fact invasions which her cousin's friends made into
their household. Melissa loved the background of
beauty and security which her aunt's surroundings
afforded.

"Well," said Asshur presently, over his third slice
of bread and jam, "I came to see if you didn't want
to go with me to the Ice Carnival day after to-
morrow, 'Lissa. Yes, I know your skating ain't so
much, but with my strong arm at your service, you

ought to pull through. What do you say?" He stood up, his long, perfect figure towering above her, his eyes dancing in his dark face, his teeth shining.

Melissa glanced at Harry, hesitated. A week ago he had asked her and she had turned down his invitation flatly. She wanted to skate, she loved the exercise, the hot pulsing of blood, the airy, crazy talk of the boys and girls around her, but she did not like Harry and his warm clinging fingers, his insinuations, the look in his small reddish eyes portending, she couldn't imagine what.

If Asshur had only asked last week!

Still why should she forfeit her fun for Harry who would never mean anything to her? She turned her glance back to Asshur. "Well, since you've asked me so prettily, Mr. Lane, I don't believe I mind accepting. Yes, I'll be glad to go. What time will you be here?"

"About eight," rejoined Asshur happily. Harry, he was sure, had come to make the same request and he had outsmarted him! "Be sure you're ready, 'Lissa. Come on, Robbins, since you are here, make yourself useful. Get in that wreck of yours and carry me down to Spring Street."

"You must be dreamin', fella," Harry retorted. "Carry yourself down there. I'm going to stay here a moment with Melissa. Don't you imagine I might want to see her, and see her without your spoiling the scenery?"

"Well, s' long," replied Asshur, unfailingly good-natured. "Well, Melissa," he teased as she followed him into the hall, "I see you showed your real

good sense in promising to go with me. You know
that's what Harry came here for, to take you. If
I was a girl I wouldn't want to be in your shoes for
the next quarter of an hour. He sure is jealous, just
don't let him scare you. If he does, see me, that's
all."

Melissa nodded. "All right, Asshur, see you in
school to-morrow." But she was strangely nervous
within as she turned back to the warm sitting-room.

Harry rose, glowering at her.

"You know I asked you first, Melissa."

"I know you did, Harry, but last week I didn't
think I wanted to go."

"But when you changed your mind you could
have sent for me."

Her temper flared. "I don't know that I am to
regulate my actions to suit your convenience, Harry
Robbins."

"It might be funny if you had to regulate your
whole life to suit me, mightn't it, Melissa? You
know I want you Melissa. I'll get you yet."

"If my father were living you wouldn't dare talk
that way to me, Harry."

"If your father were living, you wouldn't be
here," he retorted, threatening, enigmatic. His
whole being seemed suddenly portentous with evil.
"Look out, you may have to come to me after all,
my girl."

"I don't know what you're talking about," she
told him, "but I know I do want you to go home."

He slipped out the door. She waited until she
heard the throb of his engine, the violent clashing
of gears shifted by a too hurried hand.

Vaguely but thoroughly frightened, she ran upstairs and began to study her lessons.

Aunt Sal called her to supper. Afterwards she washed the dishes while Laurentine draped a velvet gown on the dress form. The peace and security of the household enveloped her. After all, what could Harry do? And anyway there was always Asshur.

Drying her hands, she went back into the sitting-room, opened the piano, old-fashioned but still sweet of tone. She played some of the season's favorites, then an old love song and finally a spiritual, "Didn't my Lord deliver Daniel?" Aunt Sal sitting quietly in a corner listened to the mighty strains, knew that her niece was playing it for her, smiled at peace in the darkness. The offspring of her own and Judy's stormy past were safe and doing well. She thought of Phil Hackett—she could not tell much of his disposition but if he gave her daughter, her precious baby, a name and protection she would lie down and let him walk over her body. As for Asshur Lane, young as he was, she could picture him already as the rock he might be to a woman in the weary land called life.

.   .   .   .   .

Melissa in bed thought again of Harry Robbins and his veiled threats. And again she thought "Well, anyway there's always Asshur." But in her heart she knew she did not want Asshur. Asshur was clean, Asshur was kind, Asshur had a lion's courage and fortitude. But Asshur was going to be a farmer. A most successful farmer, she had no doubt, he would own a big, rambling house some day; he would have acres, cows and chickens, a Ford runabout, perhaps later a larger car. If she married him they would come into town on Saturday afternoons, perhaps they would go to a movie. Being colored and living in Jersey they would sit in a special section reserved for their kind. Asshur wouldn't mind, he'd laugh his big, hearty laugh.

"Times will change. It won't always be like this, 'Lissa. Our children will sit where they please in this very theatre, perhaps you and I will ourselves some day."

No, she didn't want that life even though it would be a thousand times more wholesome, more secure, more decent than that life she had known with her mother in Philadelphia. Even though unlike the lives of her Aunt Sal and cousin Laurentine it should have no hidden places, no secret sense of shame. There were two colored doctors in Red Brook, both of them were married, one of them had two daughters, Kitty and Gertrude Brown, girls of about her own age. Melissa had seen one of the girls in school; Kitty was in her French class, but even so Melissa barely knew her. Dr. Brown and his family attended Reverend Simmons' church and once Kitty and Gertrude had been in a church play. Melissa had had a part too. The last three rehearsals were held in the Brown home, one of them while Mrs. Brown was having a bridge. The street outside was lined with cars of colored ladies who had driven out to Red Brook from New York, Newark, the Oranges, Trenton, Bordentown. Two of them had been driven in by their chauffeurs.

The place was full of the excited high-pitched

chatter of well-to-do, well-dressed women. Melissa caught the sheen of colorful gowns, flashing jewels. The rich tones of the dresses brought out the gold and yellow and cream flesh tints of their possessors. Melissa had never seen anything like this before. Not even Laurentine had been asked to cross this threshold.

"She'd outshine 'em all in dress and looks if she was here," thought Melissa staunchly. "But I guess it's too late for her now to get in with this bunch. Well, it's not going to be too late for me. Some of these days," she promised herself, glimpsing the lovely ladies as she ran up the stairs in Kitty Brown's house, "I'll be right along with you. Nothing doing, Asshur Lane."

CHAPTER VIII

LAURENTINE stood before her long mirror putting the finishing touches to her costume. She was to go driving with Phil Hackett and the anticipation of it filled her with a sort of wild excitement. "I'm going to surprise you," he said over the telephone. Of course that remark might mean anything or nothing. In spite of her steadiness and of the restraint to which she had long since accustomed herself, the girl chose to believe the remark meant a great deal.

She glanced at herself in the mirror smiling with an unwonted coquetry. As a rule she was distant to the point of haughtiness. No matter what her feeling she did not, she felt, dare to exercise any of the "come-hither" quality employed by most young women.   But she was beautiful, she knew it, she acknowledged it, and if she married Phil she would exercise the spell of her beauty on him to its fullest extent.

Still pleased with the vision, she studied herself. Her slender, well-moulded figure showed to every advantage in a dress of green developed in silk and wool, its uneven hem-line reaching in places to her ankle.   Her stockings of tan and her dainty yet sturdy, slender shoes of brown and tan snakeskin afforded just the necessary contrast.   Above the trim dress rose her slender, proud neck and her small, perfect head.   Her black, waving hair parted smoothly in the middle and drawn to the conventional flat knot in the nape of her neck gave her a slightly foreign look which was accentuated by her long, black, oval ear-rings.

She picked up her rouge but excited anticipation had already given her a beautiful flush, so she put it down again, applying her lipstick ever so slightly. The bell rang and, pulling on her tiny, smart, green felt hat, she got hastily into her green cloth coat with its high mink collar that fitted so beautifully, so snugly.   If her trade prospered for the next two years as it had in the past, she would be able to treat herself to an entire coat of the beautiful fur.

But it would be fun, it would be marvelous to receive such a coat from Phil.   With her taste, with her skilful fingers and his money she would be able to show Red Brook what dressing really meant. She would show Mrs. Brown and the wife of Dr. Ismay such perfection as they had never seen.   Phil visited these houses sometimes, she knew. But she had never crossed their thresholds. They would be glad to cross hers. But she would always be kind, be courteous. "Oh God, you know all I want is a chance to show them how decent I am."

Aunt Sal's soft voice floated up the stairs. "Mr. Hackett's yere, Laurentine." She came running down pulling on her soft, white gloves.

.   .   .   .   .

Hackett rose as she entered the room. He was a big man with the peculiar floridness and dapperness which marks the sport everywhere. Laurentine did not like this quality in him. Yet underneath that surface flashiness lurked, she suspected, a steely determination, a forthrightness which would stop at nothing to achieve a desire. She had seen something of the same quality in her mother and Aunt Judy and even more recently in Melissa. She herself was without it. She could be proud, she could suffer. That was all. Perhaps she would not have to suffer much longer.

His first words after his perfunctory greeting dashed her somewhat exalted mood. His greetings were always perfunctory, barely cordial, for this woman moved him terribly and he had to hold himself in leash. Laurentine suspected as much.

He said: "You know I told you I'd have a surprise for you. Look."

She followed his finger pointing through the upper glass of the door to descry a sleigh in the road. This was his surprise—and she had expected—what?

Still, as he helped her into the smart little turnout,

her spirit, crestfallen, rose again. What man would put himself to the trouble and expense of procuring this elegant, well-cut vehicle and the two prancing horses with their jingling bells, unless he were trying especially to impress and to please his lady. She smiled happily into the crisp whiteness of the winter afternoon.

"Be patient, Laurentine," she chided herself. "You've waited twenty-four years for this, can't you wait longer?"

They flashed, jingling merrily, across the humming town through the Romany Road, a short cut in the woods, to the turnpike and on toward Pompton Lakes. Laurentine was happy and Phil was devoted. Mrs. Brown coming out of the meat-market to get into her runabout over which her husband was mounting guard, stared, called "hello" to Phil and stared again—at Laurentine. Mr. Gathers turned out, in his truck. Mr. Stede and Johnasteen passing on foot, waved at her cheerily, ungrudgingly, glad, Laurentine thought, of her good fortune. When they came to the Romany Road her long constraint seemed to drop from her. She sang first the old sleighing song:

> Jingle bells, jingle bells,
> Jingle all the way.

And afterwards she hummed and sang snatches from the popular songs which Melissa played, amazed at herself for remembering them so well. Phil was entranced, delighted. "I had no idea you were like this," he told her. She might have replied that she didn't know it either.

On his admiring gaze, she grew surer of herself, even provocative. They passed some red winter berries and she ordered him to stop and pluck her a spray.

"No, no, not that one. I want that one highest up." It was almost beyond even his great reach but he caught it finally, pulled it down and hacked it off with his jack-knife. She accepted it calmly with the air of one who knows she has only to ask to receive.

Around the turn of the road they came across a lunch-wagon run by a Greek who sold them unbelievably good, hot clam chowder. Laurentine perched on the high stool feeling the admiring glances of the other customers, all of them men, on her trim figure, on her marvelous face. But her own glances were for Phil only as he hovered about her gallant, assiduous.

When they emerged the stars were out. Hackett lit the two red lanterns on the front of the sleigh. They cast twin shafts of ruddy light before them all the way in, like crimson streamers irresistibly tugging her gently on toward happiness.

Suddenly he began to talk. "You know, Laurentine, I'm not satisfied with my life here. I could have struck out for a big city long ago, Philadelphia, Chicago, New York, but I believe there's more chance for me here if I can just manage it. I can't go on like this—Phil Hackett, son of the ash-man. Dad's all right, he sure let down his buckets where they were, as Booker Washington used to say. He's a smart man and he's done a lot for his family."

He drew on a cigarette in silence.

"But that's not enough for me. And the pool room isn't either. And yet, Laurentine, it's been there in the pool room that I've learned most about men and I'd like to run them, control them, pull wires."

She was bewildered and showed it. "I want to get into politics. I know no colored man's gone in for that yet, at least not in this town nor yet in this county. I don't know as Jersey's even a good state in which to nurse such an ambition. But that's my ambition and I'm in Jersey and I'm going to have a try at it here.

"I thought—I wondered—" He stopped, and Laurentine's heart stopped too.

They went on in silence then, feeling suddenly very close, very near. It was eleven when they came jingling down the quiet street to stop before her gate. He walked to the front door with her, pulled off his fur cap, and stood holding her two hands, his rather splendid head inclining toward her.

"It's late and you must be tired. I won't come in. I'm—I'm very happy to-night, Laurentine."

She smiled at him and passed in. Aunt Sal was sitting, her hands on one another in her lap, in her favorite corner in the dining-room. As Laurentine entered she made no move except to raise her head, expectant, patient.

Her daughter passed an arm about her shoulders, pressed her face against her mother's. "I think it will be all right—soon, mother." These two had always been chary of their caresses. Upstairs she took off her coat and hat and stood again before the mirror.

She had so wanted his kiss—bestowed with love, with ardor, with respect. Yet she knew that his reticence had really been the finest expression of that respect.

But she had wanted that kiss!

"If I weren't such a fraidy-cat. If only I could have brought myself to flirt a little," she murmured.

.   .   .   .   .

In the morning he telephoned before ten, his voice abject with confusion. "I won't be able to see you to-night, Laurentine. I forgot I promised long ago to go with Dr. Brown and a party he's getting up. I'm sorry—I promised,—er—I promised before I thought. I hope you don't mind?"

She knew he was going with the Browns and the Ismays. But why should she care? It was enough to know that he felt it incumbent on him to explain his movements, to apologize for them in so far as they took him away from her. "Of course I don't care, Phil. Have a good time."

His voice came back relieved. "You're a great girl, Laurentine. I tell you what. Suppose you make an engagement to go with me to the Ice Carnival next year? How's that?"

"Fine!"

"I'll see you to-morrow then? And I want to talk about—an omission in our—er—farewell—last night on the porch. And some other things too. Like that?"

"I think I might, Phil."

"Good-bye Laurentine."

"Good-bye Phil."

.   .   .   .   .

The afternoon brought a great mass of hot-house flowers. "H'm," said Johnasteen Stede who, under the pretense of believing that the package contained a long-awaited length of crêpe Ginette, managed to view both blossoms and card before they reached Laurentine's hands: "H'm, ain't never see no such flowers sent from one colored party to another, no suh, not since I been b'on. Colored people gettin' more like w'ite folks every day. I'm tellin' you, Miss Laurentine Strange."

CHAPTER IX

REDD'S BROOK, the stream, for which the town of Red Brook had been named deserved its misnomer this night. The Electric Company which for reasons of its own was financing the Ice Carnival had festooned bunches of red bulbs from tree to tree on the banks of the stream. Bonfires and red flares made the place alive and vivid. The hot-dog and hot chestnut vendors and the blare of horns supplied the necessary noise and confusion without which no American out-door sport is complete.

Melissa and Asshur had come early. Asshur had his uncle's little Ford crammed unbelievably full of wriggling, squirming, giggling, happy, carefree high school girls and boys. Melissa in a dark blue velvet suit of Laurentine's designing and creation was in gay, almost too wild spirits. Her skirt was circular, her shapely legs and feet were encased in the nattiest possible tan leggings and shoes; her velvet beret assumed of its own volition the jauntiest possible angle.

Almost the mantle of her mother's former recklessness lay about her. Some of the older colored people had come down to view the proceedings and to exchange comments on the uncontrolled high spirits and actions of Melissa.

"There she is, there, that's her. That's Judy Strange's girl. Calls herself Melissa Paul."

"Wonder how much she knows."

"Nothin'. Why should she? Queer though ain't it, her comin' to live here!"

"Look at her. Look at that—just rarin' to go. Ain't she jes' carryin' on though! Jes' mad about the boys and they around her jes' thick ez bees."

"Tell you there's sumpin' funny 'bout this Strange blood!"

"Chile, I mean! Wouldn't want her around my husban', young ez she is!"

"Young ez she is! Ain't much younger'n her mammy was before 'er."

"Oh go 'long Mis' Tracey. You always puttin' words in somebody's mouth."

"Well, I only repeats what ev'rybody says. Well, will you-all look at thet gal!"

Melissa was no solo skater. But she was a superb natural dancer and she had the nerve and the verve, trusting herself to Asshur's strength and skill to follow him through a maze of steps and gyrations that would have done credit to a professional.

Crowds of people, both white and colored, drew up to watch them. Sidney Reamer, editor of the *Red Brook Record,* sauntered up. "Well, we have our niggers with us always. That's a pretty good exhibition, isn't it? The fellow's some kin to those Lanes out Birneysville way, I hear. Farmers, I know 'em. Good substantial people. But who's that girl? Never saw any colored woman like that in Red Brook before."

James Spratlin, a grocer, answered. "Let me see. Yes, I thought 'twaz. No, she came from Philadelphy. Niece of that there Strange woman they say old Colonel Halloway set up." Reamer moved abruptly away. "What's he gone off like that for?"

"Oh man, don't you know? Don't suppose he wants to hear anything about that Strange woman, do you? Colonel Halloway's wife is his sister."

"How on earth sh'd I know?"

The ranks of fancy dancers thinned, drew apart, went skimming off like great lovely birds now lost in the shadow of the overhanging boughs of a tree, now reappearing in the bright glow of a bonfire.

In a space unusually dim Melissa skated straight into the arms of Harry Robbins.

"Oh Harry, you frightened me so!" She spoke naturally, choosing to forget his ugliness of a few days previous.

"Skate with me, Melissa?"

She could tell from her momentary contact with him that he'd been drinking. "I think I'd better not, Harry. I'm afraid you're not quite steady. I've just put on an exhibition with Asshur. It would never do for me to spoil my stuff now, would it, with all the grand white folks looking on?"

His arm tightened around her. "I said I wanted you to skate with me, Melissa!"

"Oo! What's that?" she asked innocently, looking intently over his shoulder.

He was too bemused to recognize the palpable ruse. Involuntarily his arm went slack, he turned his head to look.

Her tantalizing laugh floated back to him as she fled skimming, skimming back to the safe brilliant lights and Asshur.

"Harry's down there, Asshur. Better get some of the fellows to get him home. He's drunk, I think. Don't you go after him."

"I can manage him, 'Lissa." He headed in long, graceful glides for the lurching Harry.

"Now Robbins I'm not joking. I want you to keep away from Melissa. Get me? She's my girl and I'm not going to have her bothered. You heard me."

He thought he heard Harry say: "Your girl? Anybody's girl."

"What was that?" asked Asshur, his voice suddenly dangerously calm.

"Oh nothing," Harry suddenly alive to his peril began to bluster. "Get the hell your hand off of me, Lane. Who do you think you are, orderin' me around, God A'Mighty?"

"No, but the devil if you get me started."

Reverend Simmons came up. "Now boys, boys don't start nothin'. Too many white folks here for that. We don't want this kind of thing closed to us."

"Well, make him keep his damned mouth off me then."

Asshur, momentarily pacified, made no retort. "I don't want to start anything, I'm tellin' you, Reverend."

"These hot-heads," Reverend Simmons complained to the first colored man he met who happened to be Phil Hackett.

"What's the matter?" asked Phil, smiling and showing his splendid teeth.

"I'm sure I don't know," replied the minister irritably. He wished he'd never left the South for this parish. Knowing how quickly the most ordinary fight could develop into a riot, he was nervous and watchful and too old, he felt, for this searching atmosphere, this sharp, penetrating night. He wished he were home in his comfortable slippers before his bright gas range. He would be glad when the festivities were over.

. . . . .

The excitement was increasing, the crowds growing denser. New parties kept joining the company, the Reverend Simmons withdrawing discreetly well beyond the hither edge of the bank, wondered if the ice would hold. But oldest inhabitants assured him of its safety. Dr. and Mrs. Ismay, Dr. and Mrs. Brown, a Mrs. Barron of Newark, Phil Hackett and Kitty Brown came up and spoke to the minister.

Kitty glanced about restlessly, anxious to find some one of her own age and interests. If her mother thought she was going to stodge through the evening, she told herself rebelliously, with this old bartender or billiard player or whatever he was, this old Phil Hackett ancient enough to be her father—well, her mother was mistaken, that was all. She caught sight of Melissa and Asshur, Ben Davis, Mary Tucker and a few others. Ordinarily she made little pretense at mingling with the boys and girls of Red Brook, but anything was better than being bored to death with one's elders.

"Mummy there're some High School boys and girls over there. Think I'll join them for a few moments."

"All right dear, but be careful. This is the first time you've been skating this winter. Better let Mr. Hackett take you over."

Well, she could shake him later, she thought, darting off irritably. But Phil was up with her in a moment, had caught her hand and they were making their way across the pond straight by Sidney Reamer, to whom Phil often went for advice.

"Evenin', Mr. Reamer."

"Evenin', Hackett. Haven't seen you for some time. Suppose you drop in to-morrow."

"All right, sir. Any special time?"

"About five would be O.K. Suit you?"

"O.K. for me too, Mr. Reamer."

.   .   .   .   .

Harry Robbins put his flask back in his pocket. He was mad through and through. Melissa had tricked him, had tricked him and there she was laughing, pirouetting, sharing a hot dog with Ben Davis, though a moment before she had been with Herbert Tucker and a moment later she would be laughing and jesting with Asshur, like the worthless creature she was. Anybody's girl! His girl too since he wanted her. Wanted her with a devastating desire that balked and wasted him. He'd show her.

Somewhat unsteadily he skated over, laid his hand over-familiarly on her arm.

"C'mon Melissa; you're gonna skate with me now. You've skated with everybody else. My turn now."

Melissa was pale under her ruddy skin. "I don't wish to skate with you, Harry. I never promised you . . . let go my arm. Let go, I say, don't you dare to touch me again."

His drunken grasp tightened. "Don't touch you! Say, that's a good one." He pointed his finger at her, inviting the attention of the suddenly gaping crowd. "Who's she, not to be touched? Lord, that's funny, givin' herself such high and mighty airs."

Asshur strode forward, his dark face ashen. "You know I gave you fair warning. Take your hands off her."

"Why should I? How do you know how many hands have been on her? Why should she rate herself so high? Her aunt was a slut if ever there was one and everybody in Red Brook says that her mother—" Asshur's mighty fist struck him down.

Not a soul intervened. Harry lifted a face grotesquely smeared with blood. "Look here, Lane, you'll pay for this. You can't get away with this, you big black devil." He was almost crying now. "Besides you've lived here only a year. I've been here all my life. . . . I know what I'm talkin' about."

Asshur yanked him to his feet. "What in hell *are* you talkin' about? Here, come here." He drew him apart from the crowd. "Now spill your lie man and be sure you make it a good one——"

Trembling with cold and rage, Harry began whispering, putting his hand on Asshur's arm to steady himself. Asshur listened, his brow darkling, a muscle in his tight young cheek working convulsively. Then he drew back and without warning, at that terrific short range he struck Robbins again.

The young fellow lay like a log, his feet on the ice and his head in a deep bank of snow on the edge of the brook. Still not satisfied, Asshur turned him over and struck him again and again. He was like some one mad, in a frenzy. Phil Hackett dashed across and pulled him away. Strong as Asshur was, Hackett was heavier and stronger.

"You've punished him enough, Asshur. My God, man, do you realize you've almost killed him? And he's not worth swinging for."

Asshur walked to Melissa, took the trembling girl by the arm and started off toward his Ford. "You fellows'll have to get home some other way. There'll be a bus out this way in a few minutes." He took off his own and Melissa's skates. "There, that's better! Gee! I hope my car hasn't frozen."

They rode home in silence, Asshur helped her out at the gate.

"All right now, Honey?"

"Yes and thank you, Asshur. I won't ask you in."

"No, and it's too late for you to be havin' com-

pany anyway, Melissa. Good-night, girl. See you
soon."

"Yes, oh yes! Good-night, Asshur."

.   .   .   .   .

Phil Hackett, guiding Kitty back to her mother,
met Mr. Reamer again at the edge of the crowd.

"Kind of a nasty affair, Hackett. They say that
girl they were fighting over is some sort of kin to
Sal Strange."

"Yes," said Phil reluctantly, "I believe she is."

Reamer swallowed hard. "It's not, it's not her
daughter, is it? No, no, she'd be too young."

"No," said Phil shortly, "it's her niece."

"H'm, well whoever she is, she's like the rest of
them. Hackett, you know me, a broad-minded man
if ever there was one. But I tell you there's bad,
there's vicious blood in that bunch. The town
would do well to get rid of 'em . . . remember, I
want to see you, Hackett."

"Yes, I'll remember. Got to get this young lady
to her mother now, Mr. Reamer," indicating Kitty.

The girl made a face after the editor's retreating
figure. "What's the matter with him? What kind
of blood's he got in his veins. Calling a girl vicious
just because two jealous boys got to fighting over
her." She made an impatient gesture with one
hand. "He must be all wet. Personally I think it
was great if you ask me."

.   .   .   .   .

Hackett saw the Browns and Ismays into their
respective cars, refusing the lift which Mrs. Brown
so ardently offered him.

"No, think I'll stay around here and find out where Robbins got his liquor. Then I'll catch a bus home. Don't worry about me, I'm all right."

He watched the cars out of sight, caught a bus and twenty minutes later was sitting distraught and anxious in his father's office behind the large, still brightly lighted, billiard parlor.

Reamer was his one sole means of entrance into this field which he so desired to invade. It would be a case of a not quite equivalent tit for tat. Undoubtedly Reamer hoped to profit by his—Hackett's—co-operation. But he could go on without him. But Hackett was helpless without Reamer. Every one knew how persistently hipped Reamer had remained all these years on the subject of his sister's humiliation at the hands of Sal Strange.

And he had been thinking of asking the daughter of Sal Strange to marry him.

"Ain't it the devil the way I never thought of that before?"

Another very small, scarcely recognizable thought, a very beast of a thought began pushing its way through his inner consciousness rearing its ugly head.

"That fellow Robbins certainly was persistent about insulting—what was her name, Millicent, Melissa Paul. Paul h'm!"

Was there anything really he wondered in this story of "bad blood."

.   .   .   .   .

In the morning awaking from a troubled sleep after having half formed a shameful resolution he bethought himself of a freshly unpleasant eventuality. At nine he got Sidney Reamer on the telephone.

"Hackett speaking, Mr. Reamer."

"Yes, good-morning Hackett."

"About that nasty affair on the ice last night. You're not going to put that in the *Record* are you?"

"Why not, Hackett? It's news. Properly featured it might serve to rid the town of that nest of—of those damn Strange women."

"Yes. Well I hadn't thought of that. I was thinking of this young Lane's uncle, Ceylon Lane. Pretty strong out Birney Way you know."

"Yes but Hackett—here's a chance——"

"I know, I know. But I ask you is it good politics to let a purely personal matter interfere in your larger plans?" He manœuvered skilfully. "Suppose I let old C. Lane know that you killed the publicity because of your regard for him?"

"Well there's something in what you say—there's a good deal in it. Well I'll think about it."

"I think you'd better give me your word now sir. I've just had a call from Lane senior," he lied smoothly. "I know he'll want to find out what's what. He's not one to ask favors, but you can count on his acknowledging them."

"I guess you're right about that, Hackett. Well —I'll keep it quiet, you may depend on it."

"Good business, Mr. Reamer. See you later."

.   .   .   .   .

He hung up the receiver, stared moodily at the mysterious instrument.

He could do this much for Laurentine. He

could do this much but by God if he were going to get ahead at all in Red Brook he could do no more. No more.

CHAPTER X

LAURENTINE came down to her sewing-room just as Phil Hackett lifted the receiver to telephone Mr. Reamer. It was Saturday and she would have a long, full day before her. Four gowns had to be delivered to-day. Two of them genuine creations. She would have to be behind Matilda Gathers and Johnasteen Stede at every turn; she might even have to do some of the actual stitching herself—a rare experience for she attended usually only to the designing, cutting and fitting.

But she was glad the day would be full—that meant swifter passage of time and at nine o'clock Phil would probably be here. She glanced at his flowers rearing their lovely heads still fresh and odorous in a vase in the sitting-room. That reminded her. She must speak to Melissa. If her young cousin planned to have company to-night she must have them in the dining-room, in the kitchen; if girls, in her bedroom, anywhere, anyhow as long as they kept their distance from her and Phil. She would wear her red dress. It had short sleeves and a shallow round neck, not too low. It was not too elaborate either as though one were deliberately dressing up, as it were.

She even had on a red house dress this morning, trim and snug and perfect, a little dressier than usual for this time of day. True Phil had never run in during the day time. He had indeed never run in at all; his visits had always been precluded rather irritatingly by a—well, not a warning—but at least by a notification over the telephone. Nothing like the informal visits which Melissa received all the time from Asshur and that rather nasty—what was his name?—Robinson boy or something like that. Well, things happened like that when you were very young. Boys and girls felt and acted as though the world were made expressly for them. That was why she must warn Melissa about the sitting-room. She thought of an odd expression which she had read in a fashion book displaying the latest and most absolutely recklessly revealing sports wear for very young women: "Youth must be served." She supposed that applied also to things other than sports wear.

"Not that mine was ever served," she reflected in a momentary rebellion.

"That's all over, Laurentine, Laurentine," she was saying silently, "do you realize it?" No one glancing at her beautiful, still face could have dreamed of the hot blood, the rushing thoughts swirling within her.

"Perhaps later, this time next week, he'll be dropping in. He'll come in; why, he'll come in to lunch." She looked suddenly across at Johnasteen Stede and smiled, almost laughed outright.

Johnasteen anxious to pour forth her news, to register impressions for a future retailing, plunged in.

"Ain't seen Melissa this mawnin' Laurentine. She ain't sick?"

"No, I don't think so," said Laurentine listening with the very surface of her consciousness. "No of course I know she isn't. It's Saturday. She's gone to market for mother."

"She tell you about the big fuss last night down by the brook?" Johnasteen had not been near the Carnival. Mr. Stede, her father, had gone to bed at eight, Saturday being a day of many and difficult chores for him. Miss Stede furthermore had had to be at Laurentine's at eight-thirty in the morning but she knew of the entire incident, knew every word and if put through a cross examination would have made a better witness than Melissa herself whose bewilderment had dimmed everything but the actual fighting. "No," said Laurentine again. . . . Perhaps he'd telephone . . . any moment now. . . .

"Why no Johnasteen—was there a fuss?"

"Yes," said Johnasteen happily, "that there Harry Robbins and that big Asshur Lane that's always a hangin' around here after Melissa. . . . Why Matilda Gathers do you know you stuck me! . . . Why look Laurentine, she drawed blood. . . ."

"Some accident," said dignified Laurentine slangy for once because she was happy and young. "My goodness, look at the blood! Put some witch hazel on it there's plenty in the bathroom. . . . Harry and Asshur got in a fuss? I'm not so surprised. Boys seem to quarrel for the fun of it."

The Italian girl across the street, now, she was just about Laurentine's age, they had been in High School at the same time—the colored girl couldn't remember their relative status—she had a beau, a young druggist. In the nature of things he must be as busy, even busier than Phil. And he was at her house two and three times a day and of course every evening.

Well Phil would be like that too.

.   .   .   .

At one o'clock Melissa after answering an imperative door-bell returned wide-eyed to Laurentine. She had been rather listless all morning, even pale. But she was excited now, flushed and even a little anxious.

"Mrs. Ismay's in the sitting-room," she reported to her cousin who was eating dreamily from the dainty tray which Aunt Sal sometimes brought her on busy days like these.

"Mrs. Ismay?"

"Yes, Mrs. Ismay, the doctor's wife, not Mrs. Brown, you know," Melissa stammered stupidly, "she's the other doctor's wife. But this one is——"

"Mrs. Ismay, I think you said," Laurentine finished for her, smiling. "Well what's the matter with you this morning? Not awake yet?"

"What do you suppose she wants Laurentine?"

Laurentine couldn't be persuaded to guess. "But you'll find out as soon as I've finished my lunch."

Presently she was in the sitting-room looking at Mrs. Ismay, a thin, brown-skinned rather elegant woman talking with the precision, the broad "a" and the culture of the Boston which had been her home.

She plunged into her errand. "I've heard so

much of your establishment and of your work Miss
Strange—of your creations rather, and I wondered,
—I wondered——"

"Yes, Mrs. Ismay?"

"I wondered if you'd have your girls make two
or three gowns for me." She had meant to order
only one, but this girl's bearing, her real queenliness
she told her husband later, confused her.

Laurentine hesitated. She had never had a colored customer, chiefly because they had never come.
Before Melissa's arrival few of her own people had
ever crossed her sill, so persistent had been the
legend which set her and her mother as people
apart.

And then her prices were beyond the means of
most of her group. But this woman, this lady, she
said looking at her more intently, could pay. She
really was a lady. No wonder Phil Hackett enjoyed the company of people such as these. . . .
Phil—how would he like the idea of his wife being
the dressmaker of one of his fine friends? Afterwards when Mrs. Ismay was her friend she could
bestow a favor on her as a token of that friendship.

So she said very slowly, and very nicely: "I hope
you won't misunderstand me Mrs. Ismay. I've
never had colored customers. Some of my other
customers wouldn't mind it a bit. Others would
very much. You know how Jersey is. I can't afford
to trifle with my living."

"No," said Mrs. Ismay, "of course you can't. I
think you're very sensible and I understand you perfectly. Did you make that gown you have on? . . .
It is beautiful. I wish things were different—What

a beautiful girl you are. I"—she hesitated—"I wish there were some way in which we could meet again."

"I wish there were," said Laurentine quite simply. Of course she had heard of Laurentine Strange and her mother Sal Strange. She bowed her visitor out. . . . Her mother for whom a replica of this kind of thing had been going on for years, would go on. . . .

But for her—for Laurentine Strange——

She ran up to her room and looked out the window at the wintry skeleton of the Chinaberry Tree. "For me it is going to end to-night."

.   .   .   .   .

By six o'clock the last stitch had been placed, the last drapery arranged. Johnasteen and Matilda had been sent on their way to deliver the dresses. They passed out the gate, each with a large box under her arm.

"Wuzn't Laurentine actin' funny to-day?" queried Johnasteen, irritably thwarted. "Acted like she was dumb or something. After all that rucus last night too."

"Dumb yourself," retorted the usually amiable Miss Gathers. "What d'you hafta bring it up for? Ain't you niggers never gonna let that old business rest? And anyway what have these girls got to do with it?"

Johnasteen's forebears had hailed from Mississippi but she had the attitude of the Puritan Pilgrims.

"Well their mothers wan't no good wuz they? And what does the Bible say about the sins of the fathers,—and mothers too that means, don't it Matilda Gathers? Everybody knows about Laurentine's mother? Ain't that very house they're livin' in the wages of sin? 'Course I don't know nuthin' about Melissa's mother but the old folks say——"

"The old folks don't say nothin'," interrupted her fellow seamstress rudely. "Didn't my father know Melissa's mother long before the girl was born. He carried her mother's trunk to the station—I c'n remember it yet—a funny little wooden affair. He says there wan't nothin' the matter with Judy Strange except that she was too lively and jolly for these dumb folks around yere."

"Hope you ain't callin' me dumb. Well then what're they always carryin' on so for and lookin' so queer and whisperin' whenever they lay eyes on that Melissa Paul? Ain't never heard of no colored man with Paul for a last name, have you?"

Matilda's succinct retort was: "Niggers makes me sick!"

"Who're you callin' nigger, Matilda?"

   .   .   .   .   .

At seven o'clock Laurentine had had her bath and was preparing to lie on the couch in her room to rest and relax against the evening's demands. But she could do neither. For the first time she thought of the possibility of an engagement ring and sat up in excitement.

A ring, its safety, its security, its promise!

Feverishly she began to dress. Everything was perfect. The red dress was ravishing, her slippers, her thin smoky stockings. Not for nothing had she observed the élite of Red Brook who came to her sewing-rooms.   She had never bobbed her hair.   It was long and thick and shining, but it went up obediently into the dense, tight flat knot which Fashion now decreed.   Phil, she thought, her face hot and flushed, would like it though when he saw it down, he would be surprised and pleased.   From some mysterious source she who knew so little of men knew that colored men liked their wives to have straight hair, "good" hair.   They had to have these things for their children . . . their children must surpass them . . . must mark a step forward . . . poor colored people, they had so much to attain to in America . . . looks, education, morals, ambition, a blameless family life!

"I have all of them except the last," she thought wincing a little.   But she had that too she remembered.   She personally had been as pure as snow, as chaste as a nun . . . no girl whose mother had been married by a hundred priests before a thousand witnesses could lay claim to a more spotless life than she.

For the first time she understood the lines which she had repeated parrot-fashion, a girl in High School:

> "The rank is but the guinea's stamp
> The man's the man for a' that."

At about quarter of nine the bell rang.   She heard her mother go to the door.   Straining she heard Asshur Lane's deep tones, heard Melissa, obedient to instruction, invite him somewhat without enthusiasm she thought into the dining-room.   Of course they wouldn't have the piano to-night, but Asshur had probably brought his ukelele. He did so often. But if he had they weren't playing, they were very quiet she thought, missing the peals of laughter which usually floated up from any room which these two were occupying. Perhaps they were studying. Melissa was capable every now and then of intense spells of seriousness. . . . She was really a nice girl —her presence hadn't been in the slightest way embarrassing. Indeed she had brought life and pleasure into this too quiet house.

The next ring must be Phil's. My but he was late. But Saturday was probably a difficult night for him.

At eleven o'clock she took off her earrings, her beads, her slippers. He wouldn't be coming now— she understood perfectly his meticulous observance of the conventions where she was concerned. She slipped off the red gown and hung it on its scented hanger in her orderly closet. Very carefully, with unconsciously exaggerated attention to details she braided her hair, washed the rouge off her face and prepared for bed. It was intensely cold out, she would open only one window, the window opening on the side yard. Perhaps she'd better put on her robe—br-rh how chilly!

She stood by the window looking down as she had earlier in the evening on the icy skeleton of the Chinaberry Tree. Presently the side door opened and Melissa stepped out with Asshur. She could hear his voice—unusually small and quiet, so different from its ordinary heartiness—telling her to run back and get a coat. Melissa obeyed, came out again and the two descended the steps, and stood for a moment in the radius of the shade which would have been cast by the Tree. Only now in place of the shade lay a carpet of uncheckered moonlight.

With no sense of spying she kept looking down on them, saw Asshur bend his tall figure, saw Melissa's hand on his sleeve.

"Now, now, they will kiss," she thought poignantly. But Melissa said merely in a dull, toneless voice, "I'm awfully sorry Asshur. . . . I must go in now. Good-night."

She could not hear his voice but she could see him mounting the side path without his usual springiness. She lost sight of him for two or three moments, then the gate clicked and the tall lean figure went slowly down the road. . . . Melissa came up to her own room.

Laurentine got into bed and lay there sleepless and tearless, sensationless. All she was conscious of was the sudden overwhelming realization that she had never stood under the Chinaberry Tree with Philip Hackett.

CHAPTER XI

HER mother she knew was watching her. She knew that look in her mother's eyes, patient, dog-like, faithful, yet somehow impersonal as though her mother were saying: "Even though I'm watching, I'm not really aware."

She was so sorry for her mother. She knew that her mother took upon herself the blame for everything which had gone awry in her sorry, hateful, bitter, futile life. Her life that was like a spoonful of nauseous medicine which she had to take every morning on arising, on awakening. And the medicine making her no better.

And once her mother stopping outside her door and asking timidly: "Is there anything I can do daughter?"

And her own falsely surprised answer: "Do for me? Why there's nothing the matter with me mother!"

But she was sick. Sick not only with wounded pride and bewilderment, but with something far worse than that—hopelessness. For what could she expect? She would live like this always, seeing herself ripen, ripen—she was twenty-four, there were many years of cruel, burning, unsatisfied life still before her. Yes she would ripen—some poet had said it—"ripen, fall and cease." It would be exactly as though she had never been; like a leaf that had fallen too early; like a flower that some one had picked and deliberately thrown away,—no worse, had carelessly dropped to be trampled on, withered. So had her mother and Colonel Halloway dropped her and she was being trampled on, withered.

.   .   .   .   .

A week, two weeks, three weeks. She who so rarely left the house never of course saw Phil Hackett. She went to church one Sunday to still the madness creeping on her from her monotonous thoughts. She hoped he wouldn't be there. Hating him as she did now, without effort or volition she never wanted to see him again.

On a Tuesday Judge Manners' wife whose daugh-

ter was to be married the next day sent her motor
for her to come and attend to some rebellious folds
which would yield only to her skilled fingers.

She sat in the car thinking, thinking, revolving
ceaselessly those last hours. Phil had taken her
sleighing on a Thursday, they had talked, they had
been happy. His words had been a promise, if ever
words constituted a promise. On Friday he
had telephoned, and his flowers had come. They
hadn't died when she had tossed them out into the
snow—she was so glad they were there for her to
throw out. On Saturday like a fool, like a fool,
she had been so happy. She pictured herself sitting
blissfully in the sewing-room building dreams.
Johnasteen was chattering about some boys quarreling; Matilda had suddenly pricked. . . .

Matilda had pricked her and Johnasteen had become abruptly reticent! Who had quarreled?
Harry Robbins and Asshur. About, of course, about
Melissa. She remembered her cousin's sudden list-
lessness, her apathy. And Phil with his fear, which
she had always sensed rather than known of being
caught in the toils of her—she had to face the
words—disreputable family.

She spoke a sudden sharp word to Mrs. Manners'
chauffeur.

"Hurry."

When she returned Melissa had not yet come in
from school. And if she did question her would she
tell the truth? Standing in her room, removing her
hat she saw Mr. Stede moving about in the yard
engaged in one of his innumerable chores. Perhaps
he would be pruning the trees—no, it was too early

to prune trees. What did she care what he was doing?

She ran down stairs seized a large tin tray, piled on it thick slices of bread and butter, some cold beef, a cup of execrable coffee.

Mr. Stede always looked well-nourished but he said that he never sought or asked for food or sustenance. He waited, he said mysteriously, for Pentecost. If food was brought to him he ate, if not he did without. Aunt Sal often humored him. To-day she would play the part of Mr. Stede's Pentecost which she suspected was his name for Providence.

He came immediately at her call, walked to the sink and futilely washed his horny hands. Not all the soaps of all the world's advertisements would remove the grime in those ridges. Laurentine sat at the end of the table and watched him while he ate. For a man professing to care so little for food he certainly showed appreciation when he received it.

He was drinking his second cup of the muddy coffee, looking at her steadily, with his faded light eyes. Even in her wretchedness, she found herself wondering whether they'd been in his youth dark and had faded light, or had been light to start with and faded lighter. In his dark face with its wispy circular beard they looked so strange. He spoke to her in his brittle voice.

"Yore ma back yet?"

"I didn't know she was out. Have something more Mr. Stede."

"I hev told you Laurentine thet I don't never ast

for no food. Of course if suthin' sweet was set before me—" His dignified voice trailed off.

"Mr. Stede, tell me. . . ."

" 'Bout what Laurentine?" His old lashless eyes held hers.

"What happened at the Carnival, what'd the boys fight about Mr. Stede?"

His intent expression filmed ever so slightly as though he had drawn a curtain.

"Nuthin' you need know about. And anyways I wasn't there."

"No, but I'm sure you know all about it."

"Ain't Johnasteen told you?"

"She tried to but I wasn't paying attention."

"Humph 'n I told her to keep her tongue in her head. Whut's the matter with these young folks thet they can't keep a tongue in their head?" He pondered over it as though it were an actual problem in engineering.

"Who was there in the crowd, Mr. Stede? I know there must have been a crowd."

He liked to gossip, it was the one passion of his old age. Struggling with his better self he hesitated, succumbed.

"Well there was them colored doctors Brown and Isma, Asma, whatever he calls hisse'f and their wives and one of their gals and Mr. Hackett." His unwavering glance met hers equally steady. " 'N a whole passel of these young high school kids, the colored ones I mean, 'n Mr. Reamer."

"Mr. Reamer?"

"Yes Laurentine."

"That's Mrs.—Mrs. Halloway's brother, isn't it?"

"Yes Laurentine."

"The boys were quarreling about Melissa. What did they say?"

"Asshur ain't said nothin' fur's I kin make out, only smashed this Robbins boy's face in and tell him to shet his dirty mouf. That boy sho' has got a dirty mouf. His father had it before him. I remember——"

"What did he say Mr. Stede?"

He was old, he had been born at the very end of slavery. He had known suffering and pain and sorrow all his life. Neither life nor persons had ever spared him anything. But he was man enough to spare her.

"Whut he said don't make no dif'funce, Laurentine. Things don't happen, e'fects don't happen because a man sez this or that. They jist happen because this is for you and thet for me." He sat lost in his newly discovered fatalism.

"He spoke about—about my mother?"

He was silent.

"And Melissa's mother?" He was still silent.

"And all those colored people, the high school boys and Mrs. Brown and Mrs. Ismay heard him?"

He stirred himself—"No come to think of it, f'um what I was told, none of them real hinckty culled folks was in the crowd. And ez for the kids they on'y heerd what they'd already heered many's the time."

"You mean the others didn't hear at all?"

"No, nobody but the right young gal and——"

"And Mr. Hackett."

" 'N Mr. Hackett. I always called him Phil myself."

He glanced about the empty table, sighed, "Well, guess I'll go back to my job."

.   .   .   .   .

So it was Melissa after all. Her first premonitions had been right. Phil had almost never seen Melissa. If she had not come to Red Brook he need never have known, never have heard of her.

.   .   .   .   .

Aunt Sal was taking off her hat in the sewing-room. Something about her manner caught Laurentine's attention.

"Where've you been, mother?"

"Out," she said vaguely.

Laurentine went round to her, placed her hand on her arm.

"You haven't been to see Phil Hackett, mother? Mother listen, you haven't done this thing to me?"

Her tone said, in addition to the wrongs you've already heaped on me.

Sal looked suddenly small and shrunken. "I thought if I saw him—I thought if I went to him as a mother—oh Laurentine, if I could only have been your father too!"

"It's all right mother. . . . You . . . you didn't say I'd sent you?"

"No, no, not that. I only said that, as your mother I thought I ought to know his intentions——"

"Oh mother, no one, just no one does that nowadays. Even millionaires don't question the young men who come to see their daughters——

"But it's all right. I know you did it for the best. Don't bother telling me what he said. I don't want to know. But mother do you think we should keep Melissa?"

Her mother stared: "What's Melissa got to do with it?"

"Everything. Why what did he say?"

"Nothing about Melissa. Only that he couldn't afford to do anything Mr. Reamer wouldn't approve of."

"I see." Her tone was absolutely even. "Let's forget it mother. There are other men even in Red Brook. And I was never in love with him anyway."

But her mother thought, "There are things in life that matter more than love. And anyway she really did love him, I know."

Laurentine thought, "If it hadn't been for Melissa this would never have happened. I wish I had never seen her. Oh God, how I could hate her!"

CHAPTER XII

ON that memorable night after the Ice Carnival while Laurentine in her room was waiting for Phil Hackett, Asshur Lane was visiting Melissa in the dining-room.

It was still very cold, a penetrating rigorous night which made delightful the auxiliary glow and warmth of the gas heater masquerading in the recesses of the deep fireplace. Asshur stood in front of it, tall and strong and even severe on his young straight legs and Melissa thought for the hundredth time how handsome he was.

His skin unmarred by Robbins' furious defense of the preceding evening was the color of a ripe chestnut, of a tint and glossiness which colored people call a "tantalizing brown." Underneath it the red of his blood showed hot and pulsing. His eyes were bold and laughing, his nose and chin sharply defined. But his crowning glory was his thick glossy hair, not straight as many of his group fancied, but very black and shining like a Hindu's, only curly.

Sometimes in spite of Melissa's determined preferences which included a man of different profession from what Asshur's would be and also of different color, a desire which any colored person could understand, her heart raced a little faster at the thought that this bronze hero with all his athletic perfection could be hers for the taking. But she was never less inclined toward that taking than tonight.

She had in her some of her mother's single-mindedness, but with more perspicuity. Melissa had seen too many lives about her ruined for lack of foresight. She did not intend for her own to be thus wasted.

The events of the previous evening had made her determine more than ever to change that position in life in which circumstances had placed her. She had not caught all that Harry had said, had not comprehended in any way his allusion to her mother.

She was grateful to Asshur for taking her part. He had, she supposed, performed a really gallant and chivalrous deed. But the commonness of the situation, the sound of the hard blows on the resilient skin of the antagonists, the jeering impertinent crowd, the knowledge that through her aunt and cousin she really was open to this sort of proceeding sickened her. She would get out of it sometime, somehow. The day would come when she would be out of the reach of these people with their horrid, narrow malice, their stupid ways, their stupider conclusions.

"Thinking that because Aunt Sal was—irregular," —of course that was putting it mildly, she admitted as much, "that I must be irregular too." Oh, she would find a way out of it all, but that way would not be through Asshur.

"You mean, you really mean you don't love me Melissa?"

She considered him a moment, weighing her words carefully. She was only seventeen, but she had the assurance of a woman twenty years her senior. Indeed it was doubtful that Melissa at thirty-seven would have the unshaken assurance of this inexperienced girl.

She thought: "Here he is the best catch of any boy in town—and I can have him. Some day I'll meet some one better than he in every way—and I can have him too." Yet even then she thought with a fleeting sorrow that she could never meet anyone finer, more innately noble.

Aloud she answered: "You know Asshur in a way I do love you." Her hard little head was amazed to hear her lips thus pronouncing the sentiment of her heart. "But that's not enough."

He told her, his young face darkling, "It's enough for me. It should be for you."

"But Asshur love isn't all there is of life. Sometimes it works just the other way, makes you miss everything else in life that is worth while. Look how many times you yourself have told me you want success, you want esteem, respect, friends."

"And I could give you all that—and why—because of love."

But she could not tell him that though she wanted these gifts she didn't want them at his hands. She craved a larger, more brilliant setting than he with his ambitions could ever provide. So sticking to her original point she said simply:

"Look at Laurentine."

He stared: "Look at Laurentine! What about her? How's her case any different from yours?"

"Different from mine?" she echoed astounded. "Why Asshur you know there's no comparison between us. You've lived here some time. Don't tell me you've never heard that old story about Aunt Sal and that old white Colonel Halloway."

He seemed for a moment to be waiting for something more. But he only said: "His whiteness has nothing to do with it. In fact in a way it might be a sort of redeeming feature. There could be less excusable circumstances than that."

It was her turn to stare now, "How could it be a redeeming feature?"

"Well," he rejoined frowning and wrestling with a big problem. "I don't know much about the case, and don't care anything about it either except in so far as it might affect the welfare of some one I cared for. But now let's see. Your aunt's about fifty isn't she?"

"Forty-five," she corrected him.

"That means she was born when the South was still in the shadow of slavery. In what state?"

"In Mississippi, in the littlest hole, mother said. Afterwards they moved to Alabama, then a cousin or somebody was taken here to Jersey by a relative of some visiting Halloway and then she sent for Aunt Sal."

"In Mississippi, a state where to this day all possible stress is laid on a white skin. Lots of colored people made a fetish of it, and of course all white people did. The whole system of slavery hung on it."

"Well what of that? You just said Aunt Sal was born after slavery."

"But that wouldn't keep her from being affected by its consequences, the hang-over and everything. Think of her a little ignorant housemaid and then this young prince coming into her life and preferring her. Sticking to her too through thick and thin. Acknowledging her to all intents and purposes before everybody. He might have sent her away, he could have had the child put in a home.

"And on the other hand she must have found something tremendously satisfying in their life together. She's been a handsome woman. She could have gone away and married. But look, did you ever think," he paused, struck himself with this new aspect of the matter, "she's remained here to be his living monument? How often do you think people would think of Colonel Halloway, how long would they remember him?"

Melissa said stupidly, "But Asshur they weren't married."

He almost shouted at her: "Well, what of it? And let me tell you my dear girl there're worse things in this world than not being married. And any man who lets the facts of Laurentine's parentage stand in his way, any colored man especially, doesn't deserve the name of man. How many of us can trace his ancestry back more than three generations? Perhaps a few thousands of all the millions of colored people in this country. A darned small percentage I'm telling you."

But Melissa was not interested in sociology. "Well, all I've got to say is I'm glad my mother was married and that I don't have to go through what Laurentine does and Aunt Sal before her. How'd we get off on all this anyway, Asshur?"

He couldn't answer her for a few moments, just stood surveying her, feeling oddly thwarted in his first love-making. Something tender, wholly masculine, but tender and solely protective, rose in him dissipating for the time all other feeling. She was so young this girl of his—he felt himself suddenly a man of the world—so ignorant, so, so cocksure. For almost the first time he saw her as she was, a slender wisp of femininity with nothing in the world to protect her but her belief, her pride in herself for having what? The ordinary heritage of the most ordinary child born in wedlock.

He stretched out two long arms, caught her

slightly unwilling hands and drew her to him. "Melissa promise me two things."

"I'll try Asshur. Now don't ask too much. What are they?"

"First that you'll always be good." He interrupted her anticipating her indignant rejoinder. "I don't mean just ordinary good, but almost stupid good. Circumspect."

But in spite of all her high feelings, her apparently reckless determination to have a good time, she loved the conventional. So she answered readily.

"I promise, Asshur."

"And secondly if you are ever in trouble of any kind, Melissa, you'll send for me."

Her voice and face were very steady: "I'll never be in trouble Asshur. And anyway, where would you be?"

"Promise me, Melissa."

"I promise, Asshur. . . . Oo-oh look it's time for you to go. I'll walk to the gate with you."

They started out the side door but he sent her back for her coat.

Shivering in the chilly night which was in such poignantly delicious contrast with the warm room within, she stood for a moment in the bright moonlight beneath the Chinaberry Tree while her cousin Laurentine looked down at her from her darkened window above.

"I'm awfully sorry Asshur."

But he intent on other matters was hardly thinking about love.

"Just remember your promise Melissa. Gee, isn't

it cold? And isn't it great out here under the Chinaberry Tree? Run in girl. Good-night."

"Good-night Asshur."

She ran in and in almost one simultaneous motion
turned the key, extinguished the fire and snapped off
the light. Then she ran up stairs and stood as Laurentine too in the room next to hers was standing
looking out at the beautiful Tree. Only her
thoughts were happy ones. She said to herself,
"Eighteen and I've had a proposal!"

The bed was so warm, so comfortable; she wanted
to lie awake and think but the sudden warmth after
the cold had made her drowsy.

Two thoughts struggled through her drowsy almost furry consciousness.

"I almost wish he was going to be a doctor."

And later in amusement tempered by an oncom-
ing rush of sleep. "As though I'd ever get in
trouble!"

CHAPTER XIII

BUT almost immediately she *was* in trouble, although of a different sort she was sure from
what Asshur meant. The fight at the brook brought
into existence certain most unexpected results. It
seemed to have revived with truly remarkable vehemence all that old story of Aunt Sal and her white
paramour. (Melissa used this term to describe
Colonel Halloway in a diary which she began to keep
about this time.)

Melissa to her complete astonishment began to
find herself suffering from the ostracism which she

supposed had been Laurentine's portion in her
younger days. From having been easily the most
popular girl in her little group, she was transformed
with a devastating rapidity and ruthlessness into an
outsider. Little clubs of which she had been a member broke up and re-formed under a new name with
the same personnel but with the exception of
Melissa. The older people, it is true, treated her
with the same hardly-veiled, slightly mordant malicious interest which they had always shown. They
plied her with questions, smiling with sly glee at her
innocent complacent answers.

"Well now if here ain't Melissa," Mrs. Epps
would say when the young girl came down to her
house for the fresh eggs which Aunt Sal had ordered. "Any more boys fightin' over you my dear?"

"No," Melissa answered frowning faintly. She
couldn't understand the wretched woman's interest.
"My goodness me," she'd tell herself, "lots of girls
must have had fellows quarreling over 'em."

"My goodness me, Mrs. Epps," she said aloud,
"didn't you ever have any boys fussing over you
when you were a girl?"

"No," said Mrs. Epps solemnly, "I never did. But
then too nobody ain't never said nothin' about my
folks. That's why Asshur lit into him, wasn't it
because Harry Robbins said suthin' about your
folks?"

"Er—well—sort of," Melissa conceded. For all
her coolness and assurance she could not cope with
things like this. She could not conceive of such
cruelty being deliberate.

"My," she thought, "poor Laurentine! How

they must dislike her! And yet what on earth does she do to them?"

.   .   .   .   .

The boys too formed a vexing problem. Up to this time it had seemed almost impossible to escape their attention. She had been to use her own phrase "pestered to death" with them. Now without warning they let her alone. The telephone once so insistent was mute after Laurentine closed up her sewing-room. This defection meant not so much to her as the defection of the girls. Asshur was the pick of the boys and there was no question but that Asshur was hers signed, sealed, and ready at least for delivery. But still all this meant a lessening of her sense of well-being, a diminution of that intense feeling of complacence which had been hers ever since she had first arrived in Red Brook.

Not that the boys were ever rude. She almost wished they were with some of the old homely roughness which once they had tendered her. On the contrary their greetings were almost too exaggeratedly polite. In the presence of Asshur Lane this deference was more emphasized than ever. She saw Asshur turn red under his chestnut colored skin and realized that he was as helpless as she. Only Ben Davis and Herbert Tucker, old friends of Asshur's, and Ben at least a former aspirant for her own special friendship, acted as always the rôle of nice, hearty, healthy boys.

Vexed and ashamed, she spoke somewhat haltingly to Asshur about it.

He was embarrassed and sore. She could see that without guessing the reason why. But he could not help her. "I don't know what's got into them," he growled. "Half the time I think Harry Robbins gets 'em goin' somehow. Expect I've got that nigger's head to bust yet. But mind you behave Melissa. Be a good girl, a really good girl, all the time. Now remember."

.   .   .   .   .

Still she told her troubled self walking home in the soft spring afternoons through beautiful, lonely Romany Road, still things could have been far worse. For much as she hated the results following on the fight at Redd's Brook, she hated the fight itself still worse.

"Sooner or later my dear," she said to herself, "you know you meant to get away from them anyhow. Well they broke off with you first and saved you the trouble of breaking off with them and feeling guilty about it all your life."

But she wrote in her diary in the round unformed writing which showed what a child she really was: "Sometimes it's just as well to watch people even if they seem to be your friends, and get ahead of them before they get a chance to get ahead of you. That might make you feel mean but it could make you feel kind of good too."

.   .   .   .   .

But these troubles faded into insignificance before a very real problem which was slowly rising before her. Spreading, to change the figure, as circles spread and spread wrinkling the calm surface of a pond, stretching on and on. . . .

Laurentine had failed her, Laurentine who had always been so kind, so like an elder to a kid sister;

the kind of sister that you read about, Laurentine, from whom she had, with the faintest touch of super-ciliousness, accepted favors—was decidedly cold to her, Laurentine, unbelievably, decidedly, incontro-vertibly, disliked her.

It had taken her a long time, busied as she was with her lessons, her little vanities, her new prob-lems with the boys and girls of Red Brook, to per-ceive this.   She had come to her cousin with her usual confidence:

"Laurentine couldn't you find just the littlest bit of time to make me a dress for the picnic? I've just seen the peachiest picture in the evening paper. You could copy it."

Laurentine frowning at a length of crêpe Ginette, could not it seemed. And expressed no regrets.

But Melissa having seen her absorbed before in problems of designing, tactfully withdrew. She had a wholesome respect for Laurentine's positive genius in this field. Melissa could sew exquisitely, beauti-fully. Her "finishing off" in this day of makeshifts was marvelous to behold. But she could not design and drape and create. She would never be able to do that. Still Matilda Gathers had been known to step into such a breach before, and could probably be de-pended upon to do so again. The dress did not worry her.

.   .   .   .   .

"Laurentine, what about letting me have that cream silk? I could just get my dress out of that?"

"What cream silk?"

"The one hanging with your things in the spare room."

"Well what about letting you have it?"

Melissa stared wide-eyed? What had got into her tranquil cousin?

"Why, can I have it?"

"No you can't have it."

"Why Laurentine! You said, why last year you said I could have it. You said: 'Maybe I'll give you that dress next year.'"

"Did I? And this year I say I won't give it to you."

Melissa persisted: "But what are you going to do with it Laurentine?"

"Nothing so far as I know."

"Are you going to wear it yourself?"

"I'm not expecting to."

"And you won't let me have it?"

"I won't let you have it."

Laurentine's almond-shaped black eyes looked full into Melissa's round unblinking green eyes of a kitten.

It was the young girl's eyes which fell first. "Why," she thought shrinking within herself under the balefulness of that stare, "Why Laurentine doesn't like me a bit. Why she hates me!"

.   .   .   .   .

Aunt Sal sitting immobile as of late she did so often, observing Laurentine, watched the girl leave the room. Her wavering step brought a rush of pity to her heart. She had been proud of Melissa's assurance in that house of uncertainties.

"Weren't you hard on her Laurentine?"

"Wasn't she hard on me? . . . Oh mother, mother let me alone, let me alone I say! And stop watching me!"

CHAPTER XIV

MELISSA thought: "She's mad, she's mad clear through. And it's because Phil Hackett don't come to see her any more. And he's the only beau she had. And she'll never get another. . . . Asshur's the only beau I have too, but I'll have others, lots more. Wait and see—oh wait and see! For one thing I won't stick around here all my life like Laurentine. I won't, I won't!"

In the hot early evening of June she sat under the Chinaberry Tree with Asshur, her weary mind suddenly calm, her hurt heart finding balm. The young man, his long legs stretched comfortably before him, slouched beside her enveloped with Melissa in a sudden penetrating peace.

"Isn't it lovely here Asshur?" She looked at the emerald grass, the indirect handiwork of a remote God through a far more direct handiwork of Mr. Stede. Some half-open roses cast their fragrance on the air adding to the lavishness of the summer beauty. And over and above all the rich foliage of the Chinaberry Tree cast its deeper shade on the pale glow of the departing sun. The boy and girl sat enveloped and surrounded in the pensive almost sadly sweet aura of the summer night.

"On such a night," sighed Asshur, looking athwart the haze of his cigarette smoke at the pale golden light filtering through the chinks of the dark green over-lapping leaves,——

"Stood Dider with a willer in 'er 'and,"—Melissa burlesqued meanly.

"Asshur."

"Uh-huh."

"Phil Hackett's stopped coming to see Laurentine."

"He has?" Asshur straightened his spine, and tapped the toe of his sneaker with his tennis racket.

"Yes."

"Think she cares?"

"Yes, awfully."

"P'raps she doesn't. P'raps she's sent him about his business. I don't see how a girl like Laurentine could be crazy about Hackett. Always seemed to be a good deal of a stuffed shirt, if you ask me."

"Well, stuffed shirt or not, he doesn't come any more."

Asshur stirred uneasily, "Well they didn't quarrel did they? Somehow I don't see proud Laurentine quarreling with anybody. Bet she gave him the bum's rush."

"Not a chance," said the practical Melissa. "Not a chance. Mighty few colored women in this town would give Phil Hackett the cold shoulder. And certainly not Laurentine."

. . . . .

But she was not quite so sure on Sunday. Laurentine went to church quite regularly now. Melissa could not guess why. Certainly she paid no attention to the minister, and even less to the members of the congregation. Serene, beautiful, cold as a statue she stood for a moment on the steps after service, glancing over the dispersing congregation. She gave no effect of lingering to be spoken to, she was just there and the place was suddenly transformed into a background whose only business was to enhance her dignified beauty and the absolute perfection of her soft green dress.

Melissa knew that her cousin was not waiting for her. She would probably speak to the minister's wife, Mrs. Simmons, and to a few girls, members of a sewing guild which she had once directed. Then she would stroll in leisurely fashion homeward and resign herself to the quiet monotony of a small town Sunday afternoon. There would be literally nothing for her to do. The moving picture theatres would be closed, there would be no company unless Mr. Gathers or Mr. Stede dropped by to inquire about chores for the following week.

Melissa wondered how she stood it. She herself once upon a time would have gone strolling with girls, or entertaining in her side yard. Now this was a thing of the past. But there was always Asshur with his selfless devotion and the unobstrusive, unfailing courtesy of Ben Davis and Herbert Tucker. It was conceivable that she might have spent the afternoon by herself in one of her sudden attacks of studiousness. But to spend the day in enforced solitude would be beyond her endurance.

It was while she was thinking of this that she saw Phil Hackett appear suddenly from nowhere, for he had certainly not been in church, and stop in confusion before Laurentine. Evidently up to that moment he had not seen her. Mechanically his hand flew to his hat, he inclined his head, parted his lips to speak. But Laurentine stepping just far enough to the side to avoid touching him walked off down the steps, apparently unconscious that such a person as Hackett ever existed.

Melissa, round-eyed, saw the dark flush mounting painfully to his brow, saw him glance about swiftly to note if anyone else had observed his embarrassment. Evidently no one had unless it was Mrs. Ismay sitting in her car outside the church yard waiting for her husband who for reasons of his own attended service every Sunday morning.

She straightened up from the cushions against which she had been lolling, and crossing the pavement met Laurentine as she passed, still nonchalant and self-possessed, through the gates. The doctor's wife touched the girl's hand fleetingly, her arm slid around her waist.

"Miss Strange,—Laurentine—do come home with me and spend the afternoon. You can telephone your mother. Dr. Ismay is going to Trenton after dinner. I shall be all alone."

Her voice rang absolutely sincere. Laurentine hesitated, yielded. She was literally at the end of her endurance. "Thank you Mrs. Ismay," she murmured. "I'll be glad to go with you. You are very kind to ask me."

CHAPTER XV

MRS. ISMAY was a little thin woman, a Bostonian by birth with all the trade marks of her native city thick upon her. It was impossible to spend an hour in her presence without becoming aware of a gentility which was innate, and of an unaffected sincerity and kindness which even her Boston vowels could not conceal. Laurentine wondered why she had not been attracted to her at first, not knowing that her own coldness and stiffness had created a rampart which few would have attempted twice to scale. But to-day she was weak. The encounter with Hackett had shaken her to her depths. Once she would have taken refuge in scorn and contempt. But to-day she could not, she wanted to relax, to cease being on the defensive; she wanted, she thought, glancing at the placid brown lady beside her, to be serene, gracious, amiable and to be all these things because of the assurance of her place in her world.

Her hostess led her into the yard surrounding a rather large, rambling house in quite the other end of the town. Laurentine knew the locality though of late she had not visited it; it lay well to the extremity of the Romany Road, a lovely, lonely walk which led through the woods surrounding Red Brook, and then debouched into a highway not far from Aunt Sal's dwelling. In Laurentine's childhood "the Road" as it was frequently called had been a famous trysting place for lovers, but the advent of the automobile had changed all this since nowadays each couple knew of a "little spot to be made in twenty minutes in a car where you could be all alone." And none seemed too poor to possess a car of some description.

This section of Red Brook had by tacit consent been handed over to the better class of colored people. Dr. Brown's residence was only three blocks away though his office was more centrally located. Phil Hackett's father had recently built a large and comfortable bungalow on a street nearby and the

Epps' family, energetic proprietors of a barber shop catering exclusively to whites, lived and had their comfortable being in this vicinity. Melissa knew this neighborhood well but its present condition was new and startling to Laurentine.

Dr. Ismay came in presently, exclaiming a little testily over his wife's failure to meet him and drive him home from church. It was a very warm day and beads of perspiration which no amount of sopping could stay, stood out all over his ginger-colored skin.

"Oh hush," said Mrs. Ismay unfailingly calm and good-natured. "You were so mixed up with your trustees and stewards and such that I finally prevailed on Miss Strange here to take pity on me and come home to dinner. I didn't know whether you were coming or not."

.   .   .   .   .

Dr. Ismay whirled around, his face a study in amazement. "Miss Strange! Where is she Millie?"

"In your office looking at those views of Jamaica; go in and speak to her."

Obediently he crossed the hall, paid his respects to his visitor and was back at his wife's side.

"Gosh-amighty," he groaned, "what a beaut! No wonder you've been raving so about her! What are you going to do with her Millie?"

"I don't know," his wife replied soberly. "It really all depends on what she's willing to let me do." She went up close to her husband. "But Robert, from all I've been able to hear, she's had a terribly raw deal, all her life. You've got to help me straighten her out.   She can't go on living like this."

"Count on me," he rejoined, speaking with resignation, "only mind, Millie, no match-making."

She went to him swiftly and put her slender arm about his neck.   "Only if I can find some one as good and dependable as you," she murmured.

"Well, that's impossible," he assured her with mock relief.   "My dear couldn't we have dinner? I promised Denleigh I'd be waiting for him at two-thirty and it's two now."

.   .   .   .   .

For the first time in her life Laurentine broke bread with colored people of her own rank and sympathies.   There was nothing remarkable about the meal or its service.   The food was wholesome, well cooked and attractively garnished.   However, the same might be said of any meal eaten in her own home.   But the lack of restraint the utter feeling of peace and content which pervaded the house created an unforgettable memory.   Dr. and Mrs. Ismay chatted of the town, of the way in which the colored population was shifting, of the tendency of the young people to leave South Jersey for Philadelphia, Newark or New York.   Outside in the street the voices and chatter of children on rollerskates shattered the Sunday quiet.   Within, a hazy veil of sunlight hung over the darkened dining-room, affording a hazy background to what, it seemed to the young guest, must be a dream.

Presently a car drove up, a man sprang out, crossed the porch and entered the room with an air of quiet assurance.   He was a tall, lean man, not young, certainly not old. His face thin and a little worn was remarkable for its air of serene tolerance. He bowed with pleasant exaggerated courtesy over Mrs. Ismay's hand.

"So glad to see you Millie, though you might have asked me to dinner." His glance moved slowly but without offense to Laurentine, dwelt for a moment thoughtfully on her face. He acknowledged the introduction, however, as remotely as the girl herself, then turned to his host.

"Come on Ismay, we've got to get going if you mean to speak in Trenton to-night. Look for us when you see us, Millie." The trio moved out on the porch and then Ismay remembering his manners called back: "Good-bye Miss Strange. I'm going to make my wife have you over every Sunday."

But the tall stranger forsaking the group for a moment walked back through the long window and stood beside Laurentine who sat thinking rather forlornly on Phil Hackett and her empty life.

"Good-bye Miss Strange," he said formally.

And she, her mind still on many things, answered with equal formality, "Good-bye Dr. Denleigh."

CHAPTER XVI

SUDDENLY the summer burgeoned. It seemed to Melissa that on one day she had been in the thick of the confusion and embarrassment of the circumstances attending the Ice Carnival and on the next she was sitting with Asshur on the last day of June under the Chinaberry Tree. They were silent watching the scorching sun's assault on the area beyond which the thick foliage of the delectable Tree did not extend. Here in this retreat were rest and cool and shelter. Melissa had brought out a tray with a pitcher and lemonade glasses, a picture magazine and a tennis racket. And Asshur, as was usual in his rare moments of inactivity, sat slouched on the small of his back, a cigarette dangling from his lips, tapping with a light staff the firm large shoe which enclosed his firm large foot.

For a moment he yielded to his sense of utter content. "You know under this tree M'lissa it's just as though we were living in a tent; on the desert you know. Burning sands and all that kind of thing."

Melissa murmured, "Suppose you're the Sheik and I'm——"

"You're my favorite wife."

She headed him off adroitly: "More likely your Christian slave. . . . Oh Asshur what a funny year we've had! You know I've lived here fourteen months and have gone through all sorts of changes. People in Red Brook are more like the weather than any folks I've ever seen." She was almost talking to herself now, unconsciously uttering secret thoughts and puzzling fancies.

"You know when I first came here every one was rather cool but not as though they meant to be. Just the way people are when they are satisfied and at ease,—not troubling about the stranger. You know what I mean?"

"Yep."

"And then suddenly everything was wonderful, just, just—I know you won't understand this Asshur

—but just the way a girl would want her life to be, outside of being rich. You know lots of fun, lots of folks, telephone ringing, walks, girls asking you to come over, boys asking you if they can come around. And you being wonderful—and serious." She glanced at his face from which he had carefully removed every trace of expression. "No need to look blank, Asshur. Don't think I've looked on you as some one to feed my vanity. I've been conscious of your nearness and decency all along. You know you really are rather a rock, Asshur."

" 'Lion of Judah' is the correct interpretation, I believe. Dad's a minister down there in Alabama, that's how I know that kind of thing. Well what about all these happenings in Red Brook? Any new developments?"

She hesitated. In a way she hated to inform Asshur who saw her always so exalted, so desirable, of her plight. But there were times when she felt so alone, so menaced.

"I feel," she said, shivering even in the hot sunlight, "so often as though something very terrible and dreadfully unusual were hanging over me. I can't express it. I just know it's going to happen."

She half expected Asshur to laugh at her. Somehow it seemed as though if he had it would have dispelled not only her fear, but the actual danger itself. But contrary to her expectation, he did nothing of the sort. Instead he straightened up from his slouching position and asked quite seriously.

"Have you felt that way long?"

"No. Only since Laurentine began to dislike me so."

"Laurentine! Hey, that's a new one! I didn't know she disliked you. I've always thought of her as being rather decent. How does she show it? How long has it been going on?"

"Ever since—now let's see—yes I think ever since that night you quarrelled with Harry Robbins." Frowning she paused a moment,—she hated to think of that evening. "And I don't know why; she's never spoken to me about it. It was just at that time Phil Hackett stopped coming to see her. At first I thought she was so disappointed about him that it just made her generally hateful. I made allowances," said Melissa in her young magnanimity, "but she's stayed the same way for months now. And anyhow, what could I have had to do with it?"

Asshur stood up, his hands in his pockets, looking rather wonderful in his brown, youthful perfection and again as on a former occasion she thrilled to his sheer masculinity. If only he weren't so set on being a farmer!

"I don't understand any of it Melissa. I like Laurentine—what I've seen of her. But I sure don't like the idea of this sudden turn she's taken against you. Tell you what—" his eyes ran the length of her smart figure in her white mesh sports dress; the red blood began mounting under his thin bright brown skin. "Tell you what Melissa, marry me now—before I go away, I can take care of you, protect you——"

"Before you go away! Where are you going? Why Asshur you never said——"

"I know," he interrupted, "I just found out myself about it to-day, that's why I've come over so early. My father runs a summer school down home, you know. He wants me to come and help him this summer and then in the fall he's going to send me somewhere to a good agricultural college—maybe South, maybe Cornell, I don't know. Uncle Ceylon's going to let me practically run his place at Birneysville when I get through." He caught her hands.

"Melissa, it would be so wonderful!"

She said stubbornly, "You know I don't want to live on a farm, Asshur." But she was conscious of a sick terror. Laurentine's dislike was bad enough. But now with Asshur gone. Her hands clung to his.

"How long will you be gone, Asshur?"

"Well, if I'm to go to school in the South, I'll probably stay right on after summer school. I couldn't afford to come up and go right back. I'm afraid we won't see each other for a year."

"For a year—Asshur!"

"Better come with me, Hon."

But her ambition was stronger even than her fear of loneliness. "Oh Asshur, I can't. When are you going?"

"Friday."

"This very week?"

"Yep. Got to go send my father a special delivery this very minute. I'll see you every day before I go." He turned abruptly and left her, the muscles in his lean cheek twitching.

The Chinaberry Tree looked down on her first real weeping.

.   .   .   .   .

She fled to her cool room. The winter draperies had been replaced by cool chintzes and meshed curtains of palest lavender. There were touches of lilac in a cover or in a pillow; a bowl of irises struck a deep, rich, purple note. She loved her room, its complete beauty, its sense of affording a haven struck her afresh, only to be lost temporarily in the realization of this new and genuine sorrow.

The mirror reflected her woebegone face. With the naïve vanity of youth she straightened out her puckered brow, went to the glass and surveyed and estimated her personal assets, her clear light brown skin, her carefully treated reddish hair, her surprising green eyes, her thin, supple figure.

"Not so bad," she murmured, her spirits rising, —"And far too good for a farmer's wife." She thought of Nina Mae McKinney, a colored girl who had reached Hollywood; she remembered the name of Edna Thomas, a beautiful, older woman who had appeared frequently on the New York stage.

"Anything, anything could happen," she told the image in the glass "if you'll just wait, Miss."

She would dress and go for a walk. As she opened the closet door, she remembered her diary carefully tucked away between the inside wall and an old heavy suitcase filled with odds and ends of sewing which no one ever disturbed. Involuntarily her hand closed on the purple bound book, into which so many of her self-revelations had gone. Crossing to her little dressing table she wrote with complete absorption.

Presently she read it over: "I *am* the captain of my fate. Here to-day I was so blue, but ever since

I've been thinking of those actresses I've felt better. Of course I can't buck this color problem and I'm not going to try because anyway I think lots of colored people are pretty well off as they are. I shall always be on top. Not now of course but at least I can keep on going.

"And that's why I won't marry Asshur though I like him such an awful lot. If I get stuck with him what chance would I have to go further? No I'll either go on the stage or I'll marry one of these professional men and get somewhere and have a good time. One thing, I won't be like Laurentine. Of course she can't help about poor Aunt Sal, but she could help letting herself get stuck in this place. Where'll she be ten years from now? I know where I'll be. Either in New York or Queen of the May in Red Brook. Believe I'll take proud Laurentine as a horrible warning."

.   .   .   .   .

But on Friday she forgot her brave words, her fine resolutions. She clung to Asshur.

"Oh Asshur, Asshur, don't go!"

"Melissa you know I have to. But if you want me to, if you really mean you want me, I'll come back Christmas,—and take you back to 'Bam with me. My father and mother would like you. We live very near Tuskegee, that's where I'm going you know. I'd be home every week-end."

Something about him spelled safety, assurance, peace—all this apart from love. Almost she yielded. It took all her courage to smile wanly, to tell him bleakly:

"I'll write Asshur,—maybe I'll be the one to come."

But he felt the great moment had passed. "The train's coming Melissa." His voice was cold. And then with a sudden rush of memory. "But mind what I've always told you, Melissa! You be good, do you hear, just as good as you can be. Don't let anything make you miss your step. And if you ever need me really, I'll come—from anywhere."

He had her by her shoulders, almost shaking her. "Promise me—you'll be very good Melissa."

That steadied her more than anything he could have said. "You know I'll be good Asshur—you know me. Good-bye darling." Her kiss was very tender. But the tears were nearer his eyes than hers.

She watched the train fade into the horizon; she could feel the excitement and the tension of the moment drop from her like a discarded garment. Rather forlornly she turned to go home.

. . . . .

Near the Post Office she met Kitty Brown frowning over an opened letter.

"Hello," said Kitty, "you here too? Come and have an orangeade." They sipped the brilliantly colored stuff, leaning negligently against the counter.

"What do you mean, me here too?" asked Melissa. "Where else would I be? Where else would you be?"

"Atlantic City usually," Kitty answered, "but Doc Brown (she frequently spoke of her father thus) wouldn't let me go this year because I failed in Latin and chemistry. That stuff!" exclaimed Miss Brown with supreme contempt. "Kept me home all summer with a tutor. Says if I don't pass it off he won't let me go to Howard next year. And I do want to go there. You have lots of fun at the colored schools. . . . What do you do with yourself Melissa?"

"Nothing," said Melissa truthfully. "I don't seem to get along with the girls here. We used to be very friendly, but I don't know what happened to them."

"Got mad because you copped most of their fellows I'll bet," said Kitty shrewdly, who bothered very little with the local Lotharios.

Melissa was truthful. "I used to see a lot of them, but they don't come around much either any more."

Kitty showed a remarkable knowledge of the doings of her contemporaries. "You don't mean to tell me that Lane boy doesn't come?"

"No," said Melissa suddenly solaced by the coupling of his name with hers, "only he's gone away, —forever, I think—anyway for a year. I don't know how I'm going to get through the summer."

"Kind of out of luck," said Kitty with unexpected sympathy. "Tell you what. Come on over tomorrow afternoon. Mother's letting me have some girls and fellows in from places around here. We'll have supper in the yard, and dance a little if it's not too hot, and play some bridge. Think you'd like that?"

"I'd love it," said Melissa, trying hard not to seem too pleased.

.   .   .   .   .

"Did my good deed to-day," Kitty told her mother that evening. "Asked Melissa Paul to my party; you know she's that girl lives down in little Italy with that good-looking dressmaker Mrs. Ismay's always shooting off about."

"She's no dressmaker; she's a modiste," her mother laughed good-naturedly. "That was a nice thing to do Kitty. It must be hard on a young girl living down there with those two funny women."

"Oh don't start that talk again. I'm sick of hearing about those Stranges and Colonel Halloway. What's it all about? You'd think a white man had never looked at a colored woman before in these United States."

She looked at her mother elfinly. "Do you think Mumsie, if I could coax Melissa to get her cousin or her aunt or whatever she is to make a dress for me that you could manœuver the price out of old Doc Brown?"

    .   .   .   .   .

Melissa moving in a daze finally completed her preparations for bed. Just before she snapped off the light, she opened her diary and wrote happily:

"To-morrow, I, me, Melissa Paul am going to a sure enough party at Kitty Brown's. Ain't that a whole lot better than riding in a Jim Crow coach from Washington to Alabam? Now I ask you, very confidentially, Mr. Asshur Lane, am I stepping out or ain't I?"

CHAPTER XVII

SATURDAY afternoon in August.   Even in Red Brook its coming brought with it that promise of festivity which marks the American Saturday in the East.   The rush of automobiles, strolling of girls and boys down Main Street, their gaily striped blazers flashing, tennis rackets poised lightly over their shoulders.   Johnasteen and Matilda closing down sewing-machines, bending alertly to pick up stray scraps of material from the sewing-room floor before darting off to secret and alluring enterprises of their own.   Upstairs Melissa dressing and primping for Kitty Brown's party.   Aunt Sal pottering with absorption in the garden accompanied by Mr. Stede whose usefulness among the flower-beds was somewhat impeded by his persistent and irrelevant interest in vegetables,—cooked ones.

"Fried onions now Mis' Strange.   Take fried onions.   There's a dish fit fur any man.   With tripe now.   With tripe they makes a dish fit fur a king, fur Mr. Booker T. Washin'ton."   His voice grew lyric.   "Of course I'm a man don't never ask for no food.   I waits for Pentecost. . . .   When I see Johnasteen jes' now, seemed to me her breath smelt oniony.   Guess she had et 'em for lunch."

"If she did," said Aunt Sal gently, "she must have got 'em herself.   I didn't put any on the table. But there is a whole mess of scallions there in the kitchen.   I bought some from the huckster this morning."   She smiled at the old man cheerfully. Presently, as he knew, she would play the part of

Pentecost and set onions before him. She was almost happy these days. Laurentine seemed to have lost her restlessness, her effect of hopeless brooding.

.   .   .   .   .

Laurentine *was* less restless these days, more normal. She saw Mrs. Ismay several times a week, was in her house usually every Wednesday and every Saturday. There was a difference of almost fifteen years between them which Laurentine found charming. It seemed to her that the elder woman had crowded every possible experience into this span. She knew life, this placid, brown person with her slightly angular figure, and big gray eyes. She had known pleasure, and sorrow and disappointment and pain and fulfillment.

"Lots of pain and lots of fulfillment," she told Laurentine on a hot, golden summer afternoon, sitting in the quiet and cool of her side porch. Sometimes on Wednesday evenings when Dr. Ismay's office was, for some inexplicable reason, packed to overflowing, the two women drove down to Newark to a moving picture, talking all the way there and talking again all the way back as though the conversation, not the picture, were the cause of their little excursion.

As indeed it was for lonely Laurentine. Suddenly her life was full of little incidents of interest. She was learning to drive, practicing on Dr. Ismay's little Ford; she was playing bridge; because now it meant something to her, she was taking up her music again, playing old, rich ballads, singing them too in a pleasant contralto voice on Sunday evenings after the Ismays had finished supper and she and Mrs. Ismay had washed the dishes. Sometimes a friend of the household dropped in—Herbert Tucker's father and mother, both of them fat and kind and jolly,—Dr. Denleigh too, sitting in a corner quietly over innumerable cigarettes, dropping a word now and then into the conversation and usually in such a position that he could note inconspicuously Laurentine's graceful elegance, her shining rippling hair, the rosy curve of her cheek just where it blended into the smooth lower plane of her apricot-tinted face.

"This," Laurentine used to tell herself lying straight and relaxed in her dainty room, "This is life, just as one would want it." She forgot about Phil Hackett, forgot her aching loneliness and her desperate yearnings, she would rise and look out the window, marking idly how the August moonlight went sifting through the thick foliage of the Chinaberry Tree. Sometimes she would glimpse Melissa in her light summer dress sitting on the hexagonal bench with some boy—probably Asshur. But she felt no pang of jealousy, of sorrow for a lost girlhood which had missed such simple joys. Some day she would have her own little group over. They would have supper, eat and drink. They would make merry under the Chinaberry Tree.

.   .   .   .   .

On this Saturday she was, as she used to be, alone. The Ismays had gone to Atlantic City for the week-end; they had invited Laurentine to accompany them. But she did not want to go. It was riches to have an invitation and to be able to refuse it; to be lonely because she wanted to be.

She would go out into the woods and read a book of Hugh Walpole's—"Fortitude" which Mrs. Ismay had lent her. It proved to be a chronicle of sorrow, bleak despair and stark courage, but she understood it and liked it. There was a little clearing in the woods well away from the road and after awhile, closing the book, she lay on the pine needles at full length looking, through the stiff branches of the tightly-wrapped trees, at the bright broad sky. Vaguely in spite of the pain which Walpole depicted, she felt uplifted, comforted. "Life is a battle; into each life some rain must fall; joy cometh in the morning." Smiling she let the platitudes race through her mind, sensing the universal truthfulness of them which made them at once both tame and vital.

Something moved with a sharp crackle over the needles, stopped. Startled she let her glance run up an interminable length of figure to rest locked in the equally astonished gaze of Stephen Denleigh. She sat up straight, her back toward the pine tree, looking in her green summer frock with her russet face as though she were part of her surroundings.

"Like a dryad, I suppose," thought Denleigh swiftly, but he said:

"You like this place too, Miss Strange?"

Laurentine nodded, a little shy, disturbed and a trifle provoked at this interruption.

"I used to play here sometimes when I was a little girl," she told him, her face clouding with the memory of her clouded girlhood.

"Oh you've always lived here then?"

"Forever and ever," she said solemnly, "and I suppose I always will."

He thought it a little odd that he saw her about so rarely and told her so. "Though it's not odd really. I don't suppose a person like you has much in common with the Snells and Eppses and Robbinses of this place."

She thought he was jesting and threw him a dubious glance. He went on: "I suppose it's the man of it, but it does seem to me in spite of my better judgment that a person as beautiful as you has a right to make her own laws. And when she adds to that beauty, refinement, and real niceness, I suppose she feels almost a queen."

Laurentine's face grew slowly crimson. She a queen! Wait until he should hear of her mother and Colonel Halloway, of their sad romance and of herself the fruit of that romance.

"I suppose," she told him slowly, "if I were really bright I'd be able to say something clever, just like that." She snapped her fingers. "But evidently you don't know anything about me or you'd never call me a queen."

He placed his little medical case under his head and lolled full length beside her, looking rather whimsically into her grave, startled eyes. "I've just come off a case down here in Little Italy. Gosh it was awful, a poor woman, the victim of such illtreatment, such bestiality—I've been practicing twelve years but it really turned my stout heart, or stout stomach I suppose I should say. I came out here to get a breath of fresh air and find you all lovely and beautiful and serene—the way a woman should look."

"I've found my line now," she laughed down at

him, liking but not esteeming his frankness, "I never dreamed, seeing you sitting so quiet and remote on Sunday afternoons at Mrs. Ismay's, that I'd be saying it to you."

"What's your line? It's bound to be a good one."

"This is it. You're a mighty fast worker."

"Add, and an honest one. I mean it Miss Strange. You know for a long time it's been impossible for me to look at a beautiful woman without going sick. But from the very first day I saw you two or three months ago in Millie's dining-room, I regained faith in an old ideal of mine."

He was very much in earnest she perceived. Amazed at the turn which the conversation had taken, she asked him gently of what ideal he was speaking.

"That a beautiful woman must be a good woman. I know you are both."

But she didn't want the discussion to converge about her; she chose the safer topic.

"Evidently you knew a beautiful woman who wasn't."

According to Mrs. Ismay he was nearly forty and suddenly the face which he turned toward her showed the imprint of the years, it became so haggard and worn.

"I should say I did. I was married once to the most beautiful woman in the world—and to the most wicked."

Her answer was unbelievably banal. "I didn't know you were married."

"Married—and divorced—by law and by death. But not completely disillusioned."

Not perceiving the appositeness of this last remark, she rose to go home.

He fell into step with her matching his long stride with her own.

At her gate he said he would like to call. She looked at him, noting his fine drawn face, his lean erect frame, his kind eyes and slender hands. Suddenly he vanished and Phil Hackett with his heavy, slow gentility took his place. Shaking her head to emphasize her words she refused him.

"No, don't call, Dr. Denleigh. I'm rarely free—I have to work very hard at my trade. And beside —do you mean to tell me that no one in this town has ever told you about me?"

"Everybody I know has told me about you," he told her, "because I've asked everybody. May I come to call, Miss Strange?"

But resolutely she told him no.

CHAPTER XVIII

"THIS," thought Melissa to herself, "this is lovely. Oh this is perfect. This is where I belong. I'd like to write mother about it—only she wouldn't understand—or Asshur. No, not Asshur! Oh good-bye, Asshur! I know I'd never meet up with this kind of life with you."

Privately Kitty Brown considered her party rather tame but to Melissa it was the last word in gayety, vivacity and fashion. The well-groomed, good-looking lads in flannels and sports shoes were marvelous. They hailed from Trenton, Newark and even New York. Several of them were students in good Eastern preparatory schools, two of them were freshmen from Dartmouth and Harvard. She knew none of them except Ben Davis and Herbert Tucker, products of Red Brook. Ben had been spending his last six months at Andover and was very impressive. But his innate niceness kept him inoffensive. He had come to the party without company and as he knew Melissa better than any girl there he was not far from her side for the entire afternoon, which made it very nice, she thought, making up her mind none the less to get better acquainted with some of these attractive young blades.

In and out among the uniformity of male attire flashed the girls in their brilliant and gay summer dresses. Cotton was in vogue and the shimmering freshness of organdy and embroidery and lace lent its special charm. Melissa in a thin peacock blue which set off her clear skin and reddish hair was completely satisfied with her own appearance. She had learned from Laurentine the value of carefulness in detail and so, because she knew her perfection, could afford to be apparently unaware of it. The other girls beautifully dressed had evidently chosen their colorful gowns with regard to their varying complexions. But not one of them could surpass Melissa in the happy spontaneity with which she expressed her joy at being among those present.

So gay and naïve and joyous indeed was she that Kitty spied in her an aide-de-camp. She came up to her guest, the center of a group of boys and girls with a rather nice-looking slender lad who wore an unmistakable air of ennui.

"Here Melissa! Take this one off my hands won't you? He's just too bored, don'tcha know?"

"I told you Kitty I was awfully tired. I was traveling all night."

"And now you're going to travel some more with these lanterns down to the end of the garden. Melissa will help you put them up won't you? Here go with her," she gave the languid young man a shove. "He answers when you call him Malory, Melissa."

Her happy guest laughed. "Let's hear you. Come Malory, Malory." She started off at a little run and the lad followed her, lanterns bobbing about in his hands as he pursued her over the slightly uneven ground.

Together they hung the lanterns, then sat down on one of the green benches scattered about to survey their handiwork. But presently their gaze wandered and came to rest on each other. Melissa saw a slender boy of five feet some seven or eight inches with rather rough, dark brown, curly hair; his skin was light brown, slightly sallow, teeth not so flashing as Asshur's but white and well kept, eyes as light as her own but gray, not green. His hands were thin and well kept, his feet were slender and arched. He wore a thin gray suit, light blue shirt and dark blue tie. She approved of him and expressed it.

"You look very nice and clean as though you'd been scrubbed," she told him nodding her head, "only why the languidness? Do you have to be that way, or are you really that tired?"

The weariness and defeat which sat so incongruously on his young face deepened perceptibly. "I am tired—I came up from Philadelphia on the bus and that kind of travel always fatigues me. But," he hesitated, "I don't suppose that's what's the matter with me. It's my family," he said desperately. "I haven't seen them all together for a long time. But I always remembered them as being dreary and melancholy and then finally as I grew older I got to thinking I must be mistaken. Yesterday I came home for good and I found them just the way I pictured them, only more so. The house is like a tomb, quiet and dark and a lot of old musty furniture and mother so depressed. Well of course she's my mother," he broke off loyally, "but the girls—well I guess you know them."

But Melissa thought she didn't know any family in Red Brook named Malory.

"Oh that's my first name. Our name's Forten."

"I don't know them either, I've only lived here two years but I've heard one of my cousin's sewing-girls mention that name. I think she used to live near them. Would you like," she asked delicately, "to tell me about them? Families are funny sometimes."

"There's nothing to tell," he said, "nothing really. Only they're always so depressed and depressing. They make me feel—ugh—so damp." He smiled at her whimsically.

"Now I should say they're just as different from you as they can be. Of course they're a lot older than you—maybe ten years or so, but I don't believe you'll be like them when you're thirty."

"I should hope not," she said shivering a little at

the thought of that advanced age. "I mean to be jolly and happy always. I mean to arrange my life so that I just can't help being gay. Let's start off right now by going back to the porch and dancing. Kitty's got a couple who are going to dance the rhumba. That ought to be great."

Reluctantly he followed her; it would have been perfect to sit and talk to this attractive, sympathetic person. But he preferred liveliness, gayety and laughter even to the recital of his own sorrows. Melissa was the embodiment of all these. Presently, his melancholia forgotten, he was enjoying himself, always in her wake, like any other normal boy. His sense of normalcy increased when anticipating Herbert Tucker by five minutes, he had gained the girl's permission to see her home.

Melissa was grateful to life, to luck, to Malory, above all to Kitty. "Oh Kitty, I've had such a good time, do let me come again." Her hostess was charmed with such genuiness. "Of course, of course, come often." She had observed Malory's undoubted penchant for her guest. "Come soon, one day next week and we'll play some contract. Night-night Melissa. 'Bye Malory."

Together they stepped out into the solemn moonlight. The night was enchanting. Malory looked about for a belated taxi but Melissa would have none of it. They strolled through dim, tree-bedecked streets, through the mazes of Little Italy to the wide half-built-up section in which the Stranges lived and to Aunt Sal's gleaming house at the far end.

"What a beautiful place!" the boy exclaimed.

"I'd like to see it in the daylight. I hope you're going to let me come to see you Melissa."

She hesitated, a little uncertain about Laurentine and her coolness. "I don't know just what to say Malory," she whispered, stammering. "My cousin with whom I live is sort of off me just now——"

"Funny about boys," he nodded with jealous approval. "Well she ought to be, taking care of a girl like you."

"No, it isn't that," she said truthfully, "she's—in some way I've managed to vex her—she isn't very happy—Oh, I just don't know——"

"Another funny family," he amended shrewdly. "Red Brook breeds 'em apparently. Well we are certainly going to see each other sometime, somewhere. I heard Kitty ask you to come over next week. Let's meet there early next Tuesday—and leave early," he added with apparent irrelevancy. "There must be lots of nice walks around here."

"There are," she told him. "I'll say good-night now Malory, and—yes, I'll meet you at Kitty's."

"That's great. Good-night Melissa."

Faintly troubled she walked up the path. Clandestine meetings were no part of any plan of hers. "Laurentine will be all right pretty soon and then Malory will be coming right here to see me and we'll sit out here and talk and talk under the Chinaberry Tree. Oh Malory, Malory!"

She went to bed without a thought of Asshur.

.   .   .   .   .

On Tuesday she went to Kitty's. She wore a white crêpe dress with a cherry colored scarf and red and white sport shoes. Her hair was all curly all over her head and she looked, she knew it her-self, exactly as a young girl should look on a sum-mer's evening walking out with her young man. She met Malory on the path coming away from the house.

"What's the matter? Did you think I wasn't coming?"

"No," he answered joyously, "I was sure you'd be coming. But evidently the Browns weren't. They're all out. Isn't it grand Melissa? We'll take a bus and ride somewhere and then we'll walk back along some nice quiet road. Are there any parks around here Melissa? I've forgotten."

There was something better than a park around. There was the Romany Road. "Do you know that?"

"I think I do," he answered doubtfully, "but doesn't just about everybody go there?"

"No, because you can't get there in an auto—at least not very well. It's a dirt road you know and everybody goes on the good roads. It's very beau-tiful there."

"How do you know?" he queried a trifle sharply. "Here let's run and catch that bus." They jogged along in the evil smelling contrivance, talking spas-modically, but both were glad when they stepped out and started back to Red Brook and their trysting place. The little clearing off the Romany Road lay in an enchanted flood of moonlight, almost as bright as day, but with a magic which the daylight never knew. Even Melissa, infinitely more practical than the lad at her side was awe-stricken with the beauty of it.

"Oh Malory, it's lovelier than I ever dreamed."

"Then you've never been here before at night, Melissa?"

"Oh no, no, only in the day-time."

"Then this is our find, and we'll keep it to ourselves. Let's sit down,—but you mustn't get your lovely frock dirty." He stripped off his gray coat and she sat on it while he flung himself beside her. "Let's hear all about you Melissa—Honey."

She was a little startled, felt suddenly like a small girl. "You're not going to get gay, are you Malory?"

He laughed whole-heartedly. "Going to get gay! That sounds like Philadelphia. No, Melissa, I'm not going to get gay. I just like you that's all and I'm very happy, and your name means honey. Didn't you know that?"

"No, I didn't. But if it does mean that, why it's all right." She was very much pleased. "And if I talked like a Philadelphian it's because I am one. I was born there and went to school there until I came here."

"You didn't, really?"

"I did, really."

"And I was born here in Red Brook and went to school in Philadelphia until I came back here to live. So you see Melissa we were meant to meet. Tell me about yourself."

"There's nothing to tell," she replied, ashamed but truthful. "I'm the child of very poor parents. My father, John Paul, did odd jobs, I think. My mother never spoke about his work. She was a seamstress and did plain sewing. He died when I was a baby and mother looked after me until I was about fifteen. Then she married again and went to Chicago and sent me here to live with her sister. I don't know why she didn't take me with her," she ended, puzzling over this phenomenon for the first time.

"I'm glad she didn't take you—I'd probably never have met you. What was she like Melissa?"

"Well she wasn't pretty, but she was clean and—and stylish, but not elegant like Laurentine——"

"Who's Laurentine?"

"The cousin——"

"I live with," he mocked. "Yes, I remember the proud one who's sort of off you. Go on about your mother."

"Well as I said she was stylish—and—and modern," said Melissa, surprised at her ability to see her mother so objectively. "And she was always gay——"

"Happy?"

"No, I don't think she was always happy, but jolly and funny—and I can see now she must have been very courageous—I don't remember ever having seen her down-hearted though we were really awfully poor. Why we were terribly poor," said Melissa surprised. "Why Malory I don't believe anything stood between us and the poorhouse but her needle. Yet she was always laughing and gay."

"*Toujours gai, toujours riant,*" he said with a gravity at variance with his words. "And she passed it on to you. That's a gift, my dear, worth more than money." He had been very cheerful but he

relapsed for a second into the irritable languor
which she had first observed in him.

"Your folks aren't very gay, Malory?"

"Gay!" He almost laughed at the preposterous
idea. "They don't know the meaning of the word.
I don't know what's the matter with them. They
have fair health—the girls Reba and Harriett are
strong, though—wiry—I suppose you'd call them.
They do private catering and make a good living.
My mother has enough for her wants—at least as
long as she stays in this place, and her father—I'm
named for him—left me a little trust fund enough
for my education—provided I become either a doctor or an engineer."

"Which are you going to be?" she wanted to
know, suddenly alert.

"An engineer. They wanted me to be a doctor,
but I couldn't. I hate ugliness and illness in people."

"Where will you, a colored man, get a chance at
engineering?" she asked, practically.

"Well, I could go into civil service and draw plans
and bridges or I might go to South America and
build them. I'm not bothered about that side of it
but I've got to stay around here a while yet and I'd
like to see my mother in better spirits. I won't let
myself worry about the girls, they seem so deliberately, sort of stubbornly, depressed."

Silent, for a few seconds, they watched the broad
path of moonlight. Then Melissa stirred.

"I know something about melancholy people
Malory. Laurentine used to be inclined that way.
But she's much better now. What's back of your
sisters' unhappiness?"

He shook his head miserably. "I don't know. I can't imagine. It seems to me as a little child that our lives were normal enough, even merry. I remember my father very vividly, a jolly, rather noisy man, pretty selfish I fancy. But there was music and life and my mother used to practice little songs and sing them too. And I can remember their doing some dancing steps together. The girls ran in and out of the house like other girls I imagine. They all made over me—I'm the youngest and I wasn't such a strong youngster—that has always been my big quarrel," he ended disgustedly.

She was all interest. "It sounds great. What happened to change it all?"

"I don't know. I remember waking one morning and finding my father gone and my mother and the girls perfect wraiths. Ghosts you know. It was as though something, some essence of living had died in them in the night. I don't know any way to describe the change. At first I thought it would pass away. My mother was always terribly upset over any absence of my father. But they never got back to their old selves."

"Not even when your father came back?"

"He didn't come back,—at least not for the better part of a year. And when he did he was as much unlike himself, as my mother was, from the gay, lively creature I used to know. He was like a man stricken—with death I guess, for he never was well again and died in a few months."

"And of course that only deepened your mother's grief."

"Yes and no," he answered musingly. "You

know I've often puzzled over that. As a child I suppose I thought she was heartbroken over his death. But of late as I look back, it doesn't seem to me that it made any difference. Whatever had happened to her left its permanent mark on her and on the girls too, even before my father died. They sent me off to school in Philadelphia not long after. I lived with an old great-aunt who lived way back in the past. Certainly she wasn't unhappy but she was old and spent her whole life recalling memories of Isaac this one who was the first colored caterer in Philadelphia and Sarah that one who was the first student at the 'Institute for Colored Youth.' Oh I'm fed up with oldness and memories and grief."

He stretched out his arms. "I want life, sun, merriment, laughter. They've almost all been choked out of me."

"Since you love them so, maybe you could bring them into your home here and put some life into your mother and sisters."

He shook his head despondently. "No that's impossible. You can't picture what the atmosphere of our house is like. It's a regular dismal swamp. Did you ever read 'Marianna in the Moated Grange'—Tennyson's, you know?"

"No I had too hard a time struggling through the 'Idylls of the King.' I never read anything else."

"Well, in there it says:

'All day within the dreamy house,
    The doors upon their hinges creak'd;
The blue fly sung in the pane; the mouse
    Behind the mouldering wainscot shriek'd,

> Or from the crevice peer'd about.
>> Old faces glimmer'd thro' the doors,
>> Old footsteps trod the upper floors,
> Old voices called her from without.'

That's like my home and my folks."

She shivered a little as she had once before.

"Oh Malory, you'll have to snap out of it. It's too sad, too blue. I suppose you have to live there, sleep there, but you must spend most of your time outside with these boys and girls around here. They're jolly and lively, they'll get rid of your ghosts."

They were walking through the sweet-scented night toward her home.

"I don't know about them, but I do know about you. You can help me get rid of my ghosts if you'll let me see you often enough. Do you think you can manage that for me, Melissa?"

She was so strong, so sturdy in her own health and practicality and courage that she felt sorry for him. "Yes, I'll manage. I'll help you. I'll love it. When do you go away, Malory?"

"Oh I'm here to stay for quite a while yet. I'm going to the High School here for my Senior year. I'm over age because I've been out a lot on account of my health. But I'm O.K. now. Poor old Aunt Viny died last June. So there was nothing for me to do but come home."

Impulsively she said without coquetry, "I'll make it really home for you."

He came so close to her then and held her hand so tight as she stood by her gate that for a second she thought he would kiss her. She was confused and planless but she knew she didn't want this lad to hold her cheaply. So hastily withdrawing her hand she stepped back, ensconced herself safely on the other side of the gate.

"Good-night Malory. Be happy."

"Good-night, Melissa. I sure will. Just thinking of you will make me that."

She let herself in thinking with a grave joy how wonderful it was to be a girl. "We really are very responsible creatures." Her thoughts veered. "It looks as though I might have a pleasant year after all. I guess I won't be so lonely after all."

Up in her room the moonlight picked out a white patch upon her lavender bedspread. A letter. The light turned on revealed Asshur's familiar writing. He had written immediately on arriving and had despatched the missive by airmail.

A little thrilled at this evidence of his interest she sat down and read. He was home, he was tired, he was blue, he missed his girl so terribly. Three pages were full of his mourning. He ended with, "Be good Melissa, remember be good until I come and after; no matter what other girls do, you be both good and careful."

His constant reiterations sent her yawning to bed.

CHAPTER XIX

DR. DENLEIGH walked briskly up the path to Aunt Sal's house, rang the door-bell with assurance and was already standing with his hat in his hand when Aunt Sal opened the door. There was no mistaking her welcome. "Your smile is certainly a cure for what ails a man," he told her gayly. "I wish I could bottle it and serve it out to my patients as an elixir. Bottled smiles,—that's an idea, don't you think? How's Laurentine? Do you think she'd let me have lunch with her ? I've got a lot of calls to make in this neighborhood this afternoon."

Aunt Sal's genial smile and expression brought back some idea of the girl she must once have been. "Come right in Doctor. Laurentine's well and I know you can have lunch with her. I expected you even if she didn't, and I'll have everything ready in a jiffy."

She led him into the dining-room and presently Laurentine came in to greet him. "How do you do Dr. Denleigh?"

"I've told you two or three thousand times Miss Laurentine Strange that my name is Stephen. Now let's hear you say it. One, two, three! Try it. Stephen! Bet you can't pronounce it."

"Don't be silly, Stephen!"

"That's it! Good! Did it break your jaw to say it? Do you feel any internal complications? I have a bargain to make with you young lady. Give a starving fellow something to eat,—only three grains of corn, leddy,—and I'll take you for a buggy-ride."

"A buggy-ride! Oh Stephen, you don't mean to say you've ordered it and it's come!"

"The girl guessed right the very first time. Look out the window and you'll see my first Ford."

They looked out at the shining tricky little dark blue sports model.

"Oh Stephen isn't it wonderful, isn't it great? Will you let me drive her?"

"In return for one large and nourishing luncheon I will."

"H'm I'm not sure of the size but of course it will be nourishing. Mother always sees to that."

"It'll be large too, Doctor," Aunt Sal assured him. The three sat down to the savory repast. It was a day in September. Melissa was in school. Johnasteen and Matilda were having their meal in the sewing-room.

"Stephen's got his new car mother. Look at him bursting with pride."

Denleigh laughed. "I am. I admit it. I had a Cadillac in Washington, Mrs. Strange, but never felt half as proud of it as I do of this little Ford."

Aunt Sal knew more of his story than Laurentine. His car, his house and his savings all had been sacrificed in a long, tireless, vain effort to save his divorced wife in her last devastating illness.

She admired his pluck and good-humored persistence. "It means a come back for you, don't it Doctor?"

"The beginning of one, Mrs. Strange," he corrected her with a glance at Laurentine.

All three of them loved these days. The man because it gave him a glimpse of the domesticity which he loved and which he so ardently yearned to possess once more. Aunt Sal because she liked Denleigh for himself and felt she descried in him the qualities she would most like in a son—or a son-in-law. Laurentine because it seemed right and natural to have some one dropping in easily, matter-of-factly—just as guests dropped in on Mrs. Ismay or on the Italian girl across the way.

Beyond this she would not let her thoughts go.

In the late afternoon Denleigh returned for Laurentine to try out the little new car. Both of them invited Aunt Sal to accompany them. But she refused, retiring to her room, first to pray, secondly to savor the exquisite rightness of being a mother waiting for her daughter to arrive home from a drive with her beau. It was Friday she would have baked fish and macaroni for dinner—perhaps he would stay. . . .

  . . . . .

Denleigh and Laurentine sped along in the warm deep gold of the September afternoon which can be so sad unless it is made rather deliberately very, very happy. He was free until eight; he was beside the woman who, he felt, carried his future happiness in her shapely slender hands. He bent his fine head which the slightly graying hair at his temples rendered so distinguished and regarded her with pride.

"You know I like to look at you Laurentine. You seem so real."

She glanced at him, her dark eyes deep unfathomable pools in the apricot satin of her face.

"I wish you wouldn't talk like that Stephen!"

"Why not? You are the realest thing in the world to me these days. You're almost the only person I know who has been able vicariously to get down to the feel of life. Of course I know you think you've suffered and in a way you have—from awful loneliness and sensitiveness, don't think I under-rate them dear girl. But you're already so adjusted to life—without having had to be broken to

bits and remoulded as most of us have to be. . . .
I think that is why I like you. You're so ready for
living and yet so intact."

She parried him lightly, "I thought my face was
my fortune, kind sir."

"I know it. And in a sense it is. And yet Laurentine although I'm a man who cares a lot about
beauty, it wasn't that, that drew me to you. Irene
had cured me of that. I wanted to like a woman
again. I needed it. But I knew I never would unless I spied in her first something deeper, more essential than physical beauty—and yet as beautiful
as physical beauty. . . . I know I am expressing
myself poorly. But that first day I saw you at Millie
Ismay's it seemed to me I glimpsed it. That's why
I came back in and spoke to you again before leaving. I wanted to find out if I had really seen what
I thought I had. And it was there. I could see it
shining through your lovely face and your exquisite
dress like a beautiful jewel in a setting, almost, but
not quite as beautiful."

She could feel herself growing pale but she said
steadily. "I don't believe you really know about me
after all Stephen. I'm just—nobody, not only illegitimate, Stephen, but the child of a connection that
all America frowns on. I'm literally fatherless."

He frowned, his face almost as pale as her own.
"What bosh to talk to a physician! Biology trans-
cends society! Is that over your head darling?
I mean to say the facts of life, birth and death are
more important than the rules of living, marriage,
law, the sanction of the church or of man."

She didn't attempt to argue this.

.   .   .   .   .

After a while she started on a new issue. "Dr. Ismay has told me about you Stephen, how you used to be head of the National Medical Association.——"

"Only of the Tri-State, my dear."

"Well anyway you were in the running for all sorts of honor. You mustn't let pity,—chivalry, stand in the way of your career. Isn't there something about Cæsar's wife being above reproach?"

"I'm not Cæsar, I don't know. I don't care. A man knows what he wants Laurentine, you can count on that. Particularly a man who's been through what I have."

She murmured something about "bad blood."

"Don't ever say a thing like that to me again," he bade her sternly. "In the first place there's nothing in it in your case. In the second you've too much sense to think that even if there is such a thing as bad or good blood, marriage would affect it. Irene—my wife—was the daughter of one of the most socially prominent families in Washington but her father and mother were self-indulgent in their ways. Irene had never seen self-control practiced. As she grew older she too indulged herself. Marriage didn't change her.

"Now about yourself and then Laurentine—for God's sake let's have done with this. I deliberately found out all I could about your mother and Colonel Halloway and from all I hear the two of them must have loved each other devotedly. You must remember the times in which he lived and the social slant. It probably never entered his head to buck the concentrated opinion of his entire group by offering marriage. But he did everything else—he let the world know that your mother was his woman. He provided for her and for you. And in any event Laurentine it was their affair. It's over and done with. We've got nothing to do with it."

But in her heart she was not sure that it was over and done with. But of this she said nothing. "I'm not sure of myself yet Stephen," she told him bravely. "I made one mistake once about marriage —that is in my mind I did," she explained in answer to his startled look, "and you admit you actually made one. We've got to go into this thing very carefully I'm afraid. All my life I've wanted things to move in the ordinary normal way in which they seem to move for other people. But after all I was born out of the ordinary and I can't expect things to go that way. If we marry and it's a mistake I couldn't survive it."

Morosely he told her he didn't remember ever saying anything about marriage.

She burst out laughing then and quite without calculation or coquetry flung her arms about his neck and kissed him.

"You did that naturally enough," he murmured, appeased.

CHAPTER XX

AFTER they had parted Laurentine kissed her mother good-night and ascended to her room not to go to bed but to thresh certain matters over in her mind. Had she but known it her hesitancy and sobriety with regard to Dr. Denleigh and his intentions were indicative of a decided growth and breadth of vision on her part. Two years ago, a year perhaps, she would have rushed forward to meet the fulfillment implied by his frank conversations, but to-day she found herself somewhat to her astonishment in an entirely different mood. Something had happened to her.

She had loved, in spite of her brave words—she had loved Phil Hackett. She would have, once she had become his wife, gone to him in a frenzy of adoration and gratitude based on her appreciation of his willingness to take her—"bad blood," disgraceful parentage and all—under his protection; to give her his name to take the place of her own borrowed one. Hackett himself would have been amazed at the depth of devotion which he would have awakened. In all probability he would never meet with its like again.

Now she knew different values. Her talks with Mrs. Ismay, her arguments with Denleigh, or rather his responses had given her a different estimate of herself. She was young, she was strong, she was beautiful; she had been, in comparison with the relaxed standards of the day, almost ridiculously careful of her name and fame. In brief she was the epitome of all those virtues and restraints which colored men so arrogantly demand in the women they make their wives.

Yet in spite of all this, her head told her stubbornly, at the first glimpse of the difficulties which association with her would bring, Hackett had thrown her over. Her heart grew sick and faint again at the memory of those other days—she must never, never let herself in again for that sort of thing. She had seen now that there was something in life besides marriage. Mrs. Ismay, she recalled, clinging gratefully to that brave exemplar, had had disappointments,—oh many of them. And she had gone ahead with her work as a trained nurse, she had become head of a nursing establishment in Boston. It was while working there with no thought of marriage that she had met Dr. Ismay, had recognized him as he had her, as her mate and the two had consummated a union which neither had ever regretted.

Laurentine pondered on these matters. She liked Denleigh, she respected him, she was able to understand and appreciate the standards, created by his sad experience, by which he measured her. But she had nothing but his word by which to gauge his sincerity. Wounded to the quick by Hackett to whom she knew she had made the strongest appeal which a woman can make to a man, she had gone with no volition of her own through sheer instinct to the other extreme.

She wanted, she craved, love, companionship, protection. Her whole nature cried out for the complementing which a true marriage affords. That was it, a true marriage. But she was incapable now of entering into that relationship unless she was sure that the man who chose her, sought her with no thought of superiority, pity, or condescension in his heart.

"No," she told herself, sternly that night, sitting by the window, beholding, but not seeing the Chinaberry Tree, "I'm not happy now, but at least I have peace and self-respect. I wouldn't be happy without them and I might forfeit both in grasping at marriage. Stephen seems wonderful, but how can I tell, how can I test him? And what right have I to test him. . . . Perhaps God will show me a way. . . . I'll have to wait and see." And sitting there by the window she prayed.

In the morning she went resolutely about her household duties. Denleigh telephoned and asked permission to call that evening. Gravely and sweetly she told him to come, feeling her heart, her very being quicken in spite of herself. For all her brave resolutions she let herself dwell on the possibility of marriage with Stephen, let her imagination feast on its sweetness.

Her mother called in to her as she left the telephone. "The fall's really coming Laurentine. I slept cold last night. I wish you'd hunt out some blankets for me for to-night. They're in your closet ain't they? Or have Johnasteen do it."

"I'll do it myself mother," she replied dutifully. She made rather a point of not asking the sewing girls to help about the house. "I'll do it right now before I sit down. They're in Melissa's closet though I think."

Melissa had gone to school. Laurentine pushed her door open half regretfully, she so seldom entered this room. "I must be kinder to her again," she thought, thinking of the pleasant times they had spent here. When her cousin had first come the older girl had often visited her to try on a dress, brush her hair, to suggest some special adornment which was to have its telling effect on the particular

swain who was arriving that evening. Quite without
jealousy or rancor of any kind Laurentine had
helped and advised Melissa, reliving, or rather
living for the first time her own vanished first youth
in the latter's spontaneity and fresh enjoyment.

Of late she had observed the girl's wistfulness
and shyness in her presence and her heart contracted
a little at the thought that she who had herself suffered so much and so consciously, should deliberately and wantonly wound that fresh, trusting youth.

"After all it's not Melissa's fault that Phil Hackett is a cad," she thought generously. She was so
happy this morning. The September sun poured
in the window, touching the articles on Melissa's
quaint little dressing table. To look at that table
always amused Laurentine. She herself could have
been taken for a Parisian model, her elegance, her
freshness, her discreet use of discreet scents and
powders. But Melissa was the frank coquette;
Laurentine could not imagine how in her environment she became possessed of a knowledge of these
first aids to beauty.

Melissa had creams, cleansing ones, tissue-build-
ing ones—of all things with her gorgeous youth!—
vanishing creams, bleaching creams, tints for darkening the eyelids, tiny brushes for eyelashes, tweez-
ers to shape her eyebrows, pastes for finger-nails,
powders in several tints. Laurentine pulled open a
drawer to descry strange combs and curling irons.
Melissa's hair in its natural state was crinkly, even
"nappy," but no one would ever have suspected it.
Smiling, her cousin closed the drawer. "She really
is a nice kid," she murmured.

The blankets neatly folded reposed in the top of the closet. She would get down three, one for each of them, Melissa should have the pale green one even though that was her own special favorite, it would blend in better with the lavender and heliotrope trimmings, she thought, glancing with artistic satisfaction at the cluster of deeply purple asters in the vase on the girl's little writing table.

Something fell out of the blanket and clattered to the floor—a small book—it lay there open on its face. Laurentine picked it up, glanced indulgently at its purple and dull gold binding—evidently Melissa spent all her small stock of pin-money on this kind of thing. She turned it over, expecting to find she hardly knew what, a poem, some cherished directions for improving the complexion—and saw her own name—"poor Laurentine."

A quick wave of distaste and anger ran over her. Without grasping the significance of what she was doing she stood and read the diary as she had never read the most fascinating romance. Read all of Melissa's silly out-pourings about her own unstained, unimpeachable integrity, read of her pity and yet, it seemed to Laurentine's angry eyes, her barely concealed satisfaction at Aunt Sal's and her daughter's sorry plight, their ancient shame. . . .

Laurentine threw the book from her as though it stung her. "The miserable—brat!" she told herself. "To think of Judy's foisting her on us . . . with those ideas in her head. And dependent on mother for every crumb of bread, for every inch of shelter. I could hate her." She stood stock still. "But you won't, Laurentine, you mustn't." She picked up the book again, thrust it into a fold of the green blanket, replaced that and another in the closet, and arranged the third on her mother's bed.

With something of her old stoic resignation, she went down to her work. But the day so happily begun was spoiled for her. She could not bring herself to respond in any but the briefest manner to Melissa's greeting when the young girl returned from school. It gave her a sense of cruel satisfaction to see the mobile, childish face cloud and quiver ever so slightly at her coldness. "Why should she care what sort of treatment she receives from 'such a worm as I?'" she asked herself, quoting an old-fashioned hymn.

But she was dissatisfied and disgusted with herself. In the evening, distraite and bewildering she amazed Denleigh with her moody restlessness. She was sparkling, capricious, remote, momentarily tender. But he didn't mind. Manlike, he rejoiced in this earnest of new fields to conquer. "Honesty and loyalty are what I'm looking for, Laurentine. I know you have both of these qualities. I don't believe I'd like it too well if you did turn out to be too sweetly reasonable."

CHAPTER XXI

ASSHUR'S letters came regularly. Boyish, completely uninspired missives they were. Following almost a regular routine, they assured Melissa of his love for her, told of his advance in his studies, and ended with his constant, and, to the girl, wearying admonishments, "to be good, very, very good."

Melissa read them through, faithfully, and answered them with equal fidelity. She owed much to Asshur. Thanks to him and to Ben Davis and Herbert Tucker, but mostly to Asshur she had tasted the joys of unalloyed belledom for almost two years. That is belledom in the particular circles in which she moved. She had, she felt, known what it seemed to be a queen.

In these days she was no longer a queen. But she felt no regret. She had never known a more satisfying existence. Save for one blot—that of Laurentine's sustained and increased chill of disapproval—she had never experienced such rapture in living.

From being queen she had become a lady-in-waiting. But a lady-in-waiting in what surroundings! Kitty Brown had "taken her up," had liked her sincerely and because the girls who had previously been her closest intimates lived, every one of them, in nearby but none the less distant townships, Melissa, by sheer force of propinquity became Kitty's chum, her pal, her right-hand man, her side-kick. She had the good sense not to presume on this, she rarely went to Kitty's uninvited, never spoke of their friendship to the Epps and Newton girls, with whom she had once been so familiar, and because in her heart she did not care who was the dominant spirit as long as that spirit provided her with plenty of good times, she made no attempt to cross her new friend even in her slightest wish.

Kitty was selfish, Kitty was wilful, Kitty was vain. But she was warm-hearted, generous, lively

and original. Her parents, once worried by the
girl's fretfulness at having to reside in a small town
after the social possibilities of New York, and assured of Melissa's essential respectability, welcomed
their daughter's new friend warmly and left the
pair for the most part to their own devices.

But it is doubtful if this alone would have suf-
ficed to render Melissa so entrancingly happy. The
real source of the genuine ecstasy which she fairly
exhaled these days was of course·Malory Forten.
Melissa had admired Ben and Herbert and had
deeply liked and even become attached to Asshur
Lane. But with Malory she had fallen deeply,
completely, overwhelmingly in love. It seemed to
her that he was all that any girl could desire. That
curious strain in her which so insisted on conventionality and mere gentility found a vast satisfaction
in Malory's slight, rather delicate figure, his low
voice, his unobtrusive, perfect manners, his neat, in-
conspicuous clothes.

Even at his age, twenty, his views were definitely
fixed. He believed in the church, which, however,
he would not attend in Red Brook because his sisters went there and he would not accompany them.
He believed in family, in the Republican party, in
moderate wealth, a small family, a rather definite
place for women. He planned to be an engineer
and follow just that profession.

As purposeful as Asshur, he lacked completely
his unconscious rival's catholicity of standard. Life,
according to young Lane, was a gift to be relished.
You might start out with a particular end in view,
but there was no reason why you should not enter

and enjoy an occasional by-path. Asshur thought he would be a scientific farmer because he liked the soil; farming seemed to him an essential industry; kingdoms, governments, business corporations might come and go but the earth and its productivity would always remain. Transportation too, he used to tell Melissa, would always be important. He thought it quite conceivable that he might be an aviator. He liked the idea of a large family.

"I should like," he told her gravely, "to have about eight children. You could have the whole world right in your own house then."

Melissa, who thought of farms and aviation in terms of dirty overalls and thick shoes and who had the modern girl's own clear ideas on birth control, used to shudder a little and change the subject. Still there was about him a breeziness, an effect of daring and more important still the promise of great loyalty, which appealed to her.

Malory was not especially daring or breezy, but he was, she was sure, loyal. His chief appeal to her was his appreciation of her essential gayety and vitality. It was so easy for her to give and so important, apparently, for him to have. Gradually the two fell into the habit of spending all their spare time together whenever this was possible. It was here that Laurentine's attitude thwarted and chafed. Melissa winced even now when she thought of that evening when she had been on the verge of asking to have Malory come to the house. She had always taken great care to do this sort of thing from the time of her first arrival, not so much out of respect for Aunt Sal as that it satisfied in herself that desire which she had to appear the well-bred, carefully protected girl.

Laurentine, after a brief period of relaxation, had become, it seemed to her, chillier than ever. Well, she couldn't help that. And after all Laurentine never had expressed herself unpleasantly on the subject of company.

. . . . .

Melissa had come in from school, her mind made up. At dinner she began, ignoring the apprehension which Laurentine's marked coolness awakened in her.

"Aunt Sal, there's a boy I see at school every day, he's been very nice—sometimes he helps me with my Latin. He'd like to come to see me and I'd like him to; it's lonely since Asshur's been gone and the other boys. Can he come?"

Her aunt looked up from her plate, vaguely astonished at the plaintiveness of her request.

"Come, why of course he c'n, if he's a nice boy. I miss Asshur myself. What did you say this new boy's name was?"

Before the girl could reply Laurentine intervened. "I don't think that would be wise, mother. Melissa can do without so much company. I used to think Asshur was around here quite too much. This is Melissa's last year in High School, it seems to me we should see that nothing interferes with her getting the most out of it. It's all right for her to go to Kitty Brown's occasionally and for Kitty to come here, but she needn't have every Tom, Dick and Harry in the town traipsing after her. . . . Excuse me, please."

She rose hastily, really infinitely ashamed of her unkindness. But she was unable to banish the thought of the diary from her mind. Melissa and her pity for "poor Laurentine!" Well, she'd soon realize that "poor Laurentine" was some one to be reckoned with!

Aunt Sal, in surprise, said: "What's happened to you two girls, Melissa? I don't remember your quarrelin'."

But Melissa, with the bright insouciance of youth, shook it off with a shrug of her slender shoulders. "I'm sure I don't know, Aunt Sal. She's had a mad on me for a long time. It's all right, don't you bother, you sweet old thing. I don't care whether he comes or not. I just asked because he was always pestering."

Humming, she set about clearing off the table. But her mind under her calm exterior was busy thinking. As though Laurentine could separate her from Malory! See him! She almost laughed aloud. There were so many possibilities, school, movies, occasionally at Kitty's, though she thought it best for purely feminine reasons to be careful about this . . . other girls, when it came to personable young men, being frequently unknown quantities. There were walks, the lonely Romany Road for choice, there were the long trips she sometimes took to deliver dresses for her cousin. Her resources were endless. She'd see Malory as often as she pleased—and of course they could write to each other. She burst into a trill of song at the thought of those letters. She'd write one to-night.

.   .   .   .   .

Afterwards she sat down dutifully enough with her cousin and aunt in the living-room and began to prepare her lessons. Malory, she knew, would telephone, she had told him she would let him know whether or not he could come to the house, never doubtful for a moment of the issue.

The telephone rang. Laurentine, who was nearest, answered it. A male voice announced himself as Tucker and asked for Melissa. Silently her cousin passed over the receiver, sat down and listened mechanically to the meaningless, somewhat slangy conversation. Melissa ending on an "oh yeah," returned to her Latin composition.

The three sat more or less in silence in the pleasant room; Aunt Sal pored over one of the modern tabloids. Reading was not the easiest of tasks for her. She liked these little newspapers that told their story so easily and comprehensively in a few dramatic pictures with just the necessary number of words beneath. Laurentine was writing to Mrs. Ismay who had gone to Boston for a while. The telephone jangled anew and again Laurentine arose automatically, placed the receiver to her ear.

"Hello," said a nice, boyish voice. "This is Malory. Is that you, Melissa?"

"Just a moment," said Laurentine. "Melissa!" The girl's side of the conversation was sufficiently innocuous. Laurentine composed herself to her writing and then paused for a moment, struck by something her relative was saying. "No, I'm awfully sorry. No, I can't see you. You see my cousin doesn't approve of my having callers. Oh yes, of course, *she* has them. Well, I will too when I'm as old as she is. Uh-huh! Well, good-bye. Yes. Good-bye-e-e."

She went back to her seat, passing on the other side of the table at which Laurentine sat writing. The older girl raised her dark, serious eyes to meet the quizzical, searching glance of her cousin's green ones.

Something like the flash of rapiers passed between them.

It was war.

CHAPTER XXII

IT was not unnatural, not even unusual that Laurentine's hostility strengthened Melissa's determination to see more of Malory. What was significant, however, was the fact that the unexpected opposition steadied her, cleared her head. She had always known what she wanted, her desire had been an unwavering, light-streaming star before her, but she had not always estimated ways and means of obtaining it. Now she reviewed both. She meant to marry Malory. He represented everything that she wanted, conventionality, security, a certain narrow beauty, definite position. "And besides, I love him, love him," she said to herself and paused in her Saturday morning task of ordering the kitchen, struck by the awful significance of those words. "And he loves me, I know it. So it couldn't be wrong, could it, God, for me to try to get him?"

She was not much given to praying, so she returned to a scrutiny of her affairs. She was as sensible as a girl of her years and experience could well be. Therefore it was not in her intention to marry at once or in secret. Plenty of time for that. With her clear vision it would never do, she realized, to be a millstone around her lover's neck. That would defeat her own purpose. No, there were four, perhaps even five years before them besides this year in High School. She would employ those years in making herself as essential to Malory as a woman could be to a man. Perhaps it would be as well to be engaged—why of course they'd have to be engaged, she thought to herself, realizing with a sudden pang of fear that for four of those five years she and Malory would have to be apart. He would be going to the Massachusetts School of Technology and she would be—where?

Unless of course she too could go to Boston—maybe she would go. But money was uncertain, she had no idea of Aunt Sal's resources, and here was this new problem of Laurentine's unfriendliness. She'd just have to make the most of this year, that was all. Not see Malory! She would see him, she would encourage him, she would enfold him with sympathy and attention and kindliness. And at the end of the school year how wonderful it would be to come to Laurentine with Malory's class ring on her third finger and say: "Cousin Laurentine, Malory Forten and I are engaged to be married."

She would make a plan and stick to it.

.   .   .   .   .

What she could not take into her calculations, poor child, was the awful pull which her newly wakened emotions would sooner or later impose upon her will. Modern youth, after all, does not differ so greatly from the youth of all ages. Melissa, in common with her contemporaries, was far better acquainted with fundamental biological facts than any girl of her age, thirty years ago. But in spite of her knowledge she was as unprepared as any of them to undergo the bewilderingly sweet agony of first love.

Fortunately she was not at that stage yet. Meanwhile life was golden, glorious. School was hard, but not too hard. Malory did her Latin carefully for her every day in advance. He himself needed only chemistry and physics. He had brought enough credits from Philadelphia with him to cover his other demands. Housework was easy—she had long since found out that playing the part of Pentecost to old Mr. Stede brought ample and satisfactory rewards in blackened stoves, scrubbed oil cloth and scoured bathtub.

Johnasteen and Matilda had both grown to like her and could find time to drape and fit the bright ends and remnants of silk and tweed which she brought them, purchased with the change bestowed on her weekly by Aunt Sal. If Laurentine had chanced to look in the girl's diary now she would have seen no reference to her own pitiful condition or to poor Asshur with his tender bi-weekly admonishments, or even of Kitty Brown. Those pages spoke now of Malory and Malory only.

. . . . .

For it was he who had transformed her life. It was he who introduced to her the joys of real companionship, the pleasures of oneness in sympathy and understanding. With Asshur and his endless tennis, rowing and skating, she had tasted the supremeness of physical well-being; she had loved being vital, and strong and young. However, he had been merely a pal. But Malory was the essential lover. He read poetry to her, the rather obvious poetry of beauty and of romance, Tennyson, Rossetti and Swinburne, what he could interpret of the intensely masculine emotionalism of Browning, the divine nebulousness of the Ode on the Intimations of Immortality. He converted the Romany Road into Fairyland. He showed her the trees, the moon, the stars and the sunset as a background for the drama of their own love, and of other lovers. He made of her a queen. With him bread and butter, houses, birth, money, clothing were necessary evils in an existence whose real object was the pursuit of compatibility, warmth, gayety, companionship and a certain almost platonic concept of love.

Neither of them knew as yet the tug of passion. The boy, as the girl, moved in a divine trance of beauty and ecstasy and thought of marriage only as a means to conserve this same beauty, this same ecstasy. In the intensity of this feeling even Melissa's hard-headed singleness of purpose wavered and blurred. At times she forgot her determination to marry this boy and when the realization of her purpose returned to her sometimes at night lying straight and still and reminiscent in her little gay bed she wept tears of joy to think that no such fixity of intention was necessary. All this and more was waiting for her. In good time it would all be hers anyhow.

.   .   .   .   .

"Malory," she told him, shivering deliberately with the delight of the nipping November weather, coming through the dark streets from the little public library, "Malory, after all, it is sort of nice that Laurentine wouldn't let me have callers, isn't it? It's just kind of wrapped us in a sweet secret, like a warm covering. If I live to be a hundred, I'll never forget this summer and fall. It is lovely, don't you think?"

The boy nodded assent, holding her gloved hand more tightly in the crotch of his arm. "Still," he added with the male desire for comfort, "it would have been a lot nicer if she had. Think what fun we'd have sitting in your kitchen this minute, snug and warm with perhaps a beaker of cocoa and a doughnut. Tell you what, Honey, it's tough on a decent guy having to meet you around like this. Why on earth did she have to pick on me? She used to let that Lane fellow come in, didn't she?" he finished jealously.

Melissa giggled delightedly. "Don't call Asshur that Lane fellow. He's a grand lad, wait till you meet him, you'll think so too. Laurentine wasn't picking on you, silly, she doesn't know you from Adam. She's just awfully unhappy all the time, that's what's the matter with her and she's started taking it out on me for the last year or so."

"What's she got to be unhappy about?"

She thought it best to be cautious. "Fell out with her beau I guess and I think it makes her kind of

sore to see me having such a good time. For she
certainly wasn't that way at first," she reflected,
"and there used to be lots of boys and girls around
here then."

"I suppose you still hear from Lane?"

"There's no way I can stop him writing, is there?
Yes, I still hear from him and answer him too. I
have to," she added honestly. "He was so kind, so
good to me before you came, Malory. This is such
a queer place to live in—blows so hot and cold.
One minute you have lots of friends and the next
minute you have none. At first everybody was
lovely and then they all sort of fell away, except
Asshur and Herbert Tucker and Ben Davis."

"H'm, a lot of boys. What're you trying to do,
Melissa—razz me? What about Kitty Brown?
Isn't she a good friend?"

"Yes, oh yes! The best friend. I'd have perished without her. But she isn't—of the town,
exactly—she's just a law unto herself. But at first
the girls were around here in droves—it was so
lively. I don't know what made them change so.
It must be something in the air. For at first Laurentine was grand to me too, and then she got so
different. If it hadn't been for Aunt Sal and Kitty
—and,—and Asshur, I'd have perished I'm telling
you."

"Asshur always gets into it, doesn't he? I suppose he asked you to marry him."

"Right-o!"

"Are you going to, Melissa?"

She went closer to him then, she laid her round,
rosy face crowned with the aureole of her soft

blown hair and her green beret, sweetly, confidingly against his rough coat. She looked up at him, in spite of herself, her whole heart in her eyes.

"What do you think, Malory?"

. . . . .

He walked down the street from her gate, shaken with ecstasy. For the first time in his life he thought seriously of money. His Aunt Viny had left him money too, but it also was all tied up; it also was for his education. "If I could only have that to do as I pleased with,—if we could just get married right away. . . . Oh, Melissa!" he groaned. . . .

The light burned dimly in the hall of his home as he entered . . . lights burned dimly all over this house, he'd discovered irritably. The second day after his arrival he had rushed out and bought a powerful bulb for his room and the bathroom, and the hall too. . . . No one had remarked on it but the dim bulb in the hall had been replaced. "I'd like to smash the damn thing," he thought with the sullenness in which dwelling in this place so often enveloped him. He let the faded-brown screen door slam to behind him. This was another source of irritation; when the summer had passed he offered to take it down, but his sisters had remonstrated.

"It's always been up there," Reba had said tonelessly.

. . . . .

As the door slammed she came now to the head of the stairs and called down. "Is that you, Malory?" Her listless voice was almost utterly without inflection.

"Yep it is. Where are you all? Gone to bed?"

"Mother has. Harriett's in her room, and I'm in mine. Be sure to lock the door before you come up."

"Before I come up! Why, aren't you coming down any more?"

"No."

All this time he'd been talking from the bottom of the stairs to the trailing gray mistiness of her figure at the top. Now he put a tentative foot on the step. "Say, what's the matter with all of you, going to bed before ten o'clock! Say, I'm going to bring a gang of folks in here one night. Fellow's got to have a little life."

She came down a step or two. "What girls and fellows? I didn't know you knew anybody."

"Don't be silly! How could I help knowing scads of people in this little place? Why, there're a couple of awfully decent fellows; Davis and Tucker," he came up a step or two, "and Kitty Brown, father's a doctor, and—" he cleared his throat, so near she seemed—"a girl named Melissa Paul, and——"

"Whom did you say—Melissa Paul?"

He tried to keep any truculence out of his tone. "Yes, why not? Do you know her?" He came nearer, peering to read her inscrutable face in the dim light.

She hesitated the slightest possible fraction of time. "No, I don't," she said listlessly, "but I've heard of her. I'm not sure she's so nice, Malory. I think a lot of boys go there. . . . Who else did you say?"

"Oh I don't know, girl named Adamson comes

from Short Hills, or Little Rocks—I don't know the names of these places around here. Believe it's Morristown she comes from. Well, what do you say?"

Her voice came steadily. "I don't believe Mother would like it." She started upstairs. "Don't forget to lock the door, Malory."

He ran down the stairs noisily. "What the heck! Reba makes me sick, she makes me sick!" he told himself savagely. He foraged in the icebox, found some cold apple pie and cheese and took it up to his bright room which his own efforts and persistence had made comfortable.

"Of all the incomprehensible ways to live! What could make people like that, I wonder?" Stonily objective, he surveyed his family in his mind. He had no criticism to make of his mother—old people were like that, he guessed—well no, Aunt Viny wasn't like that, she was gay enough with her cronies, he could hear her cackling now. But his mother, a much younger woman, was for some inexplicable reason, done with life. She was, he knew it, an empty shell.

As for his sisters—the idea of Reba's daring to criticize Melissa because boys went to see her! Of course they went to see her—so alive and bright and warm she was! Didn't moths fly about a flame? He remembered then Laurentine's edict. Wouldn't Reba be astonished if she knew that he, her cherished brother, wasn't allowed to cross her threshold?

Well, his own home would be different from this. There'd be lights all over the house, and music and

Melissa and himself and friends—yes and children.
His children! Melissa's children! . . . He snapped
off the light and lay face downward for hours in
the warm, sweet darkness.

CHAPTER XXIII

NOW that the fall was setting in, Laurentine
played bridge at Mrs. Ismay's on Wednes-
days instead of junketing down to Newark in the
little car to the movies. About seven, she would
go over to the Doctor's house, walking gravely and
happily through the quiet streets, the crackling
leaves swirling about her or breaking brittlely under
her feet. At such times her heart was singing a
little song within her. She was like any other young
woman, she thought, going off to spend a pleasant
evening with a pleasant neighbor, with no longing
or yearning in her heart, no goal to be striven for or
reached, no sick memories to be crushed down, covered with the trivial occupation of the moment.

At such times she said to herself, "God *is* in his
heaven, all's well with the world." There was
nothing during these days that she wanted changed
except perhaps her feeling about Melissa. She was
ashamed of this feeling. Yet she could not shake
it off. There were times when she was obsessed
with the idea that some time all this beauty and
peace and satisfaction in which she moved would
cease and that in some obscure way its departure
would be traceable to Melissa. She never spoke
sharply or even reprovingly to her young cousin

but in her heart lay, coiled like a tiny serpent, a little current of dislike ready to rear and strike at a moment's notice.

Sometimes Dr. Denleigh, who had opened his office in the district in which she lived, would rush over to her house in his new Ford, honk madly outside her gate, and drive her with equal madness and utter disregard of traffic signals, over to Dr. Ismay's, drop her and return to his increasing practice.

She would go in then and she and Millie Ismay would talk with the complete intimacy and interest which women absolutely *en rapport* with each other employ. Millie, who was comparatively indifferent to her appearance outside, was amazingly given over to a consideration of her indoor apparel, her house dresses and négligées. Often Laurentine brought with her one of her latest books of modes, and scraps of material used in fashioning apparel for Mrs. Judge Manners and her lovely and exclusive, newly-married daughter, Mrs. del Pilar. Laurentine would hold the cloth up against Mrs. Ismay's skin and drape with her magic fingers the stuff into marvelous fold and line, employing an enthusiasm and liveliness of interest such as she rarely manifested to her customers.

"This blue is heavenly for you, Millie. My dear, I thought of you to-day as soon as Mrs. del Pilar showed it to me. If you want me to I'll order yours along with hers, so you can get the benefit of my discount. You'll probably be the first colored woman in Red Brook to be wearing lounging pajamas!

"See, I'm going to cut them quite low. You've such a lovely back and I'll make you a little jacket to slip on when you have company. I'll make it in this Spanish Tile color. This is just a scrap, but can you get the idea?"

Mrs. Ismay was enraptured. "Oh, Laurentine, it'll be wonderful! Nobody thinks of such delightful color combinations as you, or gets such lovely lines. When I think how humbly I went to your house that time asking you to make me just the plainest sort of a dress—a mere fig-leaf as it were!"

"And I suppose I was so haughty!"

"Oh, absolutely! Frozen, unapproachable! I raved about you even then. I came home and said to Doctor: 'Positively, Doctor, that Strange girl.' . . ."

"Millie, if you start all that nonsense about me again!"

"All right then, I won't. You know I thought I really wouldn't speak to you again."

"And then you came up to me after all, that Sunday. I can imagine how lonely and forlorn I looked!"

"You didn't, you looked like a lovely statue. I wanted Doc to see you and judge you for himself. You know you really did bowl him over that Sunday afternoon."

"I don't know about that. But I know that that was the beginning of the nicest days I've ever spent in my life."

Mrs. Ismay smiled, "That wasn't because of your meeting Doctor and me, that was because you met

Denleigh for the first time. Is he coming here to-night?"

Laurentine affecting a casualness which she was far from feeling, her lovely face faintly flushing, would say she was sure she didn't know.

.   .   .   .   .

But of course he always came, as he came on one special night which Laurentine treasured in her memory. The coolness of the November weather had subsided, had stepped aside, so to speak, to allow one final gesture of departed Summer. Mrs. Ismay, in her blue pajamas, Laurentine in a deep peach dress, with still deeper tinted lace arranged in the smart, sparse fashion of the day at neck and wrists, Mrs. Brown, Kitty's mother, encased trimly in a cleverly modern black and white gown, were playing bridge with Dr. Ismay. He was impatient to be on with the game and yet half pleased too to recline, a spare, resigned figure in his chair and wait for their chatter to die down a bit and give the game a chance. It gave him a gratefully accepted opportunity to study Laurentine, whose beauty and grace always afforded him the satisfaction obtained by looking at a beautiful piece of art.

Denleigh's arrival was the signal for the game to break up. Dr. Ismay always rebelled at this. "Confound it, Stephen, why is it these women never can play after you come in? Seems to me I never have a satisfactory game of bridge any more. Here Laurentine, child, let's see that scorer!"

Laurentine obediently passed it over. She loved this moment, she loved the manner in which Denleigh after greeting his hosts and any chance guests, found his way to her side, and paused there, remained there, utterly content.

"Well," said Mrs. Ismay, "we might just as well break up. You know in five minutes, you'd be clamoring to play Black Jack with Stephen anyway. Here, I'll put this little table over here so as not to disturb him and you can bring your chair up. No, don't move Laurentine. I've got the best mousse in the world for us. I thought since to-day was so warm that we might try that kind of refreshment just once more. It seems so nice and summery."

She served her dainty repast. The men deep in their game, stopped and wolfed theirs down. Laurentine and Mrs. Brown and Mrs. Ismay ate slowly, dwelling on unimportant nothings. Mrs. Brown, remembering Kitty's overwhelming desire for one of Laurentine's creations, approached the matter obliquely.

"Mrs. Ismay's pajamas are lovely, Miss Strange. She says you designed them."

"And made them," struck in Mrs. Ismay before Laurentine could answer. "She says I'm the first colored woman in Red Brook, she believes, to be wearing lounging pajamas."

"Except myself, of course," Laurentine interposed, laughing. "I've had some beautiful green ones for two or three months now. I usually try these exotic styles out on myself before I allow my clients to take them seriously. I think Millie's are very smart, myself. You ought to have some too, Mrs. Brown. A black and white combination like that dress you're wearing would be splendid for you."

"I imagine it would be hard to get them to set right, isn't it?"

"Oh no," said Laurentine, warming to her subject. "Patterns nowadays are very easy to follow. I cut mine out myself—I usually do draft patterns for myself. But my cousin, Melissa, doesn't know how to draft, so when she made her pajamas—she usually has one of everything I have—she just bought a pattern and followed it carefully. She has a beautiful pair—brown and white they are." With some faint idea of making amends to Melissa for any possible injustice, she added graciously, "She's a clever young one."

"That's right, she is your cousin," said Mrs. Brown, rocking comfortably. "I know you live in the same house, but I never think of you as being related. Wonder why? Yes, she is clever and bright. My Kitty is very much taken with her. I just left her at my house as I came out, talking to Malory. I suppose you know him?" she asked idly.

But Laurentine said placidly that she didn't know any Malorys. Mrs. Brown, on the verge of remarking that Malory was only his first name, lost interest in the conversation as Mrs. Ismay came in with the mousse. Mrs. Brown loved good cheer and as the ice was as attractive in appearance as it proved later to be in flavor, her attention was completely diverted.

Laurentine thought in amusement: "The little wretch! I might have known she'd manage to get ahead of me. I can't have her meeting boys on the outside, though. Guess eventually I'll have

to let him come to call. I wonder who these Malorys are. I'll ask Stephen." But with the consciousness of his name in her mind she forgot all
about Malory and Melissa too, remembering only
that soon this pleasantly uneventful evening would
be over and that she and Stephen would be going
home.

. . . . .

They left at last. Denleigh gallantly crowded
Mrs. Brown into the car with himself and Laurentine. She lived only two blocks away. At last she
too had left them and the man and woman faced
each other in the tingling excitement which was
more precious to him even than to her, since he had
long since thought never to know its like again.

"I almost wish we didn't have the car," he complained. "It's such a heavenly night. I can put it
up and walk—shall we?"

But she had a better plan; a plan whose significance not even he could divine. Since the night
was indeed so heavenly, the sky so clear, the stars
so twinkling, the air so mellow and balmy, yet in-
vigorating, they would drive around to her house
and sit for awhile under the Chinaberry Tree.

She was trembling with inward eagerness. The
trivial incident had for her the force of a ritual.
She had ridden, walked and talked with Hackett,
but she had never sat with him beneath the Tree.
Perhaps silently she was pledging herself to Denleigh.

Afterwards she remembered how he looked as
he sat there. He had on a light-weight overcoat
and a soft hat which he wore well over his eyes, but

this, later, he pulled off and removing her little cap let his well-shaped head rest lightly against hers. By moving her rounded face ever so slightly, she could feel the thrilling roughness of his closely-shaven cheek against her own. She put up her hand and gently touched the little, carefully-shaped patch of hair before his ear. She felt a strange, permeating sense of well-being in being thus close to him, in being so intimate. It seemed to her she sensed for the first time the oneness which a successful marriage could bring, with no idea of its social benefits or security. Denleigh caught her hand and laid it against his lips, then moving closer to her, he sat, his arm about her, long legs stretched out well in front of him, a cigarette in his left hand, his dear face against her hair——

She thought of Melissa, Asshur, the Chinaberry Tree and almost swooned with satisfaction. But aloud she said, looking toward his shapely, sizable shoes, "You have good understandings, haven't you, Stephen?"

And his laughing answer, "The better to support you with, my dear."

.   .   .   .   .

Ah, no moments with Hackett had ever been like these—she doubted if any moments, no matter how perfect their setting, could ever have been like these with her first lover. And suddenly, she who knew nothing about men, knew completely the difference between the love of a man like Denleigh and that of a man like Hackett. Never had she felt like this. It seemed to her she needed no further proof of his loyalty—the fact that he was able to afford her this complete, this absolute sense of peace, of well-being with the world, was sufficient proof that he was as much hers as she was her own possession. And one does not mention one's loyalty to one's self.

At the next opportunity she would make him any promise he wanted. And they could marry—any time they wanted, she suddenly discovered. Almost she was ready to shout at the knowledge of her small independence. She had some few savings —why, she had a dowry, a French girl's *dot*. Suddenly she saw the value of a system which she in common with most Americans had despised. Denleigh had been heavily taxed by his former marriage, his divorce, and his wife's fatal illness. If necessary he could use her money and they would start all over again. Alone, poor. Eminently practical person though she was, she liked that. They'd have a little house—away from pitying Melissa—thank God—she smiled in the darkness—and away from her mother. But her mother would like that. She knew her mother!

If he wanted her to, she would keep on sewing, or she'd give it up, and just keep house for him. She'd cook and sew—cook food and sew on clothing which he had bought for her. She'd have to go to him for money . . . and perhaps there'd be children, his first wife had never given him a child.

"Oh Stephen, Stephen," she thought like all loving women the world over. "We're going to be so happy! Stephen, you'll be so surprised when you speak to me. . . ."

.   .   .   .   .

But although Stephen spoke, he did not speak of love. Instead he began to talk to her, as men do to the women they love and trust, about himself, about his youth, about that strange, far-off, lonely little boy which he had been, years and years ago.

"Lonely, even though I had ten brothers and sisters, Laurentine. I was the youngest. I was my mother's pet. The older children resented, half laughingly the love she bore me; my father, I see it now, was half jealous of the hold which I had on her attention. . . . She was a wonderful woman, not beautiful like you, but brave and courageous, undaunted—she'd have moved heaven and earth to get the things she wanted for her children and husband. . . . She'd have gone through hell for me."

They had been poor people in Charleston, South Carolina. But, at first, happy. His father had kept a store—he was genial, he meant well, the neighbors liked him. In a way prosperity shone on him and yet a persistent bad luck. He tried to educate his children. "But eleven children are too many for even a rich man to look after," Denleigh said musing. "The ones he educated died before he did, the others rebelled and started out in easy openings that got them nowhere. And then they died. Strong fellows too, they were."

Presently the father died—of grief and disappointment and of the ceaseless, unequal struggle forced on him by life. He knew he was dying. He called Stephen to him, the lad was but eleven. He said, "My boy, as long as you live, I know your mother will be looked after."

Laurentine fought to keep the tears back. So much responsibility for such a very little boy!

"I did look after her," he told her. "Of course I was childish, but there were things I could do. I ran errands, I cleaned house. The two boys next oldest to me worked in the brickyard. Mother wouldn't let me work there—she said I wasn't strong enough. Really I was as tough as a brickbat. But I love to think she saved me from it—I hated that kind of work and the rough men. I did work there for a brief spell but I got out of it. I played on her sympathy. I can see myself now, a miserable, snuffling brat. . . . At night I'd come home, bury my head in her shoulder and whine: 'I have the hardest time of any little chillen. . . .' My brothers teased me about it for years! . . .

"Days when she went out, she used to give me the money to buy the dinner. I had to get nourishing food and enough of it for those hungry boys, the three girls, my mother and myself. Believe me, I was some shopper!

"Know what I used to do? I used to get on the trail of hucksters and vegetable men. When they'd got to the fag end of their produce and of their own strength, I'd sidle up to them and ask them how much they wanted for what was left. I drove some mighty shrewd bargains, I tell you.

"Only sometimes you know, inasmuch as I bought whatever was left, I'd have to repeat the menu if a huckster this day was over-stocked with the same vegetables as the huckster whom I had cleaned out the day before. I can hear my brothers now revolting after the third dinner running of mustard greens.

"'You Stevie, you! Bet if you bring in any more of this grass to-morrow, we just about gonna bust yo' head!'"

He laughed. "I don't know myself how I got away from it all. Mother of course was back of it. From some place, she produced enough money to send me to Washington. My father had left her a house. She took in roomers, she ran the store. At first she used to keep me. But I picked up jobs. I was wiry and willing, fairly apt at my books. I got through High School, went to Howard, there were still six long years before me. But by that time I had got in with the fellows. We used to go away in the summer time and work on the boats. God! How my feet ached me! In the early fall I'd bum auto rides from New York all the way down to Charleston. Many a time I've done the last fifty miles on foot. My mother would wash and iron and mend for me. And I'd get back by standing in with some colored porter on the train. He'd hide me away in a baggage car. . . . But it was a great life. Seeing the obstacles loom up, disappear. Watching the years dwindle till finally there was only one . . . then interneship and the state board and the fun!"

"And the nurses."

"And the nurses! Gosh, they were pretty. And the city girls! Phew! And the tempting welcome given to young fellows, homesick and lonely and on their uppers! The Sunday night suppers, the pleasant mother, the hospitable father, the ravishing girl. . . ."

"Whom you married."

"Yes, I married her. . . . I tell you, Laurentine, I wouldn't repeat that part of my life for anything, and I wouldn't be without it. Marriage is heaven —and it can so easily be hell. She was spoilt— and to my amazement, in spite of my hard life, I realized I was spoilt. But I didn't know it until too late. My mother, my family had all thought me wonderful, you know. I thought so myself. . . . I had been so used to consulting only my own wishes, it never entered my head seriously to consider another's. She was beautiful, an only girl.

"Her father, mother, brothers had indulged her from her birth. She didn't know what self-denial, or self-control meant. I wasn't much better. And when she found she couldn't get her own way with me, she went to some one with whom she thought she could . . . and from him to another and then to another. I hated her for betraying me . . . she hated the man whose severity and lack of understanding forced her into that betrayal."

Perhaps it was the broken moonlight raining through the Chinaberry leaves that made his face look so old.

"Yet when she was dying she sent for me. Poor girl. . . . You know, Laurentine, there really *is* something about marriage."

"I'm sure there is, Stephen."

"Everybody should suffer before he marries. Suffering makes for understanding and clarity more than anything I know." He rose and looked down at her, "You'll understand me, Laurentine? You'll see me clear?"

Her answer was a vow. "Oh, I will, Stephen, I will."

"And I will, too," she told herself as she picked her way carefully through the darkened house.

CHAPTER XXIV

ON Saturday she drove into the country with him. The spell of their last talk was still on them, it seemed to surround them with an aura as sacred as a consecration. The balmy weather was continuing, though Aunt Sal had predicted a change. She came down to the gate after they had got in the car, bearing Laurentine's dark green coat with its smart beaver collar.

"Best take it with you, daughter."

Denleigh sprang out of the car, hat in hand, took the coat and held the gate open for her to re-enter.

She beamed at him loving his *petits soins.*

Denleigh waited until the straight, slender figure had gone up the path, waved good-bye and the two started off.

"She's been great stuff to you, I'll bet, hasn't she, Laurentine?"

"You can't imagine! And it hasn't always been easy."

"In a way, no. In another way, yes. After all, she's had what she wanted out of life, hasn't she?"

"Oh, Stephen, how can you ask that? Every woman wants security, unquestioned position, good standing. She's had none of those."

"I'll bet you never heard her bemoan the lack of them. I tell you, Laurentine, a woman like your mother is perfectly willing to pay the piper as far as she herself is concerned. Any suffering she's done, aside from the loss of her husband, he was really that, you know, she's done for your sake, I'm sure of it."

Laurentine looked at him in astonishment. "How can you say that? If she was suffering for my sake why didn't she take me away from here, why didn't she take me some place where I wouldn't have been known? Then I wouldn't have had to suffer and she needn't have suffered for me."

"That's easily seen into," he answered, guiding the little car past whole fields of goldenrod, gay flower-beds and the cozy homes of northern Jersey. "Why haven't *you* gone away from here long ago? Partly because you feel you owe it to your mother to remain, partly because you don't want these people here to feel they can drive you out. And she doesn't go or she didn't go (I doubt if she thinks of it now) partly because she didn't want these people to feel they could run her away, but far, far more for your father's sake."

"My father's sake!"

"Oh, yes. Women are like that. Most women love their children more than they do their husbands. But a few women love their husbands best. Both your father and mother must have been like that. Do you know anything about him?"

She answered reluctantly, ashamed and uneasy at the turn which the conversation had taken, "Only that he had fallen in love with mother when he was a boy in college and never saw fit to break off."

"Break off! And break her heart!" He was trying hard to exorcise her ghost, but this obtuseness exasperated him. "Oh, Laurentine, what are you saying? This was a true love match, the kind you read about—Héloise and Abélard and all that kind of thing. She wasn't a slave—she didn't have to yield to him. He loved her in spite of her being black and she loved him in spite of his being white. I don't advocate their line of action and yet there is something awe-inspiring. She knew—before long —that she was ruining him. He, loving her more probably than anything else in the world, knew to what he was consigning her. Yet what does he do? He acknowledges her, he provides her with a home —his building it in this town was just a flash of dare-deviltry I guess—he sees that you get an education. . . ."

"Seems to me you've learned a lot about me, young man."

"I had to," he told her soberly. "You know you spoke of bad blood. . . . My dear, there's bad blood and bad blood. . . . There's nothing the matter with yours or with your mother's.

"As I see it, the two of them were defying, not the laws of God, nor the laws of man speaking universally. Simply the laws of a certain section of America. You know if she hadn't been colored he'd have married her like a shot. Don't you think so?"

"I suppose so." She hardly knew herself; the old

familiar burden was loosening; someday it would disappear.

"Everything's all right with me you know girl. I've told you that once before. But I just want to say it to you this last one time. Come closer. . . . You know, Honey, I'm not interested in fathers and mothers. . . . I'm interested in sons and daughters. But I'm here to state that I'm the kind of man who will love his wife best."

.   .   .   .   .

He was wonderful she told him solemnly. "I do believe I'm going to be happy, Stephen."

"I shouldn't wonder. I'm beginning to think so myself." He relapsed into boyishness.

"I was such a miserable little girl," she said. "I knew I was different from other children. . . . I remember once a little girl who used to play with me stopped playing. When I met her I asked her— why." She interrupted herself. "That was the last time I ever was humble Stephen, until I met you."

"My dear brave girl!"

"You know I could cry yet over what she told me. She came to me with a little toy knife—a doll's knife made of tin, and took hold of my hand. She said: 'My mother says you've got bad blood in your veins, don't you want me to cut it out?' " Tears sprang into her eyes at the memory of that far-off little girl whose woefulness she could never heal.

He stopped the car then, his face grave and stern, he put his arms around her. "If you want me to we'll drive over to Morristown and get a license and get married to-morrow—Sunday. And Monday we'll go away to New York, to Chicago where

people are so busy, they're different. My poor
child, my baby!" He laid his face against hers.

"You're sweet Stephen—talking of marriage—
we're not even engaged I'd have you to know.
When I was a very young girl, Stephen, I was sewing in some white woman's house and she had a pile
of old-fashioned paper-back novels there. One of
them was called 'Redeemed by Love.' I read it.
It was about a girl, proud and cold and indifferent
and how her lover's love changed her. I've never
forgotten it—I thought it was so silly. . . . I understand it now, Stephen."

He said huskily: "You know I love you for your
courage, and your mind and your beauty and your
stunning figure. . . . You're a pretty chic young
woman, Laurentine . . . but above all, I'm loving
you for your sweetness, baby."

She loved that. She, "proud Laurentine,"—she
recalled the phrase in Melissa's diary. But to
Stephen she was "baby."

Melissa's diary . . . and Judy. She wondered
if in his far flung inquiries he had happened to hear
about Judy. She did not want to think of Judy.

.   .   .   .   .

They drove home at last through a dusk shot
with orange and rose colors. With the passing of
the sun the chill came down as Aunt Sal had predicted, so that Laurentine came in at her handsom-
est, her beautiful head in its smart little hat nestling
on the folds of her snug collar, her eyes sparkling,
her cheeks glowing, her whole body radiating happiness.

Aunt Sal was expecting them. There was a clear

thin clam chowder for dinner, with lots of clams in it made as only Aunt Sal could; fried oysters, hot biscuits, mashed potatoes like cream, stewed tomatoes with green peppers, after a recipe of Laurentine's, pickles, a sharp, tart, salad, marvelous coffee, damson jelly richly reflecting light, apple pie and cheese. A fire crackled on the hearth and the table was drawn up near it after a fashion which delighted Melissa who found nothing more charming in Aunt Sal's and Laurentine's manner of living than the matter of fact way in which they changed furniture about to meet a temporary convenience. Melissa's satisfaction was further increased by the fact that Johnasteen Stede's cousin Pelasgie who worked sometimes for Kitty Brown's mother was there to wait on table. Pelasgie had been among the girls with whom Melissa had infrequently hobnobbed upon her very first coming to Red Brook. But after the memorable Ice Carnival, Miss Pelasgie had seen fit to withdraw the light of her countenance.

Melissa had spent a pleasant and profitable afternoon. She had walked with Malory and she had succeeded in charming him from one of the most despondent moods in which she'd ever seen him, into one of comparative peace and sunniness. Feeling then in her rich secrecy, her contentment and her temporary triumph over Pelasgie, very much like the cat that had swallowed the canary, she turned her attention to a leisurely contemplation of Laurentine and her new-found happiness and of Dr. Denleigh, whom she rightly judged to be the source of that happiness.

He was pretty nice, she thought, helping herself heavily to the damson jelly which, though it made several rounds of the table, always came to a halt conveniently near. Rather oldish, but looks as though he might be somebody. Laurentine's doing pretty well, but of course she's had to wait forever for it. She surveyed her aunt and cousin and Dr. Denleigh with an equal and serene objectivity, answering the few remarks addressed to her by the visitor with the brief and uninterested politeness of a very little girl.

Laurentine's really beautiful to-night, she went on in her inner conversation, coolly eating hot biscuits along with the jelly. Funny how she can get that elegant foreign look without making any fuss about it. Aunt Sal is right good-looking too, she must have been a stunning girl. I believe those two will branch out wonderfully now that they're going to be happy. Laurentine's going to be happy and I know that will pep up Aunt Sal.

Well she would be happy too—with Malory. Laurentine and Dr. Denleigh could stay here in Red Brook and be stolidly, narrowly content. But she and Malory would travel . . . she remembered a phrase of Kitty Brown's . . . they would go places and do things. . . . Her whole face radiated a sudden content. Denleigh, happening to glance at her just then was startled at the transformation. He had seen her two or three times before; she had opened the door for him, he had passed her on the street and would have failed to notice her had it not been for her pleasant nod.

But to-night she was different somehow. No

wonder the Red Brook lads flocked about her . . .
what was it he had heard about one of them in connection with her?

Laurentine saw him to the door. "Oh, Stephen,
it's been such a perfect day!"

"And such a perfect ending—you don't know
what all this means to a lonely man. Warmth, comfort, cheer and the three of you so beautiful. Your
mother's so handsome and of course you've always
been the Queen of the May. . . . and even the little
one—she's not hard to look at either is she? I
never noticed her before."

"What little one—oh you mean Melissa—my
cousin?"

He half echoed Mrs. Brown's words. "That's
right she is your cousin, isn't she? I knew she
lived here with you but I'd forgotten the relationship." He frowned momentarily. What was it he
had heard? . . . Well, no matter.

He stooped and kissed her, "Good-night, Laurentine. See you to-morrow."

"Good-night, Stephen." She watched him get
into his car. . . . She was happy, happy. But that
night she woke up suddenly and remembered his
slight frown. If only Melissa had remained in
Philadelphia!

CHAPTER XXV

WINTER came slowly that year to Red Brook. The days were sharp and clear but with a bright, thin, curiously gold sunshine that picked out the bare branches and sparse leaves of trees and made them stand like etchings against the sky. And sometimes in the middle of the day there were unexpected little gusts of balminess that permitted men to go about with their overcoats unfastened and butcher's and grocer's boys to run down the street on their deliveries with no overcoats at all.

"A green Christmas," oldest inhabitants said. Mr. Stede repeated it to Aunt Sal lugubriously. "A green Christmas," he sighed, looking at her unseeingly with his strange, faded eyes. "We all knows what that means," he went on intoning, "it means a full graveyard."

Aunt Sal smiled at him, cheerfully, almost joyously. "Let's hope not this year, Mr. Stede." She stood up straight from the table over which she had been bending, chopping suet for mincemeat. Christmas was two weeks off and she was extremely forehanded. "I wouldn't want anything bad to happen to us this year, of all years,—not to anybody."

They were going to have the kind of Christmas which she had so long desired. Not only full and plenty—she had known that as long as she had known Francis Halloway—but peace and happiness, friendship. Not only the knowledge of these qualities but the outward and visible signs of them. They

were having company, real company to dinner.
Dr. Denleigh and Dr. and Mrs. Ismay. The
night before, on Christmas Eve, they would have a
Christmas tree. On Christmas afternoon, after
dinner, Melissa was to go to Kitty Brown's to a
house dance, and she,—Aunt Sal—Laurentine and
the three guests were all to go driving.

"Motoring, if it's clear like this. Sleighing if any
snow should come," Denleigh had said.

It was like the old days in old Mr. Halloway's
house years ago. There had been plans and parties
and young voices. And Frank had come home and
had glanced at her once, at her trim gracious figure,
her fine dark face with its small features. . . . At
dinner while she was waiting table she had found
his blue eyes fixed on her whenever she glanced his
way. He had said "thank you," every time she
offered him a course, every time she set a dish in
front of him. After dinner the others had rushed
from the dining-room. But he had come back and
professed to look for a handkerchief. It was there
too, carefully disposed on the floor under his chair.
His flaxen head and her black one both leaned over
to pick it up—his white hand touched her reddish
brown one, small and roughened—she had moved
it away quickly. She had seen "fresh" young white
men before.

And the next day he had come hunting her up to
mend a rather obviously ripped glove. "Dad said
you would know where the needles and things were.
. . ." Old Mrs. Halloway had gone away. . . .
He had come up and stood very close to her as she
mended the glove, and presently, do what she would,

her hands began to flutter and tremble. He had put
his own fine firm one over hers. . . .

Oh, she had known happiness, terrible devastating
happiness. "Happiness like fiah," she had told herself more than once. It had been a special kind of
happiness which many other people would have mistaken for suffering, pain and disgrace. "But it suited
me," she thought, smiling impenitently within her
wayward heart, whose wilfulness she had long since
learned to smother for the sake of Laurentine.

Now she wanted Laurentine to be happy in the
safe, normal way which she craved, because safe and
normal ways were the only ways Laurentine understood. "She couldn't be happy in my way or
Frank's," her mother thought still smiling within
herself, listening with unregistering attention to the
old man's endless memories about the winter when
there was no snow and all his cousins died.

"Wiped out same as though a plague had lit on
'em. But there! it wuz the will of Pentecost," he
mumbled, his head sinking, his wispy beard spreading circularwise over his grayish limp collar.

When Mr. Stede began to talk about Pentecost
there was only one way of stemming him. Aunt
Sal filled a cup with the delicious mincemeat, poured
a little cider over it. "If you don't think it will hurt
you so early in the morning, Mr. Stede, you might
try this and tell me what you think of it."

He took it eagerly in his horny hands that were
so hard. Melissa used to wonder sometimes how
he could make contact with the various implements
of his various callings.

"No, this won't hurt me Mis' Strange, thank you

kindly. Seems like it don't make no dif'funce whether I eats my dessert before or after. It's a mighty good arrangement, fer sometimes Pentecost directs me to the solids fust and sometimes to the dainties. You know how I am Mis' Strange, don't never ask for nuthin'—now bread, I sh'd imagine would just about cut the richness of this yere stuff."

Still smiling she cut him two or three thick slices of bread, offered him some butter.

"No, I don't want no butter, that would be too rich again." He eyed her shrewdly, meditatively, munching away with the timed rotary movement of a machine. "Looks brighter now then I've saw her look in a long while," he mused, sighing deeply to himself. "Guess I won't talk to her yet awhile." Far off he was able to descry the merest fraction of darkness in a clear sky, the merest pinprick of a cloud.

"Guess I won't say nuthin' about it jes' now," he was deciding with surprising clearness in his old, tired mind.

"It might blow over. Things don't always hafta happen—though mostly they does."

The mincemeat and the bread finished, he sighed again regretfully . . . he had never really had enough to eat though no one but Melissa suspected this. He rose, glanced at Aunt Sal benignly. Crossing the broad kitchen, he rested a horny hand for a fleeting instant on her arm.

"Yo're awful happy, ain't you?" he said with un-derstanding, "I'm glad of it for ye. If I had my way you wouldn't never be unhappy no moah." He walked slowly out to his immaculate wood-shed, almost creaking, so stiff his motions were.

She glanced after him thoughtfully. This morning she had thought only of her happiness—but she had known unhappiness, dreadful, despairing unhappiness. "Dear Master," she prayed, "don't let me know any more of it." It was as though Mr. Stede's horny finger had rested for that brief second on an uncovered nerve.

.   .   .   .   .

Melissa and Malory found in the weather only good omens. Depressed at first by their inability to see and meet each other in the ordinary way, they had fallen into an acceptance of the inevitable and daily made plans to meet as though such clandestine visits were the natural order of things.

"You can see the gods are with us," Malory had chuckled. "Whoever saw a December like this? It's made it possible for us to see each other almost everyday. Still it would be awfully nice if proud Laurentine would relent and let you have me over for Christmas dinner. Think she would?"

They were walking through the Romany Road on their way home from school. Here they would be absolutely safe for the rest of the winter and for most of the spring. Red Brook young people were not the kind to wander through the woods unless it afforded a short cut or some reward in the shape of nuts or wild grapes. The Romany Road affording neither, Malory and Melissa felt themselves as secluded as though in the privacy of their homes.

Actually they had been seen twice, and by the same person—Dr. Denleigh. Laurentine, if asked where her romance had begun would have pronounced unhesitatingly "in Millie Ismay's dining-room." But Denleigh always thought of the walk as its first setting. Often partly because he loved nature, and partly because he was an incurable romanticist, he passed through this quiet twisting path with its unexpected clearing behind tall sentinel—like evergreens. Once glancing idly through their sparse branches as he passed by in the bright September weather he had heard Malory scanning Vergil—a harmless enough diversion, he decided for a boy and girl. The lad whom he didn't recognize had a nice open face he noticed—there was something a little feminine, womanish about it, he thought, as though it might break under strain. . . . And again he had caught sight of them far up in the clearing on a bright, windy December morning, the leaves swirling about them making a magazine picture cover as they stood almost touching each other, absorbed in feeding two very tame, very greedy squirrels.

Ordinarily he would have thought nothing of seeing the two thus together, in fact he did think nothing of it, except to reflect that Melissa probably had duties at home and was putting them off as long as she could. But of late since he had become such an intimate of the Strange household, his mind stirred uneasily at the realization that Melissa, attractive girl as she was, seemed to have no callers. There was something suspiciously docile it seemed to him in her placid acceptance of a long evening within doors, poring, he could see through the half-open sewing-room door, over her lessons, or playing parchesi with Aunt Sal with a sort of indifferent, suspended brightness . . . as though she were, cheerfully enough, passing away the time between two periods of interest.

"As though she were waiting for the time to pass until she could connect up with something more vital, more real," he thought. "I wonder how often she and that young fellow meet," he said to himself. "I wonder why he doesn't come to the house? If I thought he was up to any tricks I'd break his neck, I don't care whose boy he is. I wonder if I ought to tell Laurentine. I wouldn't have this kind of worry happen to her now for anything after the life she's had."

He began to notice then that he never met them together on the street, never saw them together in church which he as a good citizen of the community attended regularly, never saw them at a movie. This flattened him out considerably. And then one week just before Christmas he ran into Doctor Brown's house for a moment, paused at the door of the living-room whence merry voices were issuing, to come upon a medley of noise, music, a confusion of high pitched young voices. Kitty Brown was dancing slowly, sinuously with the boy whom he had seen in the woods with Melissa, and Melissa herself was dancing with another lad, Herbert Tucker, whom Denleigh remembered talking to at a basketball game. And the very next day he had met Tucker and Melissa on North Street coming from school. Tucker's arms were full of books and Melissa's were quite empty. "Hello, Doc," she had grinned up at him.

So that was that. The little minx! Probably since she was just a young girl, and a mighty sharp looking girl too, she wasn't allowed to have company but of course both she and the boys made the most of spare moments on the outside. Doubtless next week he'd come across her walking out with some one else.

.   .   .   .   .

Malory and Melissa, unconscious of course of Denleigh's half-shamed espionage, went on blissfully "eating their cake and having it too," as the boy said with no especial significance.

Melissa put a damper on Malory's suggestion about Christmas dinner. "No, she wouldn't let me invite you. Oh I don't know, maybe she would. But I'd never ask her. I'll never ask anything of Laurentine again, anyway, not long's I live. But I've thought of something grand, Malory. Johnasteen and I rode way out to Pompton Lakes last week, had to deliver two dresses. And after we got there Johnasteen was awfully thirsty—we'd had fish for dinner. So we found a little shack back from the road, where they had soft drinks. It was very nice, a fire and everything. The man had a counter in one room and some little tables in the other, and he said, 'Don't you girls wants to eat a sandwitch or something with your sassparella? You c'n take it right in and eat it at them tables there.' I suppose he wanted us to know that we could eat there even though we were colored. So we told him no. So he said 'Well anytime you're out this way and want to stop in, you can. We're gonna have good things around Christmas time, turkey, fixin's and every-th'g!' " Breathless she paused in her mimicry.

"So let's go out there the day after Christmas and have our own Christmas dinner. I'll bring some celery—I know he won't have any of that—and some nuts and some cranberry sauce if I can manage it. Won't that be fine, Malory?"

He thought it would. "Just the same this kind of thing is awfully silly, Honey. Of course it would be impossible for things to go on like this if I were going to be here after this year. I'd just have to come to your house to see you. This isn't fair to you anyway. I can't imagine what your cousin's thinking about."

"Well, of course she doesn't know we see each other. I guess she doesn't even know you exist," Melissa interposed sensibly. "Though anyway I don't see what she's got to do with me. My mother sent me here in care of Aunt Sal and not to be governed by Miss Laurentine Strange!"

"Strange, Strange, is that her name? Look here, I wonder if she's the little girl used to come to see my sisters sometimes when I was a little bit of a fellow. I used to call her Stranger, I remember . . . she only came for a little while I think, now as I look back—maybe a summer or so. And then I never saw her again . . . everything in my life seemed to change about that time. Strange, Strange! You don't think that's the same girl?"

But Melissa, suddenly remote, thought not. She'd never heard her cousin mention any Fortens. "She —she was educated in Newark you know."

"Oh, perhaps she came from there. Well it

doesn't make any difference anyway. No cousin can separate us, can she, Melissa?"

"No Malory." Her voice was faint . . . he'd been away so long, he had left when he was such a baby. Probably he knew nothing of the story of the Halloways and the Stranges. People would take it for granted that he knew and so wouldn't mention it to him, and yet probably he didn't know,—unless those awful sisters of his told him. Malory cared a lot about class, about family, she knew. Cared for it differently from the manner in which she did because he had always had it. She always listened with admiration and envy when he spoke of his great Aunt Viny and her grandfather who had been a caterer in colonial Philadelphia.

She must get him away from the subject of Laurentine. "How are your sisters, Malory?"

"Oh awful," he groaned, stopping in front of the clearing. "Let's go in here, it's so bright and warm. Oh, I've got something to show you!" He ran over to a clump of bushes, felt among their roots, and pulled out two stained old horse blankets. "I found them up in the attic and sneaked them up here last night. Here, sit down." Gently he placed her on one, and bundled her up in the other. "There, you can always be warm as long as there's no snow on the ground."

He stretched out himself on the other half of the rug. "You know Melissa, this really is too wonderful. . . . This clearing is our home isn't it, Honey, and the sky is our roof. . . . We'll have a home of our own some day too Melissa." His face clouded, "As unlike my home as possible. God!" he exploded. "You can't imagine what my home is like. Mother isn't what you'd call an old woman. I'd swear she wasn't a day over fifty. But she just sits and stares off into space. The girls read cook books and talk over recipes—they're private caterers you know—as though they were telling ghost stories. Harriett practically never opens her mouth to me. Reba just says, 'Good-morning, good-night, I wish you'd pick up your clothes off the bathroom floor, Malory. Did you get the socks I put in your room? Don't stay out too late, Malory!'"

"Oh Malory, she must say more than that!"

"I'll swear on a stack of Bibles she doesn't."

.   .   .   .   .

He might have added that of late she had taken to following him to the front door evenings, as he flung impatiently out of that deadening atmosphere. She would press her face against the wires in the screen door, her faded green or gray dress disappearing into the faded coloring of the door so that her head, as always, seemed suspended bodiless in air. "You're—you're not going out to see any girls, Malory?"

And his impatient response: "What would I be going to see any girls for? See enough of them at school—they're all over the place. Goodness, can't a fellow go out for some air, the way you keep this house shut up!"

He hated to tell a lie!

.   .   .   .   .

"We haven't any radio in the house, any piano, . . . unless a fellow, or Kitty Brown calls me up now and then, the telephone rings only on business.

. . . You know Melissa, I'm twenty-one next June. I'll be my own man then. My Aunt Viny left me a little money, to go to school with. But I'm well and strong now, there's nothing to hinder me from working in the summer—other fellows do. We'll get married. You can come up to Boston with me— We'll get a couple of rooms and have a home. . . ." He put his arms about her enveloped as she was in the clumsy covering. "We might get married before then—in secret."

"We could. And you could go away and I'd stay here and sew for Laurentine and send you money and help you." No she wanted to get away from Laurentine, away where Malory would never hear of that story. "Or no, I'll go to New York and find work there."

"New York indeed! You'll go to Boston with me and live with me and make a home for me."

"I might keep a boarding-house," she said doubtfully, "I'm a good cook." She warmed up to the subject. "We'd just take students and give them good home-cooking. Then I wouldn't be any expense."

He laughed down at her indulgently. "You funny little tucked-in squirrel—you look like one to-day Melissa, your eyes are so bright and sharp. A boarding-house indeed! No wife of Malory Forten will ever keep a boarding-house, or sew, or do anything else. I expect to take care of my wife myself, all by myself, thank you."

"Malory, that's so silly! I could help just at the start."

"Neither at the start nor at the finish."

"Then we won't be able to marry for quite some time."

"We'll marry in June," he told her firmly. "So make the most of these last six months, little Lady-bird!"

Coming out of the woods where the road debouched suddenly into the end of Owen Street, they came face to face with Harry Robbins.

Malory who knew him slightly, said "Hullo Robbins," and would have passed on.

But Robbins looking as though he had seen an unexpected vision gave him the barest nod, turning to the girl with a slowly dawning, unmistakably malicious satisfaction spreading over his countenance. Taking off his hat, he bowed profoundly almost sweeping the ground.

"Well, Melissa," he smiled, his rather prominent eyes goggling straight out of his head. "Well Melissa!"

Malory drew her aside. "Nasty, unpleasant sort of chap," he said carelessly. "Always makes me think of something crawling."

"Yes, doesn't he?" said Melissa. It was all she could do to keep her teeth from chattering. "I think we'd better separate here Malory." She barely returned the pressure of his hand, so eager she was to get away.

.   .   .   .   .

"I wish I could get away from Red Brook and everything and everybody in it!" Well in six months time she would. That wasn't her original idea, but perhaps it was just as well to follow it. She would marry Malory the day after their commencement and go away with him. Somehow, someway she would manage not to be a drag on him. Harry Robbins and his hateful tongue! Still nothing very much could happen in six months.

To her astonishment when she came out of school the next Monday she met Harry Robbins at the corner of the block. She stared at him completely nonplussed. She had not been able to see Malory the preceding Sunday, they rarely saw each other in school, never left the building together, so she had been looking forward to their meeting this afternoon with great eagerness. Now she would not see him at all she knew, for Harry was quite capable of walking all the way home with her. She'd have to enter the house to get rid of him and once in she'd have no excuse for leaving it again.

Bowing cordially—politeness she knew in his case was the best policy,—she tried to walk past him. But he blocked her, not ungently, one hand at her elbow, the other reaching for her books.

"I hadn't seen you for such a long time, Melissa," he said civilly, "that I thought I'd come by to-day and walk home with you." Silently she surrendered her books. It would be the first time she'd ever disappointed Malory. What would he think!

"I'd been wondering what had become of you since Asshur left," the smooth evil voice went on, "I kind of figured that he'd made you promise to keep to yourself 'til he came back. But I see it's not Asshur, it's that Forten fellow." She looked at him wordlessly.

Suddenly he brought his prominent brown eyes to bear directly on her. "I been thinking about you steadily since Saturday—I been figuring—I kind'a got it worked out that your Aunt and your cousin don't know that you're running around with him."

How could he know that, she wondered fearfully trying to keep her consternation out of her eyes. But he had seen them flicker momentarily and he went on, a hard note of triumph in his mocking voice.

"Oh you don't fool me, Melissa. I know too much about you and yours." He changed his tone, the triumph vanished into a mean attempt at ingratiation. "Now I don't think you treated me any too well, when you and I were going together, you even kind of sicked Asshur Lane on to me. I don't mind admitting I've got a grudge against him.

"But I've none against you Melissa, and the proof of it is I've come to tell you that nothing in the world would give me more pleasure than to see you marry Malory Forten. If you have any trouble finding a place to meet, you can come to my house. Nobody lives there but me and dad."

Still she was silent. He looked at her smiling his false smile. "Well, no one could speak fairer than that could they, Melissa?"

They had reached their gate now; he had ruined her day for her. She told him: "Good-bye, Harry, I have to go in right away."

"All right, I'm going. So you won't say anything? Well that's all right too. Well remember you have my best wishes."

She walked slowly up the path, stopped for a moment under the Chinaberry Tree which somehow made her think of Asshur. Almost she wished he were here now, he was always so strong, so capable, so full of resources. "He'd smash his face in," she thought with sudden savage satisfaction. . . . But of course if Asshur were there, there'd be no Malory. Why in a way she was longing for Asshur to help straighten out these strange new difficulties which were besetting her and her relationship with young Forten.

"And of course Asshur wouldn't help me there," she told herself clear-headedly. "But he *would* help me," something, stronger than her head, asseverated over and over again. . . . Strange how she could never picture him as failing her, even though she so signally was about to fail him.

She opened the side door, walked through the little vestibule into the brilliantly-lighted sewing-room. Ordinarily she removed herself quickly from Laurentine's domain, but to-day she flopped wearily into an easy chair.

"Tired?" asked Johnasteen sympathetically. "Home kinda early ain't you?"

Melissa said "yes" to both questions.

"Look kinda peaked," Johnasteen went on brightly. "You want me to get you suthin'?"

She could feel Laurentine's glance flicker toward her for just a second. "No," she told Johnasteen finally, "no thanks, not a thing."

Afterwards she was glad the sewing girls were there; otherwise she might have gone over to her cousin, might have gone on her knees and dropped her head in the older girl's lap, might have said: "Oh Laurentine, you're young, but I'm younger. You've had a hard time but you're coming to the end of it now. Don't be angry with me anymore . . .

whatever I've done, I didn't mean to do it. Don't hate me Laurentine, love me. Be a sister again and tell me what's happening to me? What can I feel coming from far, far away to hurt me and wound me and frighten me? What's the matter with Malory and me?"

But immediately her common sense reminded her that Laurentine didn't even know Malory, had never seen him, never heard his name. She got up wearily, went up to her room, picked up Asshur's letter which Aunt Sal always placed so carefully on her dresser and laid it down again. Then she rouged and powdered her face, washed her hands and went down stairs to dinner.

The meal over and the place ordered, she plodded with painful concentration through the fifty lines of Vergil which she'd been unable to get from Malory, remounted the stairs. Automatically she read Asshur's letter; she knew in advance practically every word he would say. Drearily but precisely she went through the rites of her toilet, snapped off her light and went to bed.

    .   .   .   .   .

That night for the first time she dreamed the dream.

CHAPTER XXVI

SHE did not dream it immediately; she did not fall to sleep immediately. Instead, lying at first tense and then relaxed in her narrow bed she sought to bring her mind to bear on Harry Robbins and his slimy generosity. What lay behind it she could not quite guess but she knew enough about Harry to realize that there lurked some evil intent. It was not like him to give her up; it was not like him to yield up anything even that he didn't want, with grace and good-will. It was indeed his would-be air of eager kindness that most frightened. She could understand his willingness to thwart Asshur, but it seemed hardly likely that he would sacrifice his own desires to that extent. No he must have some ulterior motive whose working out would satisfy the grudge which she knew he bore her.

Stubbornly she tried to fathom it out. Could it be that knowing Malory's pride in his name, Harry was hoping to precipitate the marriage and then acquaint his young rival with the story of Aunt Sal and Laurentine and their connection with her? Perhaps Robbins thought such a tale pointing to deception on Melissa's part would alienate Malory to such an extent that it would mean separation and that she would come to Harry after all for shelter and protection.

"But I never would," she told herself stoutly.

Well then what was it all about? Her tired mind refusing to cope any longer with such an unsolvable problem switched involuntarily to a discussion which they had had in her English class on the ancient Greek drama. She had meant to read up on the subject but she had been too tired. However, Miss Scarlett, her teacher had been as always very clear and precise in presenting the details. She could remember, she thought, almost every word of it, in case an examination was sprung. What had intrigued her attention most had been the pictures which Miss Scarlett had shown of the masks of Tragedy and Comedy. After they had gone the round of the class Melissa had secured them again and pored over them in an agony of fascination, fear, and repulsion.

She hated the sightless eyes, the horrid, gaping mouths, the snaky hair. Even the plane of the cheeks and the moulding of the lips seemed to carry a suggestion, in both masks, of a mad, deliberate cruelty. In particular she was at once magnetized and repelled by the hint of laughter in the Comic Mask. If anyone were ever to look at her with that vacant, leering grin, that promise of heartless mirth. . . .

"I'd scream out loud," she told herself cowering under her warm covers. She closed her eyes to shut out the image which her mind had conjured up for her, opened them again—the face was peering at her over the foot of the bed.

.   .   .   .   .

Of course it was not surprising that she dreamed, she thought, waking wanly and exhausted in the chilly little light of a December morning. Suddenly she reviewed it, hating the memory of each detail.

It seemed to her that with a heart woefully heavy and filled with fear she was walking slowly and yet purposefully along a winding road, a rather pretty road in the woods. She did not want to continue her walk, but she was forced to, something stronger than herself bearing her on.

Presently around a bend she came to an opening, a veritable open-air theatre and there far off upstage she spied what at first seemed a small figure, but as she came nearer, which perforce she had to, she came to see that the figure was not so small but so bowed and shrunken with woe, with the weight of some such terrific tragedy that it had forfeited its normal stature.

Still under the spell of her strange compulsion, she came close to the figure, she put her hand on its shoulder. She could not see the face, but yet she said, she heard herself say, without an instant's hesitation in a flat, dreary voice: "What is it, Malory?"

For all its stupor of grief, the figure whirled on her then in a very cyclone of passion and anger—and she descried not as she had expected the grief-stricken countenance of her lover, but the horrid gaping face of the Comic Mask, its mouth distorted to its fullest, reviling words issuing from those eternally open lips.

She turned and fled then in a horror and terror so complete, so devastating that it was impossible to describe it. And presently she stumbled and fell down, down into an abyss of blackness . . . she lay there unconscious,—she, the dreamer, was conscious of her unconsciousness. And finally, it seemed to her, a tall dark figure appeared from a distance and picked her up. . . .

.   .   .   .   .   .

A horrible dream! Melissa who was never nervous, who had her mother Judy's imperviousness to shock came down to her breakfast pallid and worn and preoccupied. To her Aunt's anxious question she admitted she didn't feel "so good" but she could manage to go to school. However, she hung about the house until the last moment, picking up objects and putting them down. And when she went to the door, Aunt Sal accompanying her as she sometimes did, she turned suddenly and nestled her head, as a small child might, snugly, confidingly against her Aunt's warm soft bosom, against the heart of Sarah Strange for whom life held no further fears, seeing she had met them and left them behind her.

Aunt Sal felt the touch of the young troubled head upon her all day. She hummed pleasantly to herself in the comfortable, sunny kitchen, dwelling upon the pleasant action. Her passionate, generous nature crammed by circumstances into its mould of impassivity craved an outlet. She had long regretted within herself Laurentine's lack of demonstrativeness. . . . Perhaps after Laurentine married—and left—she would find another daughter, a real little girl in this child of Judy Strange.

.   .   .   .   .

Melissa unconscious meanwhile that her own woe could be the source of such a real innocent, fundamental pleasure, meandered to school, and was reproved by Miss Scarlett for inattention in her English class. Her distraction, lessened finally by a glimpse of Malory in the student's cafeteria at lunch time, was gradually dissipated. She was still languid however, and although thanks to Harry Robbins, she had not seen Malory the day before, she sent him a note proffering no explanations, but telling him that she would be unable to see him that afternoon in the Romany Road. "Perhaps I'll never see him there again," she told herself wearily. It was too much like the road in her dream.

CHAPTER XXVII

THE weather suddenly accepting its responsibility, Christmas arrived in due time as Christmas should. Red Brook on Christmas Eve bore out the scene on the conventional Christmas card. There must be something very basic and true, Malory Forten thought, plodding his way through the soft-falling clinging snow, in a scene or a remark which was depicted or uttered again and again. Here for instance was the individual house, the moon visible over its peaked roof, its windows bright with light all over the dwelling, its children glimpsed through those same windows uncurtained and unshaded, busied about a Christmas Tree. Over beyond loomed a thin church spire, and just above him in the sky there should be—there certainly was—the star.

Somehow the accuracy, the truthfulness of the scene to type both magnified and appeased the pain in his own young aching heart. Like many boys and men, Malory had a very definite sense of what a home should be . . . perhaps if in his home there had been the warmth, the jollity and the light which one expects on Christmas Eve, he might have with sheer masculine perversity, turned both his thoughts and footsteps elsewhere and sought a far different and less suitable means of spending the occasion. As it was, thwarted, baffled, embittered by the presence of the increased gloom which the holiday season seemed to bring to his cheerless household, he would have sacrificed every hope almost that he had for the future to have been able to see enacted within his walls the scenes which he was sure were being enacted in every normal household in Red Brook that night.

In spite of continued disappointments, he had thought that Reba in some way—he had long since ceased expecting anything of his mother or of Harriett—would have responded to the supremeness of the Christmas season. After all this was his first Chritmas home, he was a boy, he was young. Great Scott, what did those folks of his have in their veins anyway! And what in God's name was the matter with them, he'd like to know! If Aunt Viny—good old sport if ever there was one—had only lived, he might have asked her. But Aunt Viny was dead now, lying straight and still under her first blanket of snow . . . could the dead feel the change in seasons he wondered, trying to think what the bare negation of life must mean. . . .

Only last Christmas Aunt Viny had given him the best party! True she would ask only the grandchildren of her own pet cronies, whereas there were one or two new (!), very new Philadelphians whom her very slightly more democratic nephew would gladly have welcomed. But after the guests arrived, Aunt Viny made it clear that they might do as they pleased; the old lady's only password to "society" being a valid claim to "old Philadelphian-ism." Having satisfied that, one might do what he wished. They had had a good time, "raising sand," (Aunt Viny's equivalent for the modern "whoopee,") dancing a discreet forerunner of the rhumba, dispensing beribboned gifts. . . .

Late this afternoon Reba had come into his room

and had placed on his bed a large flat package wrapped in a most un-Christmas-like covering of whitey-brown paper—the edges pinned together. How Malory's taste revolted at that!

"You might just as well have your presents now Malory," she said faintly. "Harriett and I will be out serving a party to-night, so we'll be sleeping late, and mother never gets up on Christmas Day. She's gone to bed now . . . if you should go out you won't disturb her coming back will you? . . . If you want me to I'll take your present in to her for you."

He'd give it to her himself when he saw her, he told her just as audibly. He was really suffering from the restraint which he felt he must put on the unreasoning anger welling within him. . . .

After she left he examined the bundle—two suits of underwear, two pairs of heavy worsted gloves— greeny-gray—with ugly, shapeless fingers, a whisk broom, a black neck-tie—a black neck-tie with small white rings in it! A tie old for a man of fifty! He left the articles reclining on their paper covering on the bed.

Melissa had given him a half-dozen fine handkerchiefs, the large size that made a fellow feel so opulent. They were monogrammed in simple, elegant lettering. With them had come a pair of heavy, short, tan gloves and a small pencil in silver and black marcasite. . . . He hadn't given her his present yet; it hadn't been completed until late this afternoon. . . . That was it, he'd go over to Melissa's this evening and hand the gift, a little monogrammed wrist watch in white gold—to whomever came to the door. No proud cousin could find fault with that! She'd probably take him for a messenger. If he could just set foot in Melissa's house to-night he would take it as an omen that next year she would be in his.

"She will, too," he vowed silently.

. . . . .

He started on his rounds early—there were candy for Kitty Brown, a copy of "Moby Dick" for Herbert Tucker whose family he liked. The Tuckers hailed him in, they made him sit down to supper. "We've got baked beans," Mrs. Tucker said hospitably, "it's so hard to decide what you're going to eat just before Christmas. You've got your mind so set on turkey and mince-meat. But boys always like baked beans."

It was great to be sitting in the warm cozy room, Malory thought, gratefully stowing away man-like portions of beans and corn-bread. They pressed him to stay. "We're not having company," Mrs. Tucker explained amiably, "we just like the family to be together on a night like this. Herbert usually goes out on New Year's Eve but he always stays home with his mother on Christmas Eve, don't you, Herbert?" She bustled out into the kitchen without waiting for an answer.

The boys grinned at each other in complete understanding.

"You know how it is," Herbert explained, whimsically resigned. He didn't really mind; his father and he had a perpetual conflict on at chess.

Malory stopped at Kitty's; met her sister Gertrude home for the holidays. A nice restful girl he

thought, with none of Kitty's aimless activity. He
pushed on to Mrs. Ismay's at whose house Mrs.
Tucker had asked him to leave a small package.
He liked Mrs. Ismay immediately, accepted her
pleasant invitation to "drop in any evening, Doctor
likes young men." He would go there sometime he
thought definitely, she seemed such a fine sort. . . .
Melissa's cousin called there too he remembered,
maybe he'd meet her and make a good impression.
. . . Wasn't it just his luck though to have absolutely no home and then to fall in love with a girl
whose home he couldn't visit either?

"Well there'll only be six months more of it," he
muttered and came to Melissa's house.

. . . . .

Assuredly this house ran true to type; its windows
were blazing, its curtains up high. Malory stepped
across the lawn in the soft snow up to, but not on,
the front porch, and peered through the window.
He saw a dark brown slender woman of about forty-
five he judged—she had small, well-defined features.
Then he saw Laurentine smiling and excited handing
Christmas trinkets to Dr. Denleigh who, mounted
on a step-ladder was trimming a fine, tall Christmas
Tree.

"Gosh what a beautiful girl!" thought Malory.
"What a wow of a girl!" He shifted his position
to see Laurentine better. Another man was standing there, middle-aged, in his overcoat, hat in
hand, apparently ready to leave. Dr. Ismay,
he saw later. Probably he had come over to bring
a remembrance from his wife. Melissa wasn't
there. He walked around to the side of the house

and saw for the first time the Chinaberry Tree with its circular hexagonal seat under it. It was only a skeleton now with here and there a leaf fluttering in the chilly night, but the moon sifting through its branches cast a pattern on the smooth snow about its base and made the tree more enchanting than ever.

Malory stopped to look at it, his quick mind visualizing it in its real glory. He said aloud what he'd said about Laurentine: "Gosh what a beautiful tree! Why didn't Melissa ever tell me about this?" He started to knock on the side door but desisted, for fear one of the others might answer him and he did so want to see Melissa.

There was another room in back—that must be the kitchen, surely she must be in there, she wouldn't be up in her room alone on a night like this.

The kitchen windows were wide but shallow and placed high. Malory looking about the yard in the clear moonlight found a soap-box and stood on it to peer in the window. Yes there she was in a white dress with a bright yellow smock; she was standing near an old-fashioned kitchen range, the oven-door was open and from it she had evidently drawn a pan of cookies.

"He tapped softly on the door. Without a moment's hesitation, she opened it. "Malory! oh Malory! Come in!"

He came in. He kissed her. His girl, Christmas Eve, the warm, safe room with its aura of living about it! "I suppose I should say, 'Together, at last.'"

She laughed with him. "Malory this is the best present! How'd you dare come?"

"That reminds me, I've got your present—was that a hint—young lady?" He began to tap his various pockets, handed her a small package, "Don't open it 'til to-morrow morning—thus sparing my blushes. Melissa Paul you wouldn't dare tell me you're making ginger cookies!"

"I certainly am; all hot and hot, and softy-like before they get cold you know. Wait a minute." She vanished through the door ran through the sewing-room, peeped into the room where the others were. She came back her face glowing. "I told them to be very good and stay in there and later on I'd bring them something. Take off your overcoat and stay awhile;" she helped him with it. "Oh Malory, Malory to think you're actually in my house. . . . I think that's a good sign. . . . I've been so troubled Malory . . . but now I believe everything will be all right."

He had on galoshes, but recklessly she bade him take those off too. He sat by the kitchen fire and she fed him hot gingerbread and cider and sandwiches which, already prepared, appeared fresh and dainty swathed in a thick white napkin. And all the time she was piling similar viands on a huge tray which she set in turn on a rolling tea table. Trundling this she disappeared again, returned for plates and glasses, disappeared for a last moment and reappeared triumphant.

"There, that ought to hold them. They won't even think of me for the next hour." She dragged up a chair beside him, rested her head in one of her rare gestures of familiarity against his arm. "Malory, isn't it too grand? Have you opened your presents yet? Did you like them?"

"Like them? Look here!" He pulled one of the handkerchiefs from his pocket and flourished it. Another pocket in his vest revealed the smart new pencil.

"You shouldn't have used them so soon—greedy!"

"I couldn't help it, Honey. Know what I've been thinking about Melissa?"

"No, tell me!"

"This time, next year, we'll be together, you and I in our own home. Say it and believe it." She said it and didn't believe it, though she wanted to.

He looked around at the kitchen, its bright orderliness, the rows and rows of shining gaily colored plates, the clever furniture, the Dutch clock on the wall. Colonel Halloway had fitted out the place thoroughly, but that was long ago. Laurentine was responsible for bringing it thus up-to-date.

"You've never told me anything at all about your folks, you know, Melissa," he said looking around him with frank curiosity. "I had no idea you lived like this. I had no idea any colored folks in Red Brook lived like this. What's your aunt's husband do?"

"He's dead," said Melissa uneasily. "Malory I hate to hurry you but I think you'd better go—see I'm going to put these ginger-snaps in your pocket." She wrapped them in a small fringed napkin. "Which I know I'll never see again," she teased him.

"You bet you won't. All right, Honey. I'll be going, but I'm so glad I came, aren't you glad? Perhaps we can manage it again."

"Perhaps," she said breathlessly. "Here I'll slip outside with you." She snatched a fleecy pink and white wool scarf from a hook, wrapped it around her rosy face in the old-fashioned style of the fascinator and stepped out into the path with him. "My boots are around on the side porch. I left them there this afternoon. I'll slip them on and walk a block with you."

But once near the side porch he remembered the Chinaberry Tree again. "Why didn't you ever tell me about it, Melissa? Here you've got your boots on, let's sit under it for a minute. Wait, I'll brush the snow off—and you can sit on the famous handkerchief. . . . Why this place is too good to be true; isn't it really just the right place for a lover—and his lass?"

"Yes, it is," she agreed faintly. Why on earth must she remember, sitting here with Malory her lover, the many, many times she had sat thus with Asshur?

"Listen, Malory, I'll have to be going in—I'll take cold and then anyway they might come out in the kitchen and miss me."

"Of course they will, better run along in. But let me tell you something, young lady. In the spring, come warm weather we're going to sit out under this tree many's the night."

"How can we?"

"Easily enough. What time do your folks go to bed?"

"Oh I don't know. Ten, half-past ten, eleven except when Laurentine's at Mrs. Ismay's or Dr. Denleigh's here."

"Well, we wouldn't expect to meet every night," he said reasonably. . . . "Say your cousin is a stunning looking girl. Why didn't you ever tell me about her? 'Fraid I might look at her too hard?"

She laughed at that. "Silly she's years older than you."

"Well, we'll slip out while the fair Laurentine and her mother are sleeping—I'll probably be here already—and we can talk and make plans. That's better than the Romany Road, Melissa, for you'll be already home then. I hate to see you starting off by yourself when you leave the Road."

She thought this over in silence. "Yes, yes, why I guess that would be better. I'm sorry darling—my teeth are chattering. Do go Malory."

Once beyond the radius of the Chinaberry Tree her uneasiness left her, her old adoration for him surged up. She put her arms about his neck in a sudden abandonment of love and regret at his going.

"Good-night, Malory. Merry Christmas, Malory."

"Merry Christmas, Melissa. Don't forget to come to Kitty's to-morrow."

"I'll come right after dinner."

"And we're having our own dinner you remember the next day at Pompton Lakes."

"Oh yes and I'm to bring the celery."

He walked off thinking it hadn't been such a bad Christmas Eve after all. "And when I know I don't have to have another one like it, I imagine this will be a very sweet and romantic memory," he told himself sensibly.

.   .   .   .   .

Melissa crept in the side door, rushed noiselessly up to her room, kicked off her wet boots and unwound her fascinator. Then bethinking herself of Malory's present reposing in the pocket of her smock, she took it out, pulled off its wrappings.

A wrist watch! In spite of herself she threw herself face downward across the bed and giggled almost hysterically. Asshur had sent her the selfsame gift, even to the design, from far off Alabama. It had arrived by special delivery just an hour before Malory came. Recovering presently, she arose and bearing the two watches under the electric light on her dressing table, she examined them carefully.

Yes, they were exact replicas—save that Asshur's watch had a tiny green jewel in the top of its minute winder, and Malory's had a blue one. And perhaps there was some slight difference in the monograms.

She took off her smock, smoothed her hair, applied powder and rouge and went back to the warm, spicy kitchen. Mr. Stede came in with a present from Johnasteen. Aunt Sal emerging from the living-room for a fresh supply of cookies found Melissa in the rôle of Pentecost, staying the insatiable old man with platters of sandwiches and cookies, comforting him with flagons of cider.

CHAPTER XXVIII

CHRISTMAS came and Christmas sped as Christmas has and will through the eastern section of the United States—a little less thrilling than its anticipation promised; a little unexpectedly fatiguing by reason of a morning spent in strenuous preparation of dinner; a little stodgy in the early evening by reason of that same dinner; a little more desirable and mysterious than ever as night turned the corner and one began to bask in the penetratingly sweet realization that all the bustle and hurry lay behind and that one could live normally for another year. Of course, for another Christmas one would do differently. . . .

Aunt Sal would have changed none of it, neither the faint disappointment of the early morning, the breathless hurry of preparation, the moment of repletion, and certainly not the relapse into peaceful content. All this she knew to be normal. She who had once flung every convention, every phase of normal living to the winds now revelled, for the sake of her child, in every action that seemed to mark her and hers as being no different from the rest of mankind.

For Laurentine, of course, the day was actually different inasmuch as she had never known a Christmas so full of the Christmas spirit, so wreathed in happiness and joy. She took part in and loved every phase of the day. Cooking was for her an enjoyable art which she had little opportunity to exercise. It was with great pleasure then that she worked side by

side with her mother, letting her artistic sense run
riot in gastronomic expression. She thought of untried combinations of flavorings; she it was who arranged the centerpiece of white flowers and bright
red haws and berries; she it was who grouped the
candles in twos, so that when the lights were extinguished at dinner, the bright spurts of flame illu-
mined the lovely old, dark room.

Even the "stodginess" that crept over Aunt Sal
and Dr. Denleigh and the Ismays after the charming
meal did not dismay her. She herself felt none of
it; in her nervous excitement she had eaten too little
to be affected by it, and rightly she interpreted it for
what it was in the others. She thought happily that
Christmas would be like this many, many times after she and Stephen had married, he replete with
content, she brimming over with the realization of
her great good fortune.

Melissa observed none of the phenomena of the
day. She was too young to philosophize. She had
surreptitiously examined all her presents the night
before anyway, so she had nothing to anticipate in
the way of thrills for Christmas morning. And far
from being wearied by the unusual amount of household activities she welcomed them, for would they
not fill in the day and wouldn't the passage of the
day bring her closer to Kitty Brown's party and to
Malory? After dinner Dr. Denleigh drove her
over to her destination—she was all in yellow and
looked just as a young girl ought to look on going to
a party, happy, vital, sparkling. You knew that
her clothes, her pretty inexpensive costume jewelry,
her dainty shoes were of no real importance in the

ensemble of her appearance. She enhanced them more than they enhanced her; fig leaves, had they been in style, would have done just as well, since their only office could be to lend the assurance which comes to one who knows she is superlatively and modishly dressed.

Malory was mounting the steps as she appeared, so the two entered the house together, handed their wraps to the watchful and sullen Pelasgie; at the entrance to the reception rooms the young man placed his arm about Melissa's slender figure and the two drifted off into the strains of a sensuous, tender, enrapturing waltz.

.   .   .   .   .

Denleigh drove back through a lightly whirling flurry of snow. The air was fine for him; it braced him, dissipating completely the slightly sickish effect of the rich food and the warm rooms. Rather leisurely he drove, savoring deliberately the comfort of home-coming, the dear joy on Laurentine's lovely face. So it would be many times in the future he mused with no thought at all for his tragic past life. Of course life was full of petty annoyances, but outside of those, there was no reason at all why he and his wife should not know a blissful, enjoyable existence. He could not think of a single possibility which might mar Laurentine's and his own serenity, he assured himself,—and flicked away as one might an insect his tiny insistent wonder as to why it upset him, frightened him a little to see Melissa, so confidently, so matter-of-factly at ease in the company of Malory Forten.

Laurentine's face did beam as she let him in; his

reception held all the promise of peace and comfort for which one could wish. Men fought and died to preserve just this sort of homelife. They would go on forever fighting and dying for its preservation. . . . And homelife itself would always go on; it would exist for ever in spite of all the disquisitions in the magazines and the Sunday newspapers to prove it was disappearing.

"We may disappear," he broke out somewhat to Laurentine's bewilderment, "as a matter of fact we, this very race, will disappear. And other races will take our place both here and in Europe, and all over the world, but certain basic things will remain. Just as the old-fashioned furniture," he tapped with his fine nervous hand, the frame of the highly modernistic arm chair in which he was sitting in the sewing-room, "has disappeared into all this angular, geometric stuff. But the comfort stays—I've never sat in a more comfortable chair, Laurentine. I didn't know Red Brook grew such things. . . . We'll have to be keeping our eyes open, won't we, for sales and bargains and what not. I suppose you'll like that Miss Strange. . . . Well, I have a confession to make. I like it, too."

From the living-room came the murmur of placid voices. Dr. Ismay was instructing his wife and Aunt Sal in the intricacies of a card game which he had brought with him from Jamaica but which he was rarely able to induce anybody to play, its tempo being considerably slower than that of any corresponding American game.

Denleigh and Laurentine in the sewing-room, he in the modernistic arm chair, she on a lower chair beside, sat before the beautiful artificial fire and talked out their plans for their new lives.

"By next Christmas, we'll be in our own house," Denleigh said confidently . . . "perhaps before many more months. Perhaps we'll put our house-warming off till Christmas. I've never had a house-warming though I've always wanted one . . . it sounds so real, so sort of—warm," he finished lamely.

"It certainly does sound warm," Laurentine conceded with equal inanity. They snickered a little over their common lack of sparkle and wit.

"It's because we're too comfortable," Stephen pointed out. "You know Laurentine I'm constantly amazed at the manner in which things, chance, happenings change one's point of view. When I was a boy, yes and a young man too, I always wanted to be different from the person I was. I imagine that the reason why I was able to triumph over my quota of poverty and lack of recognition and finally to obtain my education was because secretly in my heart I wanted to do such wonderful, difficult things that the attainment of my immediate ambitions seemed mere child's play."

Amazed, she stared at him. "Why what on earth could you have wanted to be Stephen? Certainly the road to your medical training was rocky enough."

"I know it; as I look back now, I am simply petrified with astonishment at the thought of what I tackled and overcame. But in those days I wanted to be an outstanding giant. I was sorry I couldn't have been a Crispus Attucks and strike the first blow for American Independence. I wanted to be a genuine, literal Moses for us colored people, conscious of my leadership while I was initiating and practicing it.

"I would have been glad, indeed as soon as I knew something of history, I ardently yearned to have been born back in Reconstruction Days. So sure I was that all single-handed, I would have founded a course which would immediately have brought all ex-slaves up to the highest level of any American white man, which would have established cordial relationships, equal civil rights—you know brotherhood-of-man-business completely and at once."

"And now?"

"And now," he said slowly, "I'm quite content to live anywhere, any place and do my best. I who once thought that nothing less than the halls of Congress could content me, am equally as eager to settle down in the little town of Red Brook, marry Miss Laurentine Strange, and serve my fellow man. Disappointing and yet somehow vastly satisfying," he admitted, a trifle rueful.

But she would have none of his rue. "Silly, not to see that in your way you're doing just as much as Crispus Attucks and those Reconstruction statesmen ever did. I don't know much about them, but I'm quite sure none of them grew up with the idea in mind of being great or renowned. They just 'seen their duty and they done it,' " she told him, laughing.

"You're benefitting Red Brook's colored youth marvelously, you must know that. Just think not a single colored boy around here thought of studying medicine until you and the Browns and the Ismays came into this community to show them what was what. And as for you personally, these Italian mothers round about, think you dropped. Why Mary Ricardi, the fruit woman, told me she often says a novena for you—and she's going to name her next boy after you."

"The deuce she is! Well, all I have to say is she's darn likely to have a 'next boy.' Talk about replenishing the earth! Tony and Mary Ricardi certainly believe in doing their bit."

"After all," she went on, "a man can only offer his little quota of nobility to the people among whom he lives. And if you had done nothing but what you have done for me, you'd have more than acquitted yourself."

He didn't know what she was talking about and showed it. "Here, you've sort of mixed matters up, haven't you? It's you that have ministered to me. What on earth have I ever done for you, Laurentine,—asked you to marry me? Good heavens, you don't think I consider myself as God's gift to women, do you?"

Disregarding his badinage, she answered very low: "You restored me; you made me respect myself. You made me alive to my own inner resources. No matter what fate may spring on me, Stephen, I can never be that wretched, diffident, submissive girl again. It's possible I might become a force for evil as well as a force for good. But I'll never be a tame cat again."

Much amused and yet pleased and happy, he only rejoined: "Take care not to turn into such a wild one that you'll scratch my eyes out. . . . My sweet-

est girl. . . . Laurentine just trust me, believe in
no matter what stress that I am yours as I believe you are mine and—well, we can simply face
all the punishment the world has to offer—that's all
there is to it."

"I do believe in you, Stephen," she said, her eyes
shining.

"After all, if I'd been Crispus Attucks, I'd never
have had a girl like you. So you see as I said,
chance changes us. I'd rather have you than live
the lives of a thousand Crispus Attucks. There goes
my oldest ideal." He snapped his fingers gaily.

"Let's go in with the others and see if we can get
a little good dance music out of that radio I sent you
this morning. Somebody besides Melissa has got to
remember that this is a Merry Christmas."

. . . . .

Kitty had an orchestra, a caterer and an imported
beau. Jerry Adamson had come at her behest all
the way from New York to show his allegiance and
to have it shown, and to make things go. With
Kitty's willing and surprisingly capable aid he introduced a series of new dance steps, which were
utterly unlike any dance steps that Red Brook and
its environs had ever seen. You hopped, skipped,
slid, gyrated, turned, twisted, it seemed to Melissa,
all in one. Also, you danced with your whole body
and all over your body. It was really the first inti-
mation of the Lindy Hop, though no one but Jerry
and the members of the orchestra knew this. Then
there was the rhumba. The saxophonist played and
then moaned something about playing this dance as
they did——

"On the tuba
Down in Cuba."

Melissa flushed with the heat and the excitement and the wicked music, and the unsuspected qualities of the heady potion which she had heedlessly gulped down under the impression that it was an unusually palatable variant of punch, hopped, skipped, slid, gyrated, twisted and turned until she was, Jerry Adamson told her, holding her close to his straight, handsome figure, as proficient, "more p'ficient," he mumbled a little thickly than Kitty herself. He showed a disposition to dance with her all evening. Melissa liked this. Jerry was new, Jerry was handsome, Jerry was some one's else beau she thought, forgetting how much she owed that some one else. It would be fun to show these girls from New York and Newark and Trenton, yes and to Pelasgie Stede, broodingly gathering up punch glasses, what she poor, lonely, little Melissa Paul could do simply because she was young and good-looking and—vital.

"I must have, 'it,' " she thought to herself quite simply in the unveiled idiom of the day.

But Malory did not like it. Melissa glancing past Jerry's arm saw him stalking proudly and as correctly as might be, considering its exigencies, through the measures of the tantalizing dance. His arms were about Gertrude Brown arrayed in slim sophistication in a smart black gown, which suggested what it covered as plainly as it revealed where no covering was meant to be.

Melissa had observed Gertrude's tactics before; she knew that reserved, flaunting aloofness of the older girl which said: "I have 'it,' too, don't forget that. But I'm saving it for you, you, you!" She saw the tense look which Malory's face always assumed when he was deeply annoyed, changing, softening to one of interest. Abruptly, she signaled to Herbert Tucker to cut in on her and when Malory glanced her way again she was treading the measures of the fantastic music as correctly as he. He came over to her as soon as he could leave Gertrude, a lengthy process, and asked her for the next dance.

She carried the war into his camp. "Goodness, what a washout you proved to be! Here I've been turning and twisting my head and raising my eyebrows—have I got any left or have they climbed permanently into my hair?—doing everything possible to get you to cut in on me and rescue me from that Adamson boy."

He said in simple male bewilderment: "Cut in on you? That would have been the last thing to come into my mind!"

"Oh, certainly," she broke in, "you were enjoying yourself too much with Gertrude Brown." Melissa was certainly enjoying herself. She gave him little quick bird-like glances, fanning herself the while.

"Enjoying myself with Gertrude Brown! H'm. Any interest I showed in her wasn't a patch to what you showed in Jerry, doing all that hopping and bumping and twisting——"

"I had to follow him, didn't I?" she asked sweetly. "But I didn't like it, he held me too tight." She looked suddenly all innocence, all wistful girlhood. "Come on, let's dance this together, Malory. I like to dance with you, you're so restful."

Relieved, he would have danced every number with her until the dancing stopped. But she remembered in time that she was to spend the night with Kitty and Gertrude. It would be only in this way that she could get away with Malory to-morrow to eat Christmas Dinner at Pompton Lakes. So she sent Malory off to dance again with his hostesses, paying no attention to Gertrude's carefully careless stalking and refusing Jerry Adamson's repeated invitations to dance out in the hall with him—he'd show her a few new steps,—or to sit out for a little while in his car. He assured her on his word of honor that she wouldn't be cold out there, he'd see to that.

Instead, conducting herself like a "gay, good girl," as she and Kitty privately daubed the lively, futile girl unblessed by "it," she danced again demurely with Herbert Tucker and with no visible show of reluctance in the arms of Ben Davis who danced against time. After that unequal struggle she came to rest in the offing of Doctor Brown's mother, a stout, sturdy, elderly woman, whose badly dyed black hair lent a hard and forbidding aspect to the real softness of her worn lineaments. The older woman told her daughter-in-law that she didn't know that such mannerly girls as that Melissa Paul were to be found any more. She only wished Kitty and Gertrude were more like her.

When the guests left Malory said a surprising thing. He drew aside Melissa who, secure in her assumption that she had scotched, not to say completely pacified his former irritation, was smiling up at him blandly. Holding the hand which she had extended to him in farewell tightly between his own, he said thoughtfully:

"You know, Melissa, perhaps I did neglect you a little to-night and that's how you came to be dancing with Adamson. I didn't know I did it, and I certainly didn't mean to do it. But anyway, I'm telling you again, I didn't like your dancing that vulgar dance. That sort of thing isn't—er—well, Melissa it just isn't the kind of thing I like from a girl whom I'm expecting to be my wife."

Her only answer was a faint "good-night, Malory," and an amazingly satisfactory realization that he couldn't kiss her "before the Browns and all."

He said self-consciously: "I'll be waiting for you to-morrow by the Presbyterian Church. We'll take the bus there for Pompton Lakes. You haven't forgotten, Melissa?"

"No, oh no!"

"All right, be on time. Good-night, Melissa."

"Good-night, Malory."

.   .   .   .   .

She went upstairs to her little room which opened from the large room shared by Kitty and Gertrude. She praised Kitty's party and adored Gertrude's dress, then yawning and tapping her hand against her mouth she vowed she must go to bed.

"And if I leave in the morning before you get up you won't mind will you?"

Gertrude said they wouldn't mind anything just so long as the house didn't burn down and they'd have to go somewhere to finish their much needed sleep. "Hope you didn't mind my monopolizing your young man, M'lissa."

"He isn't my young man," she lied languidly. "He comes to see Kitty and I'm around here too and it falls to his lot to take me home." It was a good sketch she thought and decided to round it off. "He never comes to see me."

Even Kitty looked startled at this. "He doesn't? Why Melissa!"

"Well he doesn't." She remembered Christmas Eve. "He's been in my house just one time and that was to bring me a package."

"Well, I do think!" exclaimed Kitty wider and wider awake. "Melissa you don't mean to say you're going to pass Malory up for Asshur Lane?"

"Who's Asshur Lane?" her sister interposed sharply.

"Boy, Melissa used to go with all the time. He's down in 'Bam now studying agriculture. His uncle's got a big place out Birneysville way and Asshur expects to run it some day," said Kitty, yawning and turning sleepy again. "Well, Melissa you certainly surprise me, but there's no accounting for tastes as the old lady said when she kissed the cow."

"No," said Gertrude slowly, "there certainly isn't." And went to bed very thoughtfully.

. . . . .

Melissa, blowing the sisters a kiss, passed into her room, closed the door and washed her face carelessly—she was sure of her complexion. But not being as sure of her hair she combed and brushed and twisted that with great solicitude, then donning a pair of gay pajamas she slid into bed. And thought.

She said to herself. "Asshur—now—Asshur knows about Laurentine and all about Aunt Sal's funny doings when she was a girl but he would never have spoken to me as Malory did about how to behave if I were going to be his wife and all." She thought, "I wonder how Malory will take it when he finds out about Laurentine and Aunt Sal and how funny most of the people treat her. It was true," she considered, staring hard through the heroically opened window at the moon which showed fainter in the grayness of the coming dawn, "it was true that the attitude of the Ismays and above all of Doctor Denleigh ranked higher than the attitude of all the remaining colored people in Red Brook except of course the Browns."

And after all none of it was Laurentine's fault. "And certainly none of it was my fault," she told herself hotly. She would, she reflected, have to tell Malory. For quite some time she had felt that was inevitable, but she had not meant to acquaint him with the facts until after they were married.

Now she realized with startling clarity that if she didn't inform Malory of her Aunt's irregularities, Malory would hold against her two grievances:

    a. The irregularities themselves.
    b. Her silence on the matter.

    •   •   •   •   •

"Asshur wouldn't be like that," her heart advised her stubbornly. "Asshur wouldn't care if I was illegitimate myself . . . as long as I was a good girl."—She thought of his letters. "Well of course any man wants his girl to be good."

Well she'd have to tell Malory, somehow, sometime—she couldn't say when. How she hated it! And the thought came to her insistently, that she wouldn't have been afraid to tell Asshur; Asshur would never let her down. Asshur cared for her, and for her only. No amount of scandal, no degree of misbehavior connected with her relatives, no libel circulated about herself would change Asshur. He would see her with his clear, strong, young eyes and somehow nothing else would enter his field of vision. Vaguely the thought of him comforted her, strengthened her.

"Well I'll tell Malory," she promised herself again. "And if he doesn't like it, he can—" But she couldn't finish the flippant phrase. She really was in love with him, and she cared immensely for the kind of life for which she had waited so wearily, and which without effort he represented. No she couldn't endure it if he did "lump it."

A branch tapping against the upper window sash and showing her the breaking day reminded her that she'd better go to sleep.

"But it hasn't been such a hot Christmas after all," she decided settling down more comfortably in her warm pillows.

.   .   .   .   .   .

Malory could hardly wait for her to mount the bus before he began his ardent apologies, "I think I was horrid, Melissa. I know I had no right to speak to you as I did last night. You didn't mean anything and I don't blame Adamson for keeping you as long as he could. You're a darn good dancer. . . .

"There's just a streak in me that makes me want my girl to be super—that's all there is to it. It's not jealousy exactly. I don't seem to want her to be looked at, or talked about—I guess in my mind I sort of want her to be quiet, almost mousy. . . ."

Startled she turned her gay young face toward him. "Why how can you say that Malory? It's precisely because I wasn't quiet or mousy that you became interested in me. Why think of that first day you met me at Kitty's. I was the noisiest thing, and I was all over the place——"

"Yes and that's the way I want you to keep on being," he assured her with a vehemence that struck her, all child as she was, as being too pronounced for the occasion. Of course she couldn't see into his mind and discern the pictures of the deadly, discouraging morning he had spent in the brief hours separating them since the night before.

He had come downstairs, he had thanked his sisters for their gifts, and had stood rather confidently, expecting some comment on what he in his innocence had selected for them. He had gone to some pains and self-denial to buy each of them a chiffon velvet dress—a black one for Harriett, rather severe and elegant, and a beautiful, brightly dark blue one for Reba. There was a lovely crescent-shaped buckle of brilliant green stones on Harriett's and a graceful fall of creamy lace on the one he had chosen for Reba. He had surreptitiously borne two of their gowns to the store to be sure of the fit and the salesgirls had shown real, if amused, and slightly pitying interest.

Reba remarked now on this morning after Christmas that the gowns were much too fine, that there was no place they could use them—"since we never go anywhere," said she without regret. To-morrow she would take them back and the money would probably keep them in underwear and stockings, "and things," she ended vaguely, "for a year."

Stunned and hurt and bewildered he stood while his mother, down early this morning, raised expressionless eyes and thanked him for the package he had sent her. "I haven't opened it yet, son, but I'll get around to it sooner or later. I know it's something very nice."

The utter lifelessness of the scene made him deathly sick. He could, he thought, swoon—or even vomit,—with the disgust it brought him. He remembered, when, as a very little boy, he had gone with his Aunt Viny, all joyous expectancy, to spend a day on a pleasure boat up the river. And as soon as the boat began to move he had become violently ill . . . even when they placed him in a berth he could not get rid of the horrid feeling which enveloped him. It had frightened him so, to think that not even lying down could relieve his indisposition. . . .

This morning he had gone back to his room without tasting his breakfast, he had sat in his arm chair with the gay chintz cover which he had pathetically picked out—"the wildest thing you have in the store," he had told the clerk—and had let a sort of frightening stupor creep over him. Frightening because it made him afraid that the awful secret curse which enshrouded his mother and sisters might some day—soon—enshroud him. And then he had thought of Melissa, so bright, so blithe, so alive . . . and he had caught up his hat and coat and dashed out into the gay December sunshine, only to remember with a catch in his throat that almost brought him to tears, that last night he had actually chidden her. He, Malory had dared to rebuke Melissa! Very much as though the gray, cold earth had dared to rebuff the sun!

He was really very contrite.

Melissa, happy and confident once more, smiled at him. She was infinitely relieved. Even so she would have to tell him, she decided. But even after she did it would be all right. "He needs me," she said to herself over and over again, not guessing the cause of that need. "He needs me and so everything will really be all right. Any coothead could see that."

They were both of them divinely, devastatingly hungry. Malory because in his disgust he had walked off without anything to eat, Melissa partly because she had been too delicate to invade the Brown's kitchen if no one was there, partly because she was afraid to tackle Pelasgie Stede if she were in charge.

"She dislikes me," she told Malory. "I don't know why."

"And I know you don't care," Malory answered. "Who cares about the Brown's maid?"

The day was fine and bright and sharp, the bus was only a third full and ran briskly and with a most engaging crunch over the fine dry snow. On the

banks of the road beneath the brown trees it lay
compact and undisturbed, like a smoothly laid
blanket. The sky was very blue, some school-
children in bright red caps and mittens scurried into
the woods, their skates in their hands toward some
not too remote frozen little stream. Two of the
little boys had new sleds.

"If only we had skates or a sled!" Melissa sighed
to Malory.

Presently it was their stop and right about the
bend was the little white road house and the hospitable Greek. He was pock-marked and wore a
villainous red stuff muffler about his throat, but he
was a good chef, heaven alone only being able to
solve how he had come by his knowledge of American cookery.

They went into the little back-room and the Greek
built a fire in the blackened chimney and piled on it
logs damp enough to sizzle. And they ate turkey
soup with onions in it, and roast turkey and stuffing
with chestnuts, cranberry sauce, stewed canned corn,
tomato and lettuce salad. Melissa had forgotten
to bring her little package of celery which the Brown
girls discovered several days later in her little room
and wondered how it had got there. But the Greek
with composure and nonchalance produced some
very white and hard, and Melissa pronounced it
better than what they had had at home.

Malory declared they had eaten for hours. And
afterwards they walked six of the fifteen miles home
along a path in the woods which ran almost parallel
with the road. Both of them were on wings, and

happier, they felt than they could ever possibly be again in their lives.

Melissa voicing some indefinable doubt said: "It must be all right Malory for us to love each other and to get married—we feel so good about it."

He stared at her. "All right? Why I should say! Oh gosh, Melissa to think that you should be in the world and I should be in it too, the same years, the same place—we might so easily have missed each other. And here you are just the girl for me."

She asked wonderingly: "How can you possibly know that?"

"Because you are me—I'm you. I recognized you the moment I met you. You're the other part of me—like—like a shell and what it contains. I had in me all these dark, vacant spaces, and you had the gifts with which to fill them—light, richness, life itself,—why Melissa, if I were to lose you now, I guess I'd die. And we see things alike, we're both proud and we're both ambitious, we both want the best. We both realize that the world is full of beauty and loveliness and we both mean to get our share of them."

Standing there in the little woods all sharply etched in white and brown they kissed under the last brilliance of the dying winter sun.

Afterwards they found the bus and rode home almost in silence. Fortified with magazines and the memory of his dear girl and the beautiful day, Malory felt he could endure the dank, gloomy house. And anyway his room would be bright and gay.

Melissa stole in through the side door and

scampered up to her room. Presently she came down to the kitchen to find Aunt Sal looking in the ice-box. "Hello! That you Melissa? Did you have a good time? Laurentine's gone over to Mrs. Ismay's, so I let the girls off. How'd you like to have just a mite of turkey—it's always so good the second day, or here's some ham and the greens we had left from the day before Christmas!"

Melissa opined that she'd had enough turkey for one while. "Think I'd like the ham and greens. Let's have it out here in the kitchen, Aunt Sal. I'll make some teeny, weeny baking-powder biscuits, just enough for you and me," she said smiling happily. She liked to be alone with Aunt Sal. She wished she dared confide some of her precious secrets to her—to Aunt Sal, who she knew must be able to keep secrets safe and well.

CHAPTER XXIX

IT had been a lovely day, a perfect day, a most satisfactory day and yet that night again she dreamed her horrible dream.

Again she saw the road; she saw herself running, running to overtake that queer, shuffling figure. Again she had the feeling that she knew who the figure was and again dreaded worse than she dreaded death to have it turn around. Long before daybreak she awoke; there were beads of sweat on her brow, indeed there was a fine perspiration over her whole body. For a while she lay there, spent and exhausted . . . thinking not so much of the dream as of what would become of her, if this sort of thing continued . . . shivering at the thought of how terrible it would be if this dream should be realized.

And suddenly she knew it would be realized. She said to herself: "This is really going to happen. I wonder what will become of me then." And with that thought came the memory that Asshur, she was sure it was Asshur, was also in the dream . . . if the reality of it ever came to pass, undoubtedly he would be in that reality. Her shivering ceased, she lay quiet, revelling in the warmth of the cozy bed and in her knowledge of the comfort which her room contained. She snapped on the light and with relief, picked out its dear accessories, the comfortable arm chair, the purple and gold hangings flapping slightly in the chilly morning breeze entering the half-opened window, the familiar little dressing table with its secret store of cosmetics. . . . She must get some more powder, she would get two shades, ochre and white, that would make just the right combination for her; she had seen Gertrude Brown mix them and she and Gertrude were of about the same color.

Thinking on such commonplace things she grew vital and normal again. . . . It was Christmas Week, she didn't have to go to school the next day, didn't even have to get up very early if she didn't care to. It was fun lying here in the "stilly night" —she had been struck by the words which she had read in a poem prescribed for supplementary reading in her English—it was fun to be thinking, living, breathing softly, consciously, like this, just keeping oneself alive. . . . She wondered why Gertrude

Brown never wore green, she ought to look very well in it; "even better than me," she decided, dispassionately critical. . . . She wondered, drowsily, if Gertrude Brown really liked Malory. . . .

Malory!

Her heavy lids flew wide open. Malory! Why hadn't she thought of him? Why hadn't he appeared both in her mind and in her dream to rescue her from this terrifying crisis, this portentous happening that crouched, she was sure of it, just round the corner of her future, waiting like a dragon, to devour, not her life, but her happiness, her peace, her sense of well-being?

And after a while it was borne in on her why Malory could not come to help her . . . shivering, she put her head under the covers and lay there as in an ague for a long while. But finally, she emerged calmer, and spoke aloud to herself once more in the eerie silence of the early day.

"Asshur will be there." She called his name softly to the corners of the dainty room. . . . Reassured, she arose, and throwing her violet robe over corn-colored pajamas, went over to her dresser and drew out a packet of letters—Asshur's. On her way back to the warm bed she stopped at the little dressing table, pulled out Asshur's wrist watch and fastened it with slim shaking fingers about her amber-tinted wrist.

So, she was safe.

.   .   .   .   .

Morning found her restored and refreshed. She opened eyes on a bright sun that showed dazzlingly on the snow that lay in the back yard. The branches

of the Chinaberry Tree which she glimpsed right
well from her window though the tree was more
directly below Laurentine's, bore feathery ruffs of
the powdery substance—Melissa thought she'd
like to stand under them and knock the stuff off and
feel it fall cold and stinging against her warm
cheek. . . .

She glanced at the watchband which surprisingly
clasped her wrist, and remembering her fantastic
fears of the night before, took it off smiling. As
though anything could happen! "Dear old Asshur,"
she murmured and forgot him again.

To-day she would not see Malory. After she had
finished her household stints she was to go over to
school and see a performance of certain acts of "*Le
Voyage de Monsieur Perrichon.*" Probably none of
her friends would be over there, excepting Ben
Davis, Malory being long since beyond the enjoyment of such elementary stuff. He had had a pretty
stiff course of the language in Philadelphia and was
now reading Loti and even Proust. French did not
come easily to Melissa, her ear played her unexpected tricks but she was immensely tickled by
Labiche's little masterpiece, so she had read and re-
read several times the few scenes which were to be
enacted, and anticipated a good laugh.

On the whole she was glad not to be seeing
Malory to-day. Not because he wearied her, she
always wanted to see him, but because she hated so
to be deceiving Aunt Sal. She did not mind it in
the case of Laurentine; Laurentine had brought this
situation on herself but her aunt was different. More
than once the young girl thought of confiding in this

woman who without ostentation had already moth-
ered her far more than Judy. But something
curiously delicate held her back. Aunt Sal she knew
could have no objection to Malory, a fine, decent
upstanding lad, her aunt would have said, but the
two young people meant to marry in June and
Laurentine's mother might not like Melissa to marry
before her daughter.

Dr. Denleigh, it was true, was constantly at
the house, there was no mistaking what his intentions
were; he was no Phil Hackett. But on the other
hand it did not look as though a wedding were in
immediate prospect. Melissa knew how much time
would be consumed in preparations for the wedding
which she would have had, had circumstances been
different.

She bustled about this morning, lively and singing
the latest song hits: "Give Me Something to Remember You By," "Lady Play Your Mandolin,"
and an old melody of her childhood, "It Had to Be
You." This was one of the days she enjoyed so
much just because she was grateful for her youth
and good-fortune and eminent decency, for her
pretty home and above all for her dazzling prospect.
. . . But she was just as glad to postpone seeing
Malory until to-morrow.

So dressed in her little snug brown suit, with the
chic, snug fur collar, and her little fur muff, her
clever little hat with its green feather pulled down
well over one eye, she went alone to the school play.
On her way she passed Dr. Denleigh driving carefully in his car. He thrust his head out the window
and shouted, "Probably I'll see you to-night."

"And how nice that is for Laurentine!" she thought to herself wistfully, plodding on and on through the streets whose whiteness the sun had turned into slush. The play was charming; the boy who took the part of Perrichon was amazingly, unaccountably good in his rôle. Ben Davis was there and he came and sat beside her and the two laughed with the unfettered heartiness of youth. Afterwards he walked home with her. She was reviewing how to give him his congé when they reached her gate. And unbelievably when they arrived Aunt Sal came to the front door and beckoned them in. "How do you do, dear?" she said to Ben, "I hope you've had a very merry Christmas!"

She pressed him to stay to supper and he accepted her invitation and ate great quantities of food and a lot of cocoa and afterwards French bon bons which Aunt Sal called "Christmas candy." She said it was nice to see him there and urged him on to a fourth piece of cake, and in answer to his apologies she said it did her good to see him eat. It reminded her of Asshur.

"Oh yes," said Ben, "how is Asshur? He's given all us fellows the air, but I guess you hear from him, Melissa."

Melissa unaccountably blushing, said she did, and Laurentine noting her rising color thought: "Perhaps she does care about him after all. Perhaps my not letting her have company hasn't been so hard on her." And relieved, she too joined in the light talk.

Later Dr. Denleigh did come in; the five of them played parchesi and whist from which last

Melissa or Ben alternately "rose and flew." The one who did not play, performed distractingly on Melissa's ukelele. Melissa recalled snatches from the farce which they had seen that afternoon and rolled them off; Ben donned his overcoat, stuffed his own and the Doctor's mufflers under it and converted himself into a rotund, portly Perrichon, speaking execrable French. Laurentine recalling little scraps of her own High School French, applauded whenever she caught a single recognizable word. Denleigh, whose own French was pretty good, abetted her. Aunt Sal, understanding none of it, enjoyed it most.

They passed a shockingly noisy, agreeable evening. When Ben rose to go Aunt Sal told him he must look in often and Laurentine said, "Yes, do come—soon."

Melissa went with him to the door, waved him good-night, thinking: "What a break that would have been for me, if that had only been Malory! . . . Poor Malory! I suppose he's sitting all hunched up at home, alone, with those terrible sisters. My, it's certainly been one swell day!"

. . . . .

As a matter of fact, Malory that evening deserved any other epithet than the word "poor." About six o'clock he'd strolled into the village somewhat forlornly to hunt up a magazine, the intention formulating rather slowly in his mind to go in later and try some chess at Herbert Tucker's when he heard a nice voice say:

"And what are you about wandering 'lonely as a cloud?' "

The words he knew couldn't possibly be meant for him, but curious to see who was quoting Wordsworth in the midst of the streets of Red Brook, he turned to reconnoiter. Having done so he found himself looking four-square into the eyes of Gertrude Brown.

She dropped him a curtsy: "How now Mr. Forten? Whither away, if a mere maid may ask?"

"Nowhere, Miss Brown. And may one inquire your errand in these parts?"

"Nothing," she said, smiling and showing very white teeth, "if not to catch up stray young men and carry them home to supper."

He said guilelessly and regretfully: "Oh I'm so sorry. I've had my supper."

"Well, come along then and watch us eat," she laughed at him. "You're not absolutely bound to partake of food just because you see us doing it. . . . Sure you haven't anything better to do?"

Nothing he could think of, he assured her, would be better anyway. Pleased and charmed he followed her home to a sparkling, bountiful table where after all he did break bread. And above all he had the pleasure of some good man talk with Dr. Brown. For all his scoffing he was missing the stout old codgers who had persisted in calling on Aunt Viny up to the very end—seeing in her incomprehensibly the sprightly young girl of their pasts. . . . Since coming to live in his gloomy, manless home, Malory had missed the stiffish arguments of those elderly fellows, their dogmatic asseverations, their quips and jests of another day.

Of course it was lovely, it was great being with

Melissa but "Oh boy, isn't it good to get into this regular home life!" he thought. He noted with sharp pleasure the little sparring bouts between Kitty and her father, the lazy, wise interpolations of Mrs. Brown, the apposite witty shrewdness in Gertrude's remarks.

"A smooth girl," he thought to himself. "Gertrude's a shrewd girl, but mighty nice."

It was the first time he'd ever seen the family like this, all together, not entertaining, completely themselves, relaxed and at ease like people in dressing gowns and slippers.

After supper they played the radio. Dr. Brown wanted to hear Amos and Andy and surprisingly some race-track news; Kitty switched all this off as quickly as possible, got some jazz and practiced a few intricate steps which she said she had picked up from Jerry Adamson. Mrs. Brown, wrapped up in a paper-covered book, forgot them completely. Even Gertrude puffing fastidiously on a cigarette dipped into the evening paper, of which she generously offered him half.

He was not quite sure that he liked to see women smoke, but Gertrude did her smoking as she seemed to do everything, easily, naturally.

By and by she tossed the paper aside, picked up a fat volume, and indicated a seat at her side.

"Ever see these?" she asked him. The book was one of verses by Hardy. "You looked as though you liked poetry and you look as though you read it well. Read me some."

He read well and with pleasure Hardy's homely

verses with their strangely turned diction, their rugged sincerity.

When the time came to go he thanked Gertrude warmly for a wonderful evening. "You can't guess what it's been for me."

"Well," said Kitty to her sister after they had gone upstairs and while they were making ready for bed: "I *am* surprised! The sophisticated, the ultra Miss Gertrude Brown falling—and how!—for a country bumpkin."

"He isn't a country bumpkin," her sister retorted. "You know that as well as I. And anyway Kitty lay off him. I like that lad."

"Oh yeah!" said Kitty derisively, "And so does Melissa Paul like him and unless I am very much mistaken Mr. Malory Forten likes her."

"Well," replied Gertrude amiably and without relevancy, "stranger things have happened."

. . . . .

Malory thought to himself in the curiously vivid phrases of modern youth: "What a girl! Of course different from Melissa, but still and all smooth, smooth, and what-a-girl!"

He thought about her a great deal that night and many other days and nights. She had about her what he greatly admired, an air, poise, self-assurance. She was well-trained too, and not, as many young people are, ashamed of that training. On the contrary it was so much a part of her that not to show it would have been a deliberate alteration of her integrity. Malory liked and respected this quality. In his new found need for life and cheer he had forgotten the promptings of his own intense but narrow standards. Melissa, now, he considered dispassionately, gave no promise of possessing or ever succeeding to a similar development. She would never be a finished product; he would always have to mould her and shape her. Not that that in the deeper inner consciousness of the true male was so undesirable. After all she was really very dear.

Unwittingly, Melissa, the very next time she saw Malory emphasized this dependence of hers. She had had to go to Newark for Aunt Sal, and Malory, meeting her in Madison, accompanied her, and the two went together to a movie. The scene depicted Commander Byrd's visit to the South Pole and Melissa so clearly needed information with regard to penguins, ice floes, "huskies," sledges and what not that her companion quickly regained his opinion of her as the most charming girl he had ever known.

Add to this the fact that during an intermission the heightened illumination revealed Melissa with her abundant, bright hair brushed back plainly and smoothly in little girl fashion, as being so childish, so confiding that his instinct to protect received an unexpected fillip. Moreover, she was thinner for no better reason than that she had overeaten of the Christmas plenitude and so was forced for a day or two to fast. Naturally she said nothing of this and the unaccountable fragility made its appeal. . . . The frightfulness of the dream recurred to her too when she saw Malory and made her cling to him and bend toward him with the manner of one who says: "Here I know is security." All in all a combination bound to flout Gertrude's momentary intrusion.

.   .   .   .   .

Gertrude telephoned him that night. She was leaving the next day, she said. The volume of Hardy which adroitly she had lent him the night before, would be, she was sure, quite safe with him. He need not bother mailing it to her, but if he would just be kind enough to copy out "Welcome Home" and send her that. It was one of her favorites.

Malory thought again that she was an awfully nice girl. No trouble about her. Lots of other girls would have had him traipsing with the book back to their houses before they left. Or more annoying yet would have had him send the volume, and there'd be all that wrapping up to do, and going for stamps and having it weighed and waiting interminable moments in line at the Post Office and all. There were so many foreigners in Red Brook and they were always buying postal money orders when one entered the Post Office, making the purchase of even a two cent stamp a matter for consideration.

He certainly appreciated her giving him permission to keep the volume and of course he would copy the poem for her. "And send a line with it telling you how I like it," he added unconscious that his suggestion followed hers as the night follows the day.

Her cool, clear voice with its barely perceptible hint of satisfaction in it replied that that was mighty fine of him. "I'd certainly like to hear from you though I must confess I'm a very poor correspon-

dent.   But we won't dwell on that. . . .   Good-bye
and Happy New Year, Malory!"

Smiling he hung up the receiver, ensconced himself in the arm chair with the volume in question, all
ready for a pleasant hour of reading.   But before
long his thoughts were wandering far from the ven-
erable poet.   He was thinking that this would be
indeed a happy New Year because he himself would
make it so. . . .   The possibility of his own potenti-
alities in this field had never before occurred to him.
Hitherto he had only wished for such a condition
never consciously taking steps to insure it.   But now
he himself Malory Forten would bring it to pass.

And while his little gas heater hummed and sput-
tered he fell to thinking in its cheerful light of how
differently placed he would be this time next year.
Away from this hateful, dismal place, at school in
Boston, studying, talking with clever people, married
to and living with Melissa, gaining warmth and
mellowness from her cheerfulness and radiance . . .
he went to sleep thinking how much he loved her
and, apart from love and its implications, how very,
very much he liked her.

.   .   .   .   .

Once at his Aunt Viny's he had heard a crony of
hers relate with some detail the chronicle of a young
girl, the grand-daughter of a mutual friend of their
childhood days, and how her marriage conceived
and entered upon with such high hopes had withered
and broken.

"And for no reason at all," said Mrs. Crockett,
"except that a lot of people were jealous of her
happiness and so had wished her ill luck."

He had been a boy of seventeen then, indifferent and incurious regarding the subjects of most of the conversations that wound endlessly on between his great-aunt and her host of aged friends. But this idea had struck him.

"Why Mrs. Crockett they couldn't bring Evie bad luck by just wishing it."

"Oh couldn't they though!"

"Why how ridiculous! Why Aunt Viny you know that couldn't be true."

Aunt Viny without removing for one second her faded glance from contemplation of the "busy-body" which adorned her second story window, yet contrived to give the impression of lending to the matter her fervid consideration.

"I ain't so sure of that son. . . . There now Carolina Crockett, you can see for yourself . . . there's that man comin' out of Mrs. Harper's. And he's there every afternoon from two till four, just as punctual. And her husband don't come home till six. It's amazing the brazenness of some people. . . .

"Well Malory I don't know . . . we always feel we do better for having the good-will of those who know us. Now ain't it reasonable to suppose we might suffer a'count of their ill-will too?" She was an old woman and had seen many strange things. She had a mind and a reason of her own too. "After all ain't that the idea behind God and the devil? God has good intentions toward you and the devil has bad ones. If you follow the devil his bad intentions will get you just as surely as if, when you follow

God, his good intentions will save you." A hard-headed practical Christian she was.

The memory of this conversation had always remained, but well in back of the boy's consciousness. It would have leaped to the fore to-night if he could have seen and heard Pelasgie Stede.

Pelasgie on her way home from Newark where she had spent the day cleaning had dropped in at the movies. She was in a morose condition, partly because it went against her grain to work "for them hinckty, cullud folks, thinks-themse'fs-so-much," partly because as soon as she saw the opening scene of the picture she knew she had made a mistake. What were Commander Byrd and his exploits at the South Pole to her? Less even than she to Commander Byrd. Pelasgie had come to the theatre to see a modernized version of King Cophetua and the beggar girl.

A thrifty maiden she nevertheless sat through the end of the picture and waited for it to come on again for she had missed the first part. It was then in the brief up-blazing of the lights that she had caught sight of Melissa and Malory—Melissa, confident and yet appealing, Malory confident and protecting. And because she was young and ugly and squire-less and Melissa was young and pretty and escorted, the envy and jealousy which always lurked in Pelasgie's heart when contemplating those more fortunate than herself, flared into a sudden flame of hatred and malice which would, if it had been a palpable thing, have seared the innocent boy and girl.

"Settin' there, thet gal, one of them turrible

Stranges jes' as though she was as good as anybody," she complained to her uncle Johnathan Stede,
sole occupant of the house when she arrived. Johnasteen had gone to a "social."

The old man sitting in his rusty wrinkled clothes
before the fire, let her rave on. Very rarely did he
speak of the Stranges—certainly almost never in
their defense. To have done so would have been to
admit that they, somehow, someway were at fault
and this he would never have acknowledged. Sarah
Strange, to him, since the first day he saw her had
been an absolutely right person, a law unto herself.

"Who," fumed Pelasgie, "does she think she is?
Comin' there to Mrs. Brown's just as big as any of
them real big colored folks from New York or some
of those places! 'Tell Kitty, I'm here will you
Pelasgie' she says, 'or no, I'll run up and tell her
myse'f.' Just as though I was nothin' er nobody.

"I'm an honest girl," continued Pelasgie, "many's
the time I feels like goin' to her with her fine airs
and tellin' her I may not be the high yaller she is,
but at least if I'm black I'm honest. My family
ain't never been mixed up with white folks yit,
neither my cousin Johnasteen ner me. No ner I
ain't likely to be neither," she concluded virtuously.
Which was certainly true.

She went on, fanning her wrath. "Got Johnasteen
all wrop aroun' her little finger because she work
for her high and mighty cousin in that nice house
that ole w'ite man lef' her mother. The wages of
sin I calls it. . . . Always lookin' at the fellers too,"
complained Pelasgie whom no amount of looking at

the fellers would have availed anything. "And now that she's got this Forten boy. . . ."

The old man erect and motionless became if possible even more erect, more motionless. Something within him signaled attention.

"Whut Morton boy, niece?"

"I ain't said Morton, I said Forten; boy lives way over toward the south end way other side the Eppses. His sisters is caterers, you don't hardly ever see them—two dumb women."

Mr. Stede spoke with a certain breathlessness, somewhat at variance with his immobile posture. "She goes out with that Davis feller sometimes."

"Well she was out with this Forten feller tonight," Pelasgie rejoined shortly. "Always makin' up to him too when he's over to Mis' Brown. I do hate a girl's always makin' up to a feller. . . . One thing it can't last long. He's got to go off somewheres to school; hear him say he's goin' in June. Ain't that a funny time to be goin' off to school? Bet he's just goin' to get shet of her. Do you see him much roun' Mis' Strange house, uncle?"

"Don't see him there at all," said Mr. Stede still not turning his head but frowning intensely at the stove. "Thet gal Melissa ain't thinkin' 'bout this Forten boy, onliest one she's got on her mind is that Asshur Lane."

"Well whoever's she's got," his niece replied spitefully, "all I got to say is I hate her. I know she ain't comin' to no good end. And all I got to say is if I ever get a chance to give her a push that way I'll do it. Settin' herself above decent girls like me just because we has to earn our honest livin'." She sniffed darkly. "They's worse ways for a girl to earn her livin' than doin' housework."

"I sh'd say so," her uncle aquiesced. "Here comes Johnasteen. Wouldn't advise you to let her hear you carry on like this, Pelasgie."

She became silent then, stumping off noisily upstairs and to bed, with no mind to run counter to her cousin's stout defenses for the Stranges.

Johnasteen, heavy footed like her father went clumping about, closing shutters, locking doors. "Think I'll go to bed, father. You comin' up? You'd better, it's kinda late."

But he thought he would wait awhile. And so he sat there far into the quiet night turning over and over the bits of gossip which Pelasgie had let fall. "Things is picked up so now fer Mis' Strange, I can't bear to think of startin' up her worries agin," he mumbled into his beard. After all, what was there to dread? In six months this boy would be gone—probably never to come back. Nothing much could happen in six months. "And then Asshur'll come back, he'll give Melissa plenty to think about."

If he could only keep Pelasgie "off'n her!" There was something chilling, marrow-freezing in an ill-will so intense, so active. "After all," he solaced himself, "she don't know nothin', 'n ef she'll jes' keep her mouf shet." Sighing a little over the unlikelihood of this he went creaking off noisily to bed.

CHAPTER XXX

THAT was a lovely winter. Laurentine and Melissa looking back in later safer years on this year in which fate showed itself at its sorriest, often recalled this season, dwelt on it, relived it; Laurentine with a certain sweet poignance; Melissa with a familiar pang of terror, a prayerful sense of gratitude.

There were snow and ice in abundance, but the winter, though a severe one, was singularly pleasing and beautiful. The snow renewed itself constantly, so that everywhere were constant stretches of glistening, dazzling white. Redd's Brook proper froze deeper than it had ever been known, responding not a whit to the brilliant persistent sun which made up in glory what it lacked in warmth.

Denleigh, southern-born, had seen very little of winter sports as a boy, and had been too busy to take them on as a young man. Now suddenly he succumbed to their charm. Every moment which he could spare from his work he spent outdoors, skating, sleighing, ski-ing. Laurentine accompanied him in the first two of these activities, coming home wind-blown and rosy at night to have a final steaming cup of the delicious cocoa which Aunt Sal had left for them on the back of the stove in the kitchen. There would be a few moments of gay talk on nothing—the skates—the condition of the ice—the angle at which Denleigh wore his skating cap. And then the overpowering rush of languor spreading over her tired muscles. . . . "Oh Stephen, I'm so tired! I could go to sleep just standing up!"

Denleigh would laugh down at her, his own face shining with health and happiness. "Run up to bed, sleepy-head! See you to-morrow."

It seemed to her she had never known such joy in living, such well-being. She had, in fact, never realized that such things existed. Few dances were given in Red Brook, none had been open to her in her extreme youth, and now it was doubtful that she would have gone, if she could. The skating supplied her with the poetry of motion which her beautiful sinuousness required; she loved her awareness of the perfect mechanism of her body; even at the beginning she adored the feel of the ache in her muscles. It was a treat to know she had them.

And all this exercise and outdoor life was having its effect on her disposition. She lost once for all that diffidence which she had felt but so rarely had shown. It had always been there but now it was completely vanquished. Mingling with the crowd, passing through them with Denleigh at her side she was like a slender burnished arrow weaving in and out. Once she met Hackett, felt his burning, passionate eyes deep on hers. Her instinct, at one time would have been to turn away with a carefully simulated indifference. Now she met and recognized his gaze, responded to it with a grave bow—because she was truly indifferent.

It was as if her newly balanced and co-ordinated body had lent a similar balance and co-ordination to her mind. Nothing outside of overwhelming fundamental disasters could be lastingly evil, eternally damning in this bright, blue, cheerful, laughing world of sport. You couldn't cry, you couldn't weep with your nerves all stimulated, your mind all steady, your heart all responsive—like this. Unconsciously she saw herself differently, as the least important and yet as the most important feature in her world.

And all this time she was building up a comradeship with Denleigh, emerging from his ægis, to wear one of her own which enabled her to walk side by side with him. She was serene, triumphant, sure of her lover, for the first time in her life sure of herself.

She used to say to him: "Oh Stephen isn't it too perfect? If we could go on like this forever!"

But he wanted his wife: "It will be much more fun being married," he told her sagely, "wait and see. This way we could still be separated. Married we'll be one. No this is all very fine, my dear, but I must be much more sure of you than this. You must be surer of me. . . ."

"I wonder," she would murmur, "if I can be."

.   .   .   .   .

Melissa's joys of course were not so mature, not experienced with such introspection. Since Laurentine had taken to going about she could not of course spend too much of her time outside with Malory. She had to be discreet. But it created a new understanding between them. Melissa would leave the house with Ben, of whom her relatives approved. She would see to it that Laurentine glimpsed her skating with her young escort. And then this over, she would leave Ben and skate with Malory, far, far off down the reaches of the Brook where the willows in spring hung so plaintively. And after that there would be Herbert Tucker, and a little rival skating with Kitty Brown, who shone in this, as she did in all sports.

It was great fun, both Melissa and Malory thought, to play such indifference before others and yet to be so tinglingly aware, he of her, she of him. Under the ghostly willows when the turn of chance brought them an opportunity to visit them, they clung together for a sweet moment and kissed, then catching each other's hands they swerved back like big, lovely birds swooping and swaying until they'd reached the center of the crowd again. There they parted carelessly, to mingle ostentatiously unaware, with other girls and boys, to reunite at the end of another half-hour or so, amused, triumphant, unspeakably full of their love, of their bliss.

After it was all over, Ben would take her home, all unconscious of what had been going on under his very eyes. Once after she got in Malory telephoned her and she talked to him in laughing whispers, well aware that Laurentine and Denleigh not twenty feet away were too absorbed to know that she was even about. And once when she knew that Laurentine was not coming home but was going with her lover from the Brook over to Mrs. Ismay's for cards and a late supper, she actually let Malory in the kitchen again. And the two sat giggling, close together like bad children in the warm spicy darkness. They ate a sandwich or two, whispering happily of gay nothings, of utter nonsense, until suddenly an overpowering awareness descended upon them, stimulating and yet paralyzing; until finally Malory stammered he thought he'd better be going. Melissa nervously fumbling with the door could not turn the key in the lock too quickly after him. Skurrying upstairs she undressed in the pitch blackness, her face on fire. . . .

. . . . .

The thaw, and the spring with it, seemed to come over night. One day they were skating on the Brook, the next the ice was cracking, showing deep fissures. Little stray breezes blew from nowhere riding like feathers on stiffer, chillier, currents of air, touching the cheek with unbelievable delicacy, carrying with them some overpowering memory, some faint poignant hint of something that had happened a long time ago. And presently the heart remembered that miraculously it had been spring and miraculously it would be spring again. . . . The willows along the brook were bare and ghostly; then one day, though still bare, they were no longer ghostly, there was life in them, creeping, mysterious, pungent. . . .

"The time of the singing of birds is come," Malory quoted to Melissa. She did not know that he was quoting . . . she never read the Bible, would have been amazed to hear it spoken of as poetry.

They were walking by the Brook which people deserted after the skating season, "When spring really does come," Malory said, "the boys will be down here swimming. But we'll find some other place to go by then . . . and the next spring, why you'll be going in swimming where I go swimming. Think of that 'Lissa!"

Melissa did think of it, thought of it too often so that when they were together she was unable to conceal her sense of completeness, of possessiveness. And Malory responded in kind. Literally neither one of them spoke of the other to anyone else and yet almost anybody seeing them together at Kitty's, at a movie, standing briefly on the church portico, must know: "Here are two young people who are mightily attracted."

It was the end of February, the snow was gone, the Brook loosened; the middle of the day was deliciously balmy. Top-coats were beginning to be a nuisance, but older folks were shaking their heads and saying: "You know this is regular pneumonia weather. March is just around the corner. You know how treacherous that is!"

In the air were thoughts of kites, tops, roller-skates, spring hats . . . love.

Colored Red Brook society, a little comatose from the severity of the winter came to life, unwrapped itself, yawned, stretched, opened an eye and saw that the world was livable again, opened yet another eye and saw Malory and Melissa.

Not everybody noticed. Since Denleigh's quiet championship of Laurentine and Mrs. Ismay's unemphatic but persistent sponsoring, Red Brook had been inclined slowly, regretfully to let the Stranges alone. But their affairs had been such a delicious morsel.

Then too, Dr. Denleigh was a gentleman—yes—granted. He was a good doctor too. But not a

Red Brookian; and no more was Mrs. Ismay or that there Brown girl to whose house Melissa was always running. Asshur too was from far away—he had returned there—who knew why? And Harry Robbins, a genuine native it is true, but really of little account. But this new and elegant young stranger—young Forten now, related to those queer Forten girls! It did seem too bad for him to come in and have to get mixed up with that "passel of Stranges." True there were few girls in the town to whom he could direct his attention. Pelasgie Stede now with her funny, spotty face and her "bench" legs—that part of Red Brook that discussed such matters at length put a collective showing of hands on collective hips and laughed as only colored people can laugh, without malice, with gargantuan laughter, at something cosmically funny.

Many of them did not stop to trace the relationship of Malory to his mother and sisters. But a few of the older folks did. Mrs. Epps seeing Melissa and her young man sipping an orange drink, passed and repassed their slim unconscious backs until she had had a full view of Malory's face. Then a little aghast she entered into session over the telephone with Mrs. Tracey, two blocks away. Mrs. Tracey dropped everything and came around.

"You don't mean Malory Forten, Hannah Epps, him that was the baby when Forten died?"

"Sure do."

"Well ain't that the beatinest!"

"Sure is." Mrs. Epps was not usually duosyllabic, but in this case as she herself would have said, she was too tuckered out to talk.

"Look here, Gracey Tracey," she said finally using Mrs. Tracey's unbelievable combination of given and Christian name, "this really ain't none of our business. Guess we'd better keep out'n it. But oh my lan' won't there be an explosion some day! . . . But keep your mouth shet. I aim to."

Still even from a closed mouth it is possible to let fall a hint of mystery, of unheard-of surprises, of something with the possibility of both comedy and tragedy in it. . . . But after all one couldn't be sure.

Melissa thought she detected some slight change in her rarely met public—a colder, more intensely curious eye; a queer aloofness that had in it something different from either meanness or malice, something faintly terrifying. It made her think of her dream, from which thank heaven she had lately been completely free.

.   .   .   .   .

Of this, however, she did not speak to Malory, indeed it was a long time before she herself was convinced in her reasonable mind of what some watchful seventh sense pointed out to her as being true. The change on the face of Rev. Simmons when she approached him from priestly benevolence to momentarily stark anxiety; the completeness with which Mrs. Epps ignored Malory the day he went with her for eggs. The old woman actually stood between them, her back to the boy, questioning and drilling Melissa with a sort of severe dutifulness so different from her one time malicious curiosity that the girl was all at sea. Even Malory, with his total inability to perceive people whom he considered not

socially but cosmically inelegible, was struck by her
odd combination of rudeness and of interest. Not
liking it, he took Melissa by the arm and hustled
her out.

"That crazy old woman! Was she losing her
mind? What was she talking to you about Melissa?
She took pains not to let me hear her. What was
she mumbling?"

"I hardly know myself," the girl stammered.
"She—she—knows my folks, so I guess she thinks
she can give me advice. She—she was talking
about Asshur."

"Talking about Asshur! Well, I'll be—! Say
what's the matter with this damned town anyway?
What are they trying to do, give us the run-
around?"

They were destined to ask themselves that question very often in the difficult months that followed.

.   .   .   .   .

Mrs. Epps who had chidden Melissa on a memorable occasion for permitting Asshur to show his
preference for her so plainly, had been that day his
undivided champion. She advanced upon her subject
tacking, so to speak, like a sail-boat.

"You young girls, Melissa, can't afford to be too
keerful how you treats these boys. Sometimes hit
runes them." The young girl stared wondering
what insidious thing she might have done to Asshur
and how Mrs. Epps knew of it.

The old woman continued: "If I was young and
had a nice feller waitin' for me, eatin' his heart out,
'pears like I'd send for him—yep'n marry him too."
She went on at a great rate never mentioning

Asshur's name and yet making it clear that she was not referring to Malory, whom indeed she did not appear to see.

. . . . .

Then there was old Mr. Stede. Malory and Melissa strolling home from an evening spent in the little public library, hunting up references ran into the old man clumping down the street in his stiff, heavy boots. His eyes could not have been sightless after all for he espied them afar off and waited for them under the arc light.

"Kinda late fer you to be out, Melissa, ain't it?" he queried. The question was addressed to the girl but his eyes never left Malory's face. Instead without waiting for an answer he addressed the lad.

" 'N who may you be my boy'n how long you ben around yere?"

"My name's Malory Forten," said Malory, instinctively recognizing a person of character, "and I've been about now for some six months. I was born here though."

"H'mph," said the old man sniffing. "Well, I bids you, good-evenin'."

"And who's he?" asked Malory but without much surprise and with no resentment.

Melissa told him wearily that it was just an old man who had always worked for her aunt, "Been with her since before Laurentine was born."

Mr. Stede met Melissa the next afternoon in the back yard whence he had inveigled her to show her how nice and fresh the swing looked. "Got it done early this year; these seasons is so onchangeable now. Does your Aunt Sal know young Forten?"

He ran the whole conversation together as though the subject of Malory were the main theme for him.

"No," said Melissa rather low, "she doesn't. . . . Laurentine won't let me have him at the house, so we meet sometimes at the library and places and stroll home together." He was the first person to whom she had spoken of Malory and it made her feel better. No need either to ask Mr. Stede to keep his own counsel, none knew better than he how to do this.

"Laurentine won't let him come to the house," his strange eyes rested unseeingly on hers. "Why won't Laurentine let him come to the house? What's she got agin him?"

"Nothing. I doubt if she's ever seen him. It's me she's—agin. She's got some kind of mad on me and she doesn't want me to have any fun."

"What's she got agin you?"

"I don't know, honest I don't, Mr. Stede. Christmas, Aunt Sal invited Ben Davis to come in and he's been around two—three times to take me skating. But Laurentine won't hear to anyone else."

He ignored all this. "This young feller now, you know anything about him?"

"Nothing except that he lives way down South End, way beyond the Eppses. Lives with his mother and his two sisters—they do catering."

"Yes, I know. Is he—now—is he calcoolatin' to stay here long?"

"No, he's going away again in June right after he graduates and," she finished with sudden determination, "he's never coming back." She would never, never permit him to return to this miserable, pestering, busy-bodying hole.

He looked at her gravely. "Ef he's goin' away I wouldn't be seein' too much of him Melissy." Old as he was he could remember the way of men with maids. " 'Twouldn't do for you to set too much store on him, and him goin' away and all. You wasn't thinkin' of marryin' him, wuz you?"

"No," she said promptly, and hated herself for the lie.

" 'N I wouldn't see him too much nohow," he continued gently. "Never can tell about even the best of these city fellers. Gone to-day and here to-morrow, that's their motter. Always gone to-day. 'N don't you fergit it M'lissy. And another thing," he said delicately, "yore ant 'n yore cousin is ben had a powerful lot of trouble—most of it not their fault. 'Twould be a real pity if you wuz to add to it in any way. My advice to you Melissa would be to be good, jes' ez good as you kin be. . . ."

She smiled up at him, "You make me think of Asshur, Mr. Stede."

"Me too. It makes me think of Asshur too," he said bewilderingly. He rested a horny finger on her brown coat sleeve. "And let me tell you suthin', there's the man for you, Melissy, the man in a thousand thousand. . . ."

Melissa, half laughing, wholly provoked, expostulated. "What's the matter with this town, Mr. Stede, that it can't 'tend to its own business? Of course I don't mean you," she broke in on herself, but she was still vexed. "Here you are tellin' me to marry Asshur and the other day there was Mrs. Epps——"

He interrupted her, "Mis' Epps? She ever see you with Forten?" A red spark burned brightly in his eyes.

"Yes and she said——"

"Better run in now, Melissy. Gittin' too cold fer you out here. Glad you like the swing. Spec' to see you a-settin' out in it shortly."

．　　．　　．　　．　　．

He would go to see Mis' Epps. That Melissa should meet Mis' Epps! "It would'a ben better," he muttered into his beard, "if she'd a drank cold poison. It'd a ben better if she'd a fell in Redd's Brook. But I'll tell her, I'll tell her that M'lissy's a gonta marry Asshur. I'll tell her they both told me. Him, yes, and her too. . . ."

Late that night he left Mrs. Epps' bungalow gorged to repletion, Pentecost having been in one of its most beneficent moods. . . . He'd had to part with one or two of the choicest secrets which he had stored away in that secretive mind of his. He dared not be too obvious. Then he let it drop. . . . "Big doin's up at Mis' Strange's pretty soon. By summer I reckon. Shouldn't be surprised now ef'n Laurentine up and married that doctor feller any time now. See his pitcher up in her room one day last week. I wus up there cleanin' winders."

Mrs. Epps looked at him sharply, "That makes jus' one weddin'. What makes it so big?"

He took out a square of terrible tobacco and began to hack at it with a huge rusty jackknife, his foot in his great rusty boot with the unsightly ridges

as of cast-iron across the top swaying slowly, comfortably.

"Is Epps' spitoon handy, Mis' Epps? . . . Oh,
the little one, she's a cute trick, lotta boys callin'
her up all the time, walkin' around town with her.
Her ant don't allow them to call no more, 'count
she don't think it fair to Asshur. 'Ceptin' only that
Ben Davis boy, she let him come, yeah she shore
let him come, 'cause she knows he's Asshur's best
frien'."

Mrs. Epps said unbelievingly, "Asshur! What
about that Forten boy?" She watched him narrowly.

His gaze never wavered, his lashless lids steady
under his tangled brows. "Whut Forten boy?
Kinda slender, runty feller, one who helps her with
her farren langwidges?—She sho' has trouble with
them langwidges. 'Pears like I never see no gal
what has so much trouble as she has with langwidges. This here Forten feller he speak 'em
all the time. Yasm'm. He speak farren langwidges
with Melissy all the time. . . . Course these is secrets, Mis' Epps. B'lieve I won't wait for Sam
no longer." He pulled a letter from his pocket.
"Got to go round by the Post Office to mail this for
Melissy. She always sends me 'bout this time ev'ry
day I'm there. . . . Sho is a long ways from Red
Brook to Alabam!"

.   .   .   .   .

In her heart Melissa thought she knew the source
of Mrs. Epps' and even Mr. Stede's unprecedented
interest in her affairs. "It's that old business of
Aunt Sal and Colonel Halloway popping up again,"

she told herself disgustedly, "that's what all the shooting's for. My hat! Aren't they ever going to lay off it?"

Her mind had run like the town folks'. Dr. Denleigh, an outsider, might connect himself with the dubious Stranges. He was an unknown and then too he'd been married and presumably knew what he was looking for. If he'd found that in Laurentine—why so much the better for Laurentine, thought her complacent and unenvious younger cousin. "And besides he's an old man," mused Melissa who once had privately decided to die at the age of thirty-five rather than to attain to a doddering old majority of forty or thereabouts. Rather recently she had thought of changing this ultimatum. Mrs. Ismay and Mrs. Brown were women in their early forties and seemed to be going pretty well.

But in the case of Malory Forten, the finest young colored man as anyone could see in Red Brook, it was not at all surprising that people should resent his falling into the hands of a relative, however reputable, of the notorious Stranges. Melissa picked the adjective critically, secure in the knowledge that no notoriety could be traced to the door of either her or of her mother with her two most reputable marriages.

Sooner or later some one would make it his business to expostulate with Malory on his choice of a lady only to discover that Malory, far from requiring arguments pro and con, was absolutely ignorant of the whole affair, the lady of his choice having informed him of nothing, just nothing.

"And won't that put me in a tough spot!" thought
Melissa who went regularly to the movies and who
therefore saw all the best gangster pictures, acquired their vocabulary and, had not her mind been
so completely at another slant, might have acquired
also the common or garden variety of their tactics.

Malory, she knew now positively, was a snob.
Not in the ordinary sense. Malory would waste no
time, no thought, on persons like Pelasgie Stede
and Mrs. Epps. On the other hand, something in
him reached out with immediate respect to old
Johnathan Stede standing like a challenging sentinel
under the revealing arc light. That incident on the
whole had redounded to her credit.

In likewise he would see the intrinsic superiority so patent in Aunt Sal and Laurentine. He would
be, he had been, impressed already by the latter's
beauty and he would be just as greatly intrigued by
something finer than beauty in Aunt Sal,—if only
he could know her. But he would never be able to
forget that Aunt Sal had for years been the storm
center of the greatest scandal that had ever touched
Red Brook, that Laurentine, with her beauty and
her pride, her independence and above all her faithful reproduction of Colonel Halloway's other two
daughters, line for line, feature for feature, had
served to increase rather than decrease that scandal. . . .

Only he must be told, and that shortly. "And
by me," said Melissa stoutly. She had the insight
to see that her simple confession might be counted
unto her for righteousness. But again it might
bring with it an enveloping tarnish—she might not

appear so white, so desirable in her lover's eyes. Malory, she knew, wanted his roses dewy, his woman's reputation, not to say her virtue, unblemished and undiscussed.

"And yet," said Melissa sensibly, "if he hadn't fallen in love with me whom would he have fallen in love with, in this town?" Kitty and he were of the same class, but as far apart as the opposite, outer confines of that class. . . . Of course there was Gertrude . . . she knew Malory wrote to Gertrude, she rather thought that Gertrude looked with some favor on Malory. . . . If she and Malory should break and Malory were to go to Boston, his affair with Melissa behind him, and Gertrude still in Wellesley! Oh! she would never be able to endure that! . . . And again she thought of Asshur and remembered with pride but no comfort that in spite of his admonitions he would be ready to be anything she chose to let him be—yes were she ten times in Aunt Sal's predicament.

CHAPTER XXXI

MR. STEDE had unwittingly left with Melissa the germ of an idea. That swing now that he had just painted and was leaving out on the lawn! It was well to the rear of the house and rarely used, since Aunt Sal and Laurentine, like Melissa, chose when they sat out doors the shadow of the Chinaberry Tree. The weather was growing milder and the spring warmth was around the corner, even after sundown the air was soft and mild. Why shouldn't the two of them meet there late in the quiet night, well muffled and protected from stray breezes? In this way they would be safe from prying eyes, they could sit safely and comfortably outdoors and there would be no uncalled-for expression of opinion on the part of Mrs. Epps and others of her kind.

There were endless plans to be made these days. After all four months was little enough time for a boy of twenty-one and a girl of eighteen to make plans for the great adventure of marriage. There was money to be had, clothes to be bought, lodgings to be secured. Over and over they talked of that last day in school, when diplomas bestowed, each should feel equipped to step out into the world and therefore doubly the man or woman which they had been prior to that significant ceremony. More amply able to take care of their affairs and to emerge unhampered by acquaintances or relatives, friends or foes, into the splendid untried world.

Malory had a flair for precision. He would have liked to map out every moment of this intervening time, and to have every action hold some particular significance. In order to save they had decided to elope to Boston by bus and trolley. Malory had already possessed himself of countless maps and routes. He knew already all the stops and changes by heart. Melissa here in Red Brook was at times a little wilful, a little persistent in sustaining her preferences and decisions. But once they should have left Red Brook, the burden of the direction of their small affairs must rest with Malory. He as the man and as the director of their

little enterprise must be prepared to meet and conquer any emergency. Melissa loved to hear him
on this subject.

All these and many other things they planned
sitting late at night in the swing under the quiet
stars. Malory in his overcoat, his collar up to his
ears, explained and expounded. Melissa, her beret
close down over her ears, her little girl figure
swathed in an old gray blanket which she had found
along with Mr. Stede's other equipment in the tool
shed, listened and offered suggestions. It seemed
to her the most wonderful, the most thrilling experience she had ever encountered in her life. Not
the marriage itself—of course the thought of that
would be calculated to send any young girl into
transports. But the knowledge that they two, all
unaided, were about to snatch out of a welter of
difficulties the peace and security which they both
so much courted.

She thought of the numberless, needless objections which their elders would have contrived to
place in the way of their marrying so young. She
could not imagine what Malory's people, dim, in-
effectual shapes, would say or do. But she knew
they would disapprove. But in her own case, Laurentine had already shown her definite unwilling-
ness to subscribe to any such arrangement. Objecting
as she did to the idea of Melissa's receiving callers,
certainly she would have used all her influence, all
her oratory against marriage.

Not that she seemed to have any objection to
Malory; Melissa was sure that her cousin knew
nothing specifically of this young man. It would

be fun to see her face when she learned that the young girl had disregarded her injunctions, had not only met the youth who had been refused the house, but had even married him and gone off, far off, to live . . . she would probably never come back, yes she would, she would come to see Aunt Sal who had been so heavenly kind, and Kitty Brown and old Mr. Stede. She would probably never see Asshur again, she reflected, her throat constricting a little at the thought of that deprivation. Well of course one couldn't have everything.

What pleased her most was that, thanks to Malory's cleverness and foresight, it seemed likely that they would be able to get away without encountering any more of that strange, haunting uneasiness which Mrs. Epps' and Mr. Stede's unwarranted opposition awoke within them.

   .   .   .   .   .

Only one difficulty remained and that was to acquaint Malory with the past history of her connections. She must tell him herself, plainly, explicitly and without varnish that old tale about the colored maid, the white gentleman, the beautiful mulatto child. Sometimes it looked so easy. When Malory spoke as he often did about her Aunt's charming house, the carefully kept grounds, the spaciousness and equipment of the kitchen, she might have managed some careless rejoinder. Always in his voice at such times as these was the hint of inquiry and she might have replied: "Surely you know all about this. Aunt Sal, well Aunt Sal was just the same as married to one of the Halloways—*the* Halloways you know. Of course he couldn't marry her, so he left her this for herself and Laurentine. Laurentine's his daughter, see?"

But when the occasion did arise she was never equal to answering thus. And when she did feel nerved to it, the facts of the sorry dilemma seemed to her so towering, so startingly removed from Malory's staid sense of decency that her courage failed her after all. But she must make it plain to him. She did not dare permit him to learn of it from some one else. She knew and he knew that she knew of his belief in class, in position, in integrity.

Malory had absolutely no feeling about color. He did not resent it, he did not suffer from the restrictions which his appearance might impose on him, here and there. Of his own racial group he belonged to the cream. Others might have more money—he could make sufficient for his needs. But in birth, gentility, decency, Malory believed, complacently, no one could surpass him. He cared, save in rare instances, surprisingly little for those who could not equal him.

. . . . .

The swing had been well oiled, it moved easily and without a creak. The nights were getting milder, Melissa had discarded her blanket, Malory no longer buttoned up his overcoat. They met now very seldom out of school, reserving their talks, their planning, their rare rapturous kisses for their sessions in the swing, where they met some three or four times a week. In the darkling spring evening Malory strolled through the meadow which lay to the side and rear of Aunt Sal's grounds, vaulted the low fence of thin, twisted wire and waited in the swing.

Melissa left the house to go to the library, to Kitty Brown's, to get an assignment from a schoolmate. She made a great to-do of slamming the front gate, without even leaving the yard, then tiptoeing on the short, tender grass she stole back past the far side of the house, past the kitchen, past the tool shed and so on down the long yard until she had reached her lover. At a little after nine she came in mildly, innocently, leaving Malory still ensconced in the swing. Yawning ostentatiously she sat down at a table, glanced at a school-book, at a magazine.

Presently she said sleepily and dutifully: "Goodnight Aunt Sal, 'night Laurentine. Oo-oo-h I'm so sleepy."

The two older women would hear the door of her room close, could faintly distinguish the raising of her window. By and by it would be ten o'clock and after; the two elder women, except on the nights when Denleigh or Mrs. Ismay were there, put away their work or their books and meandered off to bed. Aunt Sal's room was in the front of the house, Laurentine's was back of it and communicating. Melissa's was farther down the long hall, nearest of the three to the stair-steps. It was great fun later, when she was sure the others were asleep, for the young girl to steal out of her room down the familiar staircase, through the sewing-room and kitchen, and so out, into the back yard where Malory would be alert, waiting. This was the most dangerous part of their evening; once these moments were past it was possible for them to sit and chat, completely at their ease, as far into the night as they would.

.   .   .   .   .

Malory, deliberate sentimentalist, grew tired of the swing and its safety, not because it was safe but because with his sure sense of values he knew that the Chinaberry Tree was the place where they really should foregather.

"It's so beautiful, Melissa; it makes it all seem like a fairy-tale."

"Yes, I know, Malory darling, but it's nowhere near as sure. The Tree is right under Laurentine's window and sometimes if the moonlight comes a certain way you can see right through the leaves and tell who's there."

"Well, she wouldn't be leaning out of her window at this hour of night, would she, like the blesséd Damozel out of Heaven?"

"I don't know anything about the blesséd Damozel," said Melissa, forgetting the Rossetti to which he'd introduced her, "but I do know she might just chance to look out one night and see us!"

"And what if she does?" he queried reasonably. "She's not the Queen of Sheba, is she, and we're not her subjects even if she is,—and after all, what's it all about? Come to think of it, I'd like to see your proud Laurentine, Melissa, and tell her what I think of her for making a nice girl like you receive her company out of doors. What's the matter with her, anyway?"

.   .   .   .   .

Well, this was as good a chance as any. With a little guilefulness, she might even contrive to make Laurentine's pitiful state enhance her own desirability. She leaned back against his arm, looked up into his face. If possible, she'd finish this up tonight.

"You know, Malory, you look awfully nice with all that silvery light about your face. Makes you look very grave and tender like—like the angel Gabriel I guess," she finished doubtfully. "Anyway it's quite a swell character and an awful important one."

"That's a very nice speech. You deserve a kiss for that. You're a swell kid yourself, Melissa. . . . But look here, let's get down to brass tacks. Not that it makes much difference now, we're so near the end of the whole business. . . . But—just what is eating Laurentine, Honey?"

Even in her fear she laughed at him, repeating his question, mimicking his nice pronunciation of his "ing-s." "It sounds so funny for you to talk slang and yet be so precise about it."

He smiled briefly. "Yes, I know—sort of takes the curse off it, doesn't it? What is the matter with her? Why on earth wouldn't she let me come to see you?"

"I don't think it was just you, Malory," she murmured, fending off the evil moment. "I don't believe she even knows who you are."

"Well, anyway, what's she doing refusing to let you meet any boys, as long as they're O.K.?"

"Well, you see Malory, it's like this," she cast about, seeking for words sufficiently delicate,—

"Laurentine's, well, Laurentine, you see, is a child of sin."

He stared at her incredulously, his jaw sagging, "What are you talking about?" His tone was almost rough, "What do you mean a child of sin?"

His roughness steadied, even though it frightened her. "I mean just that, a child of sin. You see—er —her father and her mother—my aunt—weren't married."

He didn't like it, she could see that. "Does she know who her father is? Does he live around here?" She could imagine his mind asking itself, "What colored man in this town could have been the father of that beautiful creature?" He actually thought of Brown and Ismay, but of course they were scarcely old enough—and neither one of them had any looks anyway.

"No, he doesn't,—he used to, that is. But he's dead now. He—he was a white man, he was Colonel Halloway whose father built the factory."

He was aghast. "You don't mean, why Melissa, you don't mean to say she's one of those Stranges?"

She couldn't pretend not to know what he meant. "She's a Strange—I don't know what you mean by 'those Stranges,' but anyway they're the only family of that name here."

"But, Melissa, they're, they're,—why, they're notorious, why, they're known all over. Why, I can remember as a little fellow—I was only four when I left here—they used to talk about your aunt—er —her mother. Why, I used to be afraid to come down this way—See here, did they always live down here? I remember my mother used to say to my sisters 'I never want to hear the name Strange mentioned under this roof.' She was so queer about it, her voice was—it frightened me. . . . I hadn't thought of that for years."

Melissa was paler than the silvery light warranted. "I'm sure I don't see why anyone, any colored person should have anything to say about it. She hadn't done anything to any of them." To her own amazement she heard herself taking up for Aunt Sal, excusing her, exonerating her, using and believing in Asshur's arguments.

"After all, she was only a very young girl, Malory, living in a time when—when a colored woman might be very much dazzled at receiving such marked attention from such an important man."

"She should have known better," he interrupted stubbornly.

"And after all, he must have loved her, he must have respected her. Goodness knows he was faithful enough to her in the face of everything. I imagine he'd have married her, no matter how poor or ignorant she was if only she hadn't been colored. It's only in this poor old dumb country anyway that people carry on so about color. . . ." For the first time in her life she was able to see how purely artificial, how man-made such a barrier was.

"You see he thought a lot of her . . . he left her this house and grounds, and the money to keep it up."

Moodily he gazed about him, evidently beholding the beautiful place with an altered vision.

"Naturally," he said slowly, "you'd have to take up for them. . . . Just what relation are you to the famous Laurentine?"

"She isn't famous," she said resentfully and as steadily as one may with a chin that would quiver. "She isn't famous a bit, she's a very fine lady. Not anybody," said Melissa, confused in her grammar, "is any better than my cousin Laurentine, not if she had all the sons and daughters of the American Revolution back of her—and you know Malory Forten, no colored person has that. . . . And I'd take up for Laurentine, relation or no relation. Yes, and for Aunt Sal too. Her being my mother's sister's got nothing to do with it."

"Your mother live here too, Melissa?"

"No, she didn't, she just paid one little visit here when she was a very young girl. It had all happened then—Laurentine, I've heard her say, was eight or nine. No, my mother lived in Philadelphia and so did my father and I was born there." She was suddenly sick unto death of his inquisition. . . . "I don't think you've been very nice, Malory."

He was pretty unyielding, "Why didn't you tell me all this before, Melissa?"

"Well, at first I didn't think it was necessary. After all, it's Laurentine's affair, isn't it? It isn't mine. My father and mother were honestly married," she added with that little rush of pride which the contrast of her own estate with Laurentine's always seemed to release in her.

"Well, why did you tell me now?"

She was a little evasive. "To explain to you why Laurentine won't let me have company. She's al-

ways been very strict about her own behaviour—
naturally she'd be strict about mine."

He considered a moment. This was clearly a
new and not distasteful point of view. He said
more humanly, "I'm glad you told me about this
yourself, Melissa. I can't tell you how it would
have hurt me to hear it from anybody else."

She thought: "You don't know how the way
you've taken it has hurt me." But she only said,
"I'm awfully tired, Malory. I'm going in. . . .
I feel as though I could sleep forever. Guess you'd
better not come any more this week."

He said tardily, "Perhaps I did seem a little—
tight. But I was so shocked, Melissa. I'll call you
up to-morrow."

"No, don't do that. Good-night, Malory."

"Good-night—little Princess." Belatedly gallant,
he caught her hand and kissed it.

She was tired, but for all that she lay sleepless
for hours locked in a perfect fury of reflections.
She thought, "The darn snob! Well, I'll get all
that nonsense out of him before we've been married
long. . . . My heavens, what difference does it all
make? After all, it's over. Aunt Sal and Laurentine's conduct can't affect me. But don't say I'm
not sick and tired of this whole Halloway-Strange
business. Well, Mr. John Paul," she apostrophized
the father whom she never remembered seeing, "I'm
mighty glad you took it into your head to marry
my mother. . . . Poor Laurentine!"

.   .   .   .   .   .

"Come to think of it," Malory said a few evenings later, "I'm just as glad we did get this all

threshed out the other night, about your cousin. It explains why Mrs. Epps spoke as she did that day. I must say, Melissa, that up until you told me about Laurentine, she had me quite upset."

"How does that explain anything?" Melissa asked a little stonily. Malory was very handsome to-night. He had been very gentle and tender and had brought her a little nosegay. She liked his handsomeness and she liked his little present but she was still secretly resentful of his attitude of the other night. "It makes me—why it makes it seem as though he were doing me a favor to marry me," she told herself in childish dismay, "and I certainly don't like that."

"Well, you see," Malory said a trifle hesitantly, sensing something changed in her manner, "I figure it's like this. You know what busy bodies these people are here in Red Brook. Mrs. Epps I suppose knew all about your—er—cousin's—er—misfortune. But she knew that I'd been away from home so long and that I'd left so young that probably I didn't know about it."

"Yes," said Melissa expectantly.

"Well, then she could just about imagine that someone would tell me about it some day and while she doesn't know of course that we're engaged still she may have thought that we were interested in each other and that perhaps—perhaps I—well maybe it might be different if I knew about it all. She didn't want you to be hurt, and so she advised you to think about Lane."

She said to him steadily enough though her eyes were very wan: "Is it any different?"

"No," he told her immediately, and his voice was very sincere. "At first, Melissa, I thought it was. I thought it would have to be. I was really shocked out of my senses. Of course I know as well as you that these things at least theoretically are of no importance, but actually, Melissa, every fellow does want his wife to be on a pedestal; he'd like to think of her as a little inviolate shrine that isn't ever touched by the things in the world that are ugly and sordid."

But she had done a lot of thinking within the last few days and although she had never heard Dr. Denleigh express his views on matrimony, she had come in her childish way to certain conclusions very much like his because they were equally fundamental.

"I'm only eighteen, Malory," she told him slowly because she was struggling with a big thought, "and I haven't had such a lot of experience, but it seems to me, Malory, that while all this about shrines and pedestals and things like that are awfully pretty, really beautiful, that life doesn't permit you to keep things like that in your head."

A trifle amazed and very much amused at this evidence of original thinking, he regarded her however with profound attention.

"I'm thinking that after all, Malory, if our plans do turn out all right and we do get married, even with your grandfather's and your Aunt Viny's money we'll still be pretty poor. And I just imagine that then you'd rather I'd be able to cook and sew and mend and copy notes and all that—than to be an inviolate shrine which sounds to me mighty darn useless. . . . It might be better for me then that I had seen something of real life even if I hadn't been particularly touched by it."

She was thinking not at all of Aunt Sal nor of her cousin but of her own mother. Judy had seen Melissa, when she was beginning to grow, frown with distaste at some of the rough badinage exchanged between herself and her noisy admirers. "Let me tell you something, girl; they's many a time we'd starve, you and me, if these fellers didn't like me and my fun enough to make them bring their steaks and potatoes here for me to fix."

Melissa privately determining that her own life would be different, got the point no less. Out of her pondering on these private matters she spoke:

"You've always complained about the sadness of your home life, Malory. It was partly because you thought I could relieve that sadness that you began to like me. You don't think the fact that I'm related to Aunt Sal—and mind you I don't think there's anything the matter with her either, only that she's had a bad break—is going to make me less cheerful and—and well enlivening as a wife, do you, Malory?"

He put his arms around her, dragged her up from the seat and held her close. "You blessed little logician! Listen, honey, I'm just a miserable snob. I don't even know where I get it from, Melissa. Part of your job as my wife will have to be to get it out of me. Hope you'll like that Melissa."

She looked up at him, her eyes very sweet and trustful, "I'll adore it, Malory."

"Good! Now kiss me good-night. You're

sleepy, darling. . . ." Laurentine gently raising her window so as to let in more air glanced down at the Chinaberry Tree and saw to her amazement, two figures standing in a broad white shaft of moonlight. She could not recognize the boy whose dark head was bent down over the girl's smooth, tawny one, but the girl she knew was Melissa.

CHAPTER XXXII

EASTER. "The time of the singing of birds is come and the voice of the turtle is heard in our land," Malory quoted again to Melissa. He liked the Bible, having read a great deal of it in company with Aunt Viny who took it quite literally. Since she insisted on reading every bit of it even down to all the "begats," the lad had in self-defence been forced to look for something in it aside from its religious value. Quite without any prompting he had discovered its literary and poetical beauty. It gave him a curious sense of satisfaction to have found this out unaided; he quoted it frequently as an evidence to himself of his own innate good taste; the adoption of it by others served him unconsciously as a sort of intellectual shibboleth, very much as once the frequent quoting of the Rubaiyat marked a person as possessing a certain amount of literary perspicuity.

Melissa, being almost entirely without the aforesaid perspicuity, wondered often at the choice and meaning of his selections. Such things appealed to her only if their meaning was immediately apparent or apposite. In this case, for instance, she could see no connection with spring and turtles; she had never heard of turtles possessing a voice. But she was by this time aware of the fact that Malory was endowed with many tastes which to her were incomprehensible. On the whole she rather liked her ability to be cognizant of the fact that he was different without showing resentment or jealousy. It made her feel that she would be a fine, forbearing wife whose motto might be "Live and let live." Malory was aware of this slight deficiency on her part; it both amused him and appealed to his vanity. Neither one of them was old enough or sufficiently experienced to envisage the very real joy that might be in store for two people who found in each other an exact and even sympathy along the line of common tendencies.

With Easter came the Spring Vacation, meaning many varied things to many varied people. To Laurentine it meant an extra onslaught of work plus the promise of a brief holiday. Her customers were getting ready for their exodus to seashore, city, foreign parts,—any of the places which the nomadic rich visit in order to get away from their own home no matter how charming its situation. Laurentine must turn out sports clothes, street costumes, filmy evening dresses, wisps of negligées, accessories of scarf and tie and throw such as only she could contrive.

For a few weeks, for a last few days the rush would be hectic, nerve-wracking. Hitherto the girl had, at the conclusion of such a period, merely stayed in bed of mornings for two or three hours

later, "taking it easy" for a few days. Now this
year she was to have a treat. She would go to New
York. Denleigh was to drive her over; they were
to go sight-seeing, to the theatres, they were to visit
the tops of sky-scrapers; she would meet some of
Denleigh's class-mates. Mrs. Ismay, who was accompanying her and with whom she was to stay in
New York, had arranged for a tea at the house of
one of her friends. It was to be perfect. Laurentine went about smiling, singing, dreaming.

"You're like a young girl," Mrs. Ismay told her
laughing, "you have the gift of enjoyment. People
will like that. They like to do things for folks who
are not afraid or ashamed to show their appreciation of the thing that is new or different." She
teased Stephen, "Better look out, Stephen, she'll
find a handsomer man than you yet, and go off with
him."

Denleigh smiled complacently. " 'I fear no foe,' "
he sang, quoting a song that his oldest sister used
to warble years ago at church concerts to the ac-
companiment of a reed organ.

.   .   .   .   .

Melissa grumbled a little about the exigencies
caused by the overflow of work into her cousin's
establishment.

"I was thinking," she told Malory standing almost at midnight under the Chinaberry Tree, her
arms clasped loosely about his neck, "that we'd be
having some time out to talk about our affairs. I
thought, why I even thought we'd be able to go off
for a whole day's hike,—I had planned the best
lunch! But as it is she needs me to help too, with

the finishing-off and things like that.   Of course I'm glad to do it,—Laurentine and her mother have been awfully good to me."   She rarely said "Aunt Sal" any more to Malory.   She knew he did not like to hear the relationship emphasized.   Her failure to do so, however, always left her with a curious sense of shame.   She continued hastily.

"Of course she's going to pay me.   Laurentine's awfully decent that way.   The chances are that if I were independent of her she wouldn't offer me a penny.   But being that things are as they are she pays me because she doesn't want me to feel that she thinks I ought to do it."

Malory's face hardened ever so slightly.   He assuredly did not want to hear anything about Laurentine for all her beauty, of Aunt Sal for all her kindness.   "You'll be quite a millionaire," he teased her.   "What are you going to do with your wealth?"

She hugged him with her ridiculously childish strength that afforded him so much pleasure.   "Silly as though you didn't know!   I'm going to buy house-keeping things with it.   I'm going to buy curtains, window-shades you know.   They're having the most marvelous sales right now at Barton's. And, Malory, I'm not going to buy the kind people usually buy,—horrid black or blue or brown things. Everything in our house is going to be beautiful, full of color, 'sweetness and light.' . . . See, I can quote too when it makes some sense.   They had the divinest colors.   I never saw anything like it before. . . . I'm going to get some very, very deep old-rose ones, almost red.   I saw some once in a house in Philadelphia where my mother used to go to sew.

. . . They made the light so beautiful—oh Malory you never saw anything else just like it. I'd rather have them than extra fine things to eat. And I like to cook too," she ended, a trifle prosaically.

He looked down at her, amused and touched. The moonlight sifting through the Tree gave her piquant face a delicate, fragile beauty. "Darling, I hate to tell you,—after all, we don't know the size of the windows yet. All the shades might be the wrong width. We oughtn't to throw money away."

"As though I didn't know that." She revealed the unexpectedly practical quality of the woman who is getting down to the only job in the world that seems to her really worth while,—that of building her home. "I'm allowing for that. I'm buying the largest possible sizes and then when we go into our home I take a yard stick and measure the width of the window, and you take a saw and if you've any manhood in you at all, Mr. Forten, you saw off the end of the rod to fit the space at the top of the window and you nail up one or two of those funny little gadgets that hold the rod in place. Then I take a pair of scissors and trim off the shade,—and there you are!"

Overwhelmed by such an unexpected exhibition of knowledge he made some feeble remarks about their not knowing what kind of rooms they might be able to get. "The rose curtains might clash with the paint."

But she was ready for him. "Most rooms are painted nowadays in white or cream. But if ours aren't, all I'll have to do will be to get one of those little cans of quick-drying paint,—you know you see

them in the advertisements of all the magazines.
The wife is hustling her husband off to work and
then she gets into her apron, seizes her trusty brush,
dips it into her little can, and in a moment the
whole house is transformed. That day of all days
her husband comes home to lunch, but the paint is
all dry; he looks anxiously at his coat, at his trou-
sers, not a spot! 'What a wife' he cries! Oh
Malory, that's the way it will be with us, won't it?"

"You bet!" He stooped and kissed her. "Melissa, you are the sweetest girl!"

"I'll be the sweetest housekeeper! Oh you're going to love it so. Housekeeping is lots of fun
nowadays if you just know how to go about it. Dust-
pans blue as the sky! Yellow kitchenware; Boston
baked beans,—if we're going to live in Boston we'll
have to eat baked beans,—well, we'll eat 'em out of
green ramekins. I saw some at Barton's. . . ."

"Eat 'em out of what?"

"Out of ramekins, individual green ramekins. . . ."

"Melissa, what are they?"

"What are what? Ramekins? Why they're
ramekins, like cups, only of course they aren't cups.
The individual ones are about so big." She indicated measurements vaguely with her hands. "You
know."

"I certainly don't. I never heard of them before. . . . They sound terrifying to me. Well, anyway, you're not buying any of them yet are you?"

"Why of course I am! Why they're practically
giving them away down at Barton's!"

"I bet they're paying you to take them away!

But Melissa—say, Honey, I don't care such a lot about beans. Aunt Viny used to make me eat plain boiled ones when I was a kid. Gee! Will I ever forget those Sunday dinners! But what on earth are we going to do with all this junk? We don't have a car you know. I was figuring on our sending our winter-coats ahead, general delivery, and then eloping with a suitcase apiece."

Strangely she was impressed by this romantic aspect; she wavered. "Tell you what I could do Malory. . . . It really is a shame to pass up these lovely bargains. I could take old Mr. Stede into my confidence just before I go and he'd send the things after us. . . . I wouldn't dare tell him just now because he's hell-bent for me to marry Asshur. But when he finds I'm in earnest about you, he'll do anything I ask just to help me out."

"I'm sure he would. Thus endeth the battle of the ramekins. But of course it doesn't settle the fact that we're hardly going to see each other for a week. Unless you could get your Mr. Stede to run up some gussets and seams and things for your cousin."

"Cra-a-zy! Good-night, Malory; got to get up early in the morning, Old Precious. Be a good boy and don't forget me."

"Listen to the girl talking like a wife already. Good-night Honey . . . be sweet."

.   .   .   .   .   .

To the unlimited astonishment of the Brown family, Gertrude announced that she was coming home for the Easter holidays. Kitty went over to the junction to meet her.

"Why did you do it, Gert?"

"Don't you call me Gert. Suppose I was to let the colored population of Red Brook in on the fact that you were really christened Katchen and might at a pinch be called, Cat?"

"Help! Help! . . . Changing the subject. Gertrude Brown why are you darkening your mother's doors at this time of year, much as you hate Red Brook?"

They were home and up in their room, Kitty dumping the contents of drawers and shelves wholesale on chairs and on the floor so as to afford Gertrude space for her dainty, carefully-folded belongings. Gertrude hung up the last frock, smoothed out its folds for a moment, turned and looked at her sister.

"Kitty," she said her mouth trembling a little, "don't you dare laugh. I've really got it this time. I'm in love."

"You don't mean it! But what did you come home for? To get over it? Where does he live? Boston?"

"You know where he lives. He lives right here. Now don't tell me you don't know whom I mean. I'm talking about Malory Forten."

"Were you in earnest last Christmas? I never thought that! Why I supposed you were over that long ago. Well I don't think you've got much chance there; I'm sure he's in love with Melissa Paul."

"And I don't suppose there's any chance of his falling out of love with Melissa and falling in love with one, Gertrude Brown on the rebound?"

Kitty became serious. "Ordinarily, Gertrude, you know I'd have nothing to say about what you do. But this is different; it isn't only that he's in love with Melissa. I'm sure she's in love with him."

"She said she wasn't."

"Well, what would you expect her to say? Pour out her life's secret to you, a girl whom she's spoken to about three times in her life?"

"Well how do you know such a lot about her? Has she confided in you?"

"No she hasn't and what's more I've never met him in her house and she's never spoken to me about him. I think as a rule she hardly ever sees him except right here in our home and in school. I guess I've seen them together on the street about twice."

"Well then how do you know she's in love with him?"

"How do I know I'm breathing?" asked Miss Kitty succinctly. "I know she's in love with him because I know she's in love with him."

.   .   .   .   .

This argument seeming to convince Gertrude more than her own observations, or than her sister's manner, she relapsed into a rather sulky silence. Kitty, stretched on her stomach across the bed, watched her thoughtfully.

"I don't know what you're thinking about, Gertrude," she continued after a few moments, "but I can tell you now, it isn't being done."

"What isn't being done? And anyway how can you talk? As though you didn't snatch Jerry Adamson from under Claudia Temple's very nose and she crying her eyes out!"

"I'll tell you what isn't being done," rejoined Kitty, ignoring alike her sister's lack of logic and her allusions. "This is what isn't being done. No girl like you with a chance to meet all the up and coming colored boys in the country is coming into a little hick town like this and snatch away a helpless girl's one stick of candy."

"What do you mean 'helpless'?"

"I mean she hasn't any breaks. Take Malory away from her and where is she? There's that crazy story about her aunt and that old Colonel Halloway; there's her beautiful cousin Laurentine, she's so handsome and so successful—you ought to see the things she turns out—they've all got a mad on her. Then to top it all from the things this miserable little Pelasgie Stede hints at, Melissa's mother, Judy Somebody, lived here for a while when she was young. She seems to have been a kind of high-stepper, ran around with Phil Hackett's father and a couple of other married men. Then she left here and married some fellow named Paul in Philadelphia. As far as I can make out these old hens are so mad because Judy didn't follow in her sister's footsteps that they've taken it out on Melissa ever since.

"The way I see it, Melissa's got to get away from all this and Malory's her one way out. See?"

Gertrude's sole reply was: "I thought you said she had a beau around here."

"So she did have. Well she didn't want him when he was here. Now he's gone to Alabama.

Goodness knows we have a hard enough time here in Jersey. What colored person in her senses wants to go to Alabama to live? . . . So you see Gertrude, Mr. Malory Forten is all out as far as you're concerned."

Gertrude, yawning, stepped into the bathroom and turned on the water. "Oh Kits," she called suddenly, "go down and get Pelasgie to bring up my other suit-case won't you? It's got my bath-salts in it."

"Right," said Kitty and descended.

.   .   .   .   .

"Hello!" Gertrude said to the sulky Pelasgie as she hove into sight lugging the desired suit-case. "Thanks ever so much for bringing it up. . . . You've got thinner, haven't you? What have you been doing to yourself?" She glanced down at her own svelte, shapely lines suggested through her thin kimona. . . . "And I've been getting plumper. . . . I was just wondering what I would do with that white shantung I had last summer. It's too tight for me now . . . I don't suppose you know anybody who could use it."

"If you wus to give it to me Miss Gertrude. . . ."

"Oh if you wouldn't mind taking it . . . you'd certainly oblige me . . . I think you'd find it very useful."

"Sure would, Miss Gertrude. . . . Many thanks."

Dr. Brown, busy and pre-occupied, meeting Pelasgie on the stairs wondered what made her look so different. "I don't believe I ever saw her smile before," his sub-conscious mind told him while his

conscious mind concocted formulas for the Simmons'
baby.

     .   .   .   .   .

"Just the same," said Gertrude to herself, "I'm
not going to leave anything to chance. It might
just happen that Malory doesn't care as much for
Melissa as he thinks or she may not care as much
for him. Perhaps they like each other simply because there isn't anybody else for them to like in
this awful town. . . . I believe I'll wear those
mesh stockings with this dress."

She drew on the stockings, put on a pair of light
shoes with the sides cut almost entirely away; arranged her hair with its not too permanent wave
back from her extremely good forehead and into a
small flat knot at the nape of her neck, got herself
into a crushed strawberry tinted thin wool frock
with squares of mulberry embroidery arranged distractingly about the skirt, the sleeves and neck. A
mulberry colored handkerchief and a few drops of
some devastating perfume completed her ensemble.

"Slick, I calls it," Kitty commented coming in to
freshen herself for dinner. She too in a few
moments achieved an effect of smart modernity,
choosing and putting on her garments with absolute
assurance, never hesitating, never asking her sister's
opinion for one moment about her appearance.

They went down to dinner, the pair of them, all
suave and *soignées,* to the bewilderment of their
father who could not understand whence these two
capable, sophisticated, entirely self-contained young
ladies evolved. It seemed only yesterday since

Kitty had been freckled, her front teeth missing, her elbows and knees downright rusty. Recently at a bathing beach he had seen a great deal more of his daughter than it had been his privilege to behold for many years . . . he had been amazed at her velvety fineness. . . .

And Gertrude . . . why Gertrude had been positively ugly! "And now look at her!" he had on this occasion said to his wife who sat regarding her two daughters with complacence. "She looks, the pair of them look, like princesses. How do they do it?" . . . Mrs. Brown murmured something about "blood telling in spite of everything," very much as though he had buried the precious fluid under an avalanche of refuse but it, in its bright blueness, had seeped through after all. . . . The blood in question came of course from her side of the family.

To-night he was more bewildered than ever. By some tacit agreement, they had united in pouring their charm out on him. They made over him at the table, they passed him pleasant viands; Gertrude at the close of the meal arose and lit his cigar for him. She took out her own delicately tinted cigarette holder . . . but first she leant toward him deprecatingly: "You don't mind, do you, Dad?" Well he did mind, but it was so nice to have this charming, well-dressed, dainty, deferential creature near him, with her nice voice and her quiet wit. . . . And Kitty . . . Kitty was a nice girl too, a little louder than Gertrude but with a nice boyish sincerity and prettier too, with a prettiness which he could define and understand. . . . She asked him to stay in for once . . . she'd like to play some checkers with him.

But first she went into the next room to the piano and played two or three ballads, then dashed off into a couple of old, crazy jazz favorites, singing them in her sweet crazy voice, keeping time with seductive shoulders.

>*(Boom! boom!)*
>"Hello Beautiful!
>*(Boom! boom!)*
>How'd you get so beautiful?"

What were they up to, he wondered uneasily; what were they going to ask of him? Well he wouldn't let them go to Atlantic City or to New York, that was flat. Girls had no idea of the dangers to which they subjected themselves in these days running around without their parents in these resorts, these huge cities, for he knew they wouldn't want their mother to accompany them. . . . Why in heaven's name couldn't they be satisfied to stay at home, just as they were, making music and bedecking themselves? They could ask an occasional boy in to see them; maybe one or two of them might drift over from New York . . . he'd have to speak to his wife about that . . . you couldn't draw too tight a check-rein on girls these days anymore than you could on boys.

He'd have been amazed if he had known that his state of mind was exactly the condition to which they had planned to reduce him. They didn't want to go away . . . they wanted to stay right there at home. Only Kitty meant to have Jerry Adamson, far removed from the influence of Claudia Temple, to be in that home too . . . instinctively she knew that her father would not approve of Jerry . . . she doubted if she herself would approve of him long . . . but her father would welcome ten Jerrys. if it meant her spending a long holiday at home in contentment.

Gertrude wanted to see more of Malory . . . since there were no contemporaries at whose house she could meet him, what better than to pursue her cautious stalking at home right under her parents' unsuspecting eyes? They would see in him only a young man repaying in little attentions to their daughter, the many courtesies which he had received at their hands.

Kitty proposed a game of contract, to which Dr. Brown joyously acceded and which Mrs. Brown flatly rejected. Now for a fourth. The girl had foreseen this situation. Jerry played admirable contract. When he came down as he assuredly would in a few days she would have him drop in . . . he could play with her father against herself and Gertrude; the two men would beat the two girls "forty different ways" said Kitty to herself joyously.

From that hour her father would be completely "sold" on the boy. . . . Meanwhile for to-night's contingency there was Herbert Tucker . . . she telephoned him. Young Tucker came over, played some good bridge. The doctor was to attend a little conference the next morning in Newark, to discuss a social matter with several of his colleagues. Usually the men talked, had a luncheon and then a

rubber or two of bridge before adjourning. One
of them would be unable to attend in the morning.

"If you'd like to come along, Tucker I'd be glad
to take you to fill in his place. I'd like Dr. Sand-
borne see you play that club convention." Herbert,
flushing with pleasure, said he'd be glad to go, only
he had promised to meet Malory Forten in the
Public Library in the morning at ten-thirty. . . ."

"Well we'd have to get going by ten. But that's
all right, call Forten and ask him to let you off
. . . tell him it will oblige me . . . he's a nice
fellow."

"Yes sir. Oh I'm sure it will be all right."

It was all right. Malory would oblige. "You
think you'll stay in the library until late in the afternoon? All right I may look in on my way back."

Gertrude avoided Kitty's eye. "A direct act of
Providence. It would be wicked for me not to take
advantage of it," she told herself piously.

.   .   .   .   .

Malory, glancing up idly from his article on
Kinetics, saw her delicate, amber cheek half-hidden
under the brim of her coquettish hat, let that glance
travel along her slender form enveloped in its
sheath-like gown. No colored girl in Red Brook
wore her clothes just like that. The color and arrangement of the dress were too subtle for Melissa;
the figure itself was too slender for Kitty; Miss
Strange was taller than this perfectly turned-out
stranger. Then who could it be? And at once his
sense, his memory and his imagination working in
concert replied to him "Gertrude Brown." He
rushed over to her; he had forgotten how striking-

looking she was; he had forgotten how charming
she could be. He returned the book on Kinetics to
a disapproving librarian who had gone to some
pains to reserve the volume for him.

He followed her out into the street, along an
avenue where only the very wealthy lived, a very
park of an avenue, with estates set far back, and
with so little traffic on it that they were practically
alone. Scarcely he knew what they talked about;
it seemed to him that they laughed a great deal,—
not merely healthy laughter, the happy reflex of
youth,—but laughter of a sophisticated sort which
made him feel that he had got off many very witty
remarks, clever repartee, a collection of *bons mots*.
He walked back with her as far as her gate, all
eager and polite attention in his nice blue suit, with
his carefully brushed shoes and his rather stiffly
curling short hair. He was wearing no hat.

She did not ask him in, but she let drop that she
was anticipating a very quiet vacation spent chiefly
outdoors; that she felt she ought to spend a good
deal of time with her parents; that she would be
home that evening and that she was not averse to
contract.

Malory was, but he asked just the same if he
might come in and take a hand if she was not sure of
a fourth, and she said in her nice voice: "That
would be splendid, Malory."

He went back to the library and read his article,
went home, ate his dinner and spent an hour dressing, tying, untying and hurling ties aside . . . she
always looked so jack-out-of-the-box herself, that

he owed it to himself to appear very spic and span. . . .

Again the Brown family was at home and also Herbert Tucker who had shone, positively shone, in his playing in Newark. Dr. Brown praised him so extravagantly that Mrs. Brown opined that maybe with a teacher like that, "a teacher who really knew what he was talking about," she might be able to get a little idea of the game into her head. . . . That was exactly what happened; after Herbert had laid down successive hand after successive hand and had talked very steadily for two hours, she did get a very little idea of the game into her head. . . .

Malory and Gertrude had politely refused to play, withdrawing in favor of Mrs. Brown. But there were snap-shots of scenes at Wellesley to be examined and James Weldon Johnson's "God's Trombones" to be read. And then Gertrude played. Not jazzy songs such as Kitty invariably rendered but lovely, touching things like "Songs My Mother Taught Me," and "The Old Refrain," and a hauntingly beautiful, modern tune "Falling in Love Again." The card-players in the back-room broke up, came in. Herbert Tucker in a fine baritone sang along with Gertrude. Dr. Brown leaned across the piano, humming, and was suddenly and joyously young once more.

Everything contributed bewitchingly to the realization that life was going on as it should,—in a home. And with the realization came the thought to Malory of the home which some day he hoped to make. And with the thought came the vision of

Melissa straining her eyes, fearfully looking for him under the Chinaberry Tree.

It was half-past eleven; the evening, as Dr. Brown remarked mildly, was still young; Tucker said if he would wait a while longer, he would walk a piece with him. But, declining, he caught up his hat and hastened out. He had an errand to perform for his mother he told them worriedly. He hated to leave but he hated much more to think of Melissa, after having worked hard all day, in her disappointment. He almost ran across the town through the quiet, fragrant streets that were so alluring. . . . But when he got to Melissa's house, surprisingly she wasn't there. . . .

．　　　．　　　．　　　．　　　．

No one but Gertrude had observed his confusion. She said to herself: "Why should he be so upset, and whom could he possibly be going to see for his mother at this time of night? . . . I know he wasn't going on any errand but where was he going?" . . . He was at her house again the next evening, enjoying himself obviously, but at eleven he arose and with quiet determination announced his intention of leaving. And suddenly as clearly as though he had told her she knew he was going to see Melissa. . . . But why, why, thus "clandestinely"? she said to her self. She had a great habit of using words correctly even when communing with herself; slang with her was an acquisition, a deliberate one; she really was an intellectual; if her blood had run a little less hot in her veins, she might easily have gone her ways to a nunnery. . . .

It was this habit of thinking matters out precisely

and in detail that aided her now. She bore Melissa no ill-will, she really felt, in spite of her mounting passion for young Forten, that there would be no gain in her attempting to intervene, "just so," between Malory and this girl. "But there is something queer about their meeting in secret," she said to herself and in that queerness might lie the one fact which could react to her advantage.

She thought she could understand why the Stranges, "poor things," might not want Melissa to have company. Not that they might have been afraid of her heritage,—Gertrude, reading Melissa like a wide-open book knew that nothing with her would ever outweigh the value of ultimate respectability,—but because they knew that she, a poor dependent, would have to earn her living and they did not want her to marry until she was equipped to meet life. Lots of parents and guardians were like that.

But she could not understand Malory. Malory, she knew was at heart a gentleman, no girl, if it were left to him, need feel that her fair name must be imperilled because of his heedlessness. . . . He had a mother and two "terribly respectable" sisters. What could have been easier than for him to lay the case before them and to have them invite the girl over to their house? Most people would prefer to do that rather than to have their only son and brother "running around." . . . But of course they probably were unaware that he was "running around." . . . It seemed a needless sort of mystery.

The very next day Malory deepened its needlessness. He had seen Melissa; the child was tired from

her school work, the unseasonable weather and her
steady confinement to Laurentine's sewing-room.
Added to this she had, all through this holiday been
revisited by her dream,—it had a vampire-ish quality
of sapping away her vitality—of course of this last
she had told Malory nothing. She had bade him
wearily to amuse himself as best he could without
her . . . almost, under the influence of the hateful
haunting nightmare she had said: "That's what
you'll finally have to do anyway. I don't believe
we're ever going to be able to get together."

He had never seen her washed out and lifeless like
this. Something of her depression communicated
itself to him. He felt let-down, apprehensive. . . .
In addition to this Reba had remonstrated with him
for staying so much away from the house.

"What do you do with yourself, Malory? It
isn't as though you hadn't a comfortable home."

And he had rushed out of the place banging the
rusty and rotting screen-door which irritated him so.
"You don't call this a home, I hope!" he had flung
back at her dim, futilely worried figure. The very
wrinkles, the very crowsfeet which sullied what otherwise might have been a very fair countenance
angered him past endurance. "What in God's name
has she got to be worried about? What's eating
them?" he asked himself in the insensate fury to
which they so often reduced him.

And because he hadn't Melissa to talk to and because after all, even at twenty-one, he was a badly-
frightened, unhappy, nervous, little boy, before he
knew it he had blurted his woes out to Gertrude.
Not of course about Melissa, but about his miser-

able home-life and the secret persistent misery which spread, penetrating like some malignant mist about and through everything. . . .

They were out walking in the lovely weather. Gertrude turned her clear, cool face toward him, spoke to him in her clear, cool voice. She asked him no questions, she pointed out to him how blest he was to be of a different stripe from his relatives. "You yourself, Malory, suggest such a different environment; you're going to be such a truly remarkable man with your keen mind and your appreciation of everything that is lovely." In no time she had sustained and uplifted his fainting spirit.

She took him home; Dr. Brown of course was out, and so was Mrs. Brown. It was Pelasgie's day off, but Kitty was there. . . . Her sister however refused to be a party to this campaign; she withdrew disdainfully to her room. But Gertrude didn't care . . . she was a wise woman . . . she was able to do for him what Melissa, she surmised shrewdly, had never been able to do—fix him a meal. The table, spread intimately for two, wore an aspect of spring itself with its combination of yellow jonquils and green glassware, and its daintily arranged but nourishing salad and knic-knacs.

Gertrude moved about, serene and restful, like a pastel nymph in her delicate pinks and rosy tans. "Easy on the eye," Malory thought even in the midst of his fast-vanishing unhappiness. In spite of his fondness for words and literature he liked slang, believing that it had about it an exactness, an appositeness that nothing, no other form of expression, equalled.

He stayed until just before dinner-time when he left, immensely appeased and comforted. "Of course I'd like to stay," he acknowledged sturdily in response to her delicate urging, "but I can't have your folks thinking that I've changed my lodgings." He actually went off whistling down the walk.

. . . . .

But she was not so happy. On the contrary she was infinitely depressed, immeasurably disturbed. For a long time after his departure she sat in their pleasant living-room biting her lower lip, holding an unlighted cigarette in her carefully manicured fingers. Assailed by a grave, by a serious doubt, she arose and walked the length of the room, her hand resting on her hip. "Only one thing," she told herself slowly, "only one thing in this world could make people act as crazy as that and that would be for them to be crazy. I wonder if that's it. I wonder if those Fortens are half insane and know it and don't want Malory to know it. . . .

"But I've got to know it," she told herself firmly, "I've got to find out about this. . . . Now how am I going to do it?" She was a selfish girl, but this rather unsophisticated, unsuspecting lad awoke in her the finest, gentlest sympathies which she was ever to know. "Poor Malory," she thought to herself, "even if the rest of them are tainted, perhaps I can save you . . . I'll do anything I can to help you, Malory, Malory!" . . . But what could she do?

. . . . .

The impossibility of her task never deterred her. Characteristically enough, her mind leaped to no impulse of action. Rather she sat down and took stock of where she was, what she knew, what she might learn and the time she had in which to collect her knowledge. Clearly she, who had never associated with any of the rank and file of the Red Brookians, except quite literally, Melissa, Ben Davis, Herbert Tucker and Malory himself, must find, and must find in less than a week, some one who knew all about the Fortens, some one who didn't talk and yet must be made to talk; some one who would know how to keep quiet when once that talking was over.

"In Red Brook," said Gertrude to herself quite seriously, "there ain't no such animal."

There was no use approaching Kitty, granted that she had known anything. Kitty was whole-heartedly for Melissa. Gertrude, feeling her way, had ventured some slight remark about Malory which her sister ignored. Strangely but logically enough she harked back to a former conversation which the two of them had held on the first evening of Gertrude's homecoming.

"There's no use," she said to her sister, "reminding me of what I did to Claudia Temple about Jerry Adamson. You know there's no comparison between the two cases. Taking Malory away from Melissa Paul with the odds she has against her and all, is just like taking candy from a baby and you know it. . . ." A peaceable, easy-going girl by nature, she was for once violently angry. "You make me sick, Gertrude Brown, if you ask me." . . . She mumbled to herself: "What in the devil did Pelasgie

do with my green slip? She only puts away the
things you want to wear and then she hides them."

Gertrude said evenly: "You know how mother
hates to hear a girl swear." Kitty went out and
slammed the door.

Her distaste had made Gertrude wince. Preferring, it is true, her own somewhat devious methods
to Kitty's straightforwardness, she possessed none
the less considerable admiration for her sister; she
disliked forfeiting the latter's careless good-will.
. . . Well she'd have to do without it for a season. . . . The question now was how could she,
with discretion, find out what she wanted to know
about Malory's family? It was not easy to probe
too openly into the affairs of a man whom you were
planning to marry. . . . And suddenly her sub-
conscious mind working on after her conscious attention had strayed away from the subject in hand answered: "Pelasgie" . . .

Of course, Pelasgie! Not that Pelasgie was safe,
not that Pelasgie was discreet, only that Pelasgie
properly stimulated would talk and never know that
she had been incited to talk. Pelasgie, Gertrude
rightly guessed, would talk gladly about anyone,
provided only that she might let her venom have
full sway. Pelasgie, embattled as she was against
the whole of colored Red Bank, could hardly open
her mouth about any one without immediately telling you the worst.

.   .   .   .   .

Gertrude asked her to wash her hair in the morning. The only understanding dresser of colored hair
was as far away as Morristown; Gertrude thought

Pelasgie might just as well earn that money and save herself the trip. Pelasgie thought so too. But Gertrude was doomed to disappointment. Mentioning Mr. Malory Forten's name as a bait elicited from the current hair-dresser only the remark that she was glad to see Malory "comin' eround to see you a spell, Miss Gertrude. Take some of the shine outa that high and mighty Melissa Paul, think-so-much-of-hers'ef ever-sence-you-all-tuk-'er up. But ev'ybody 'round yere know that bad Strange blood, yessir-ee."

That seemed to be that. And after all there were limits. You couldn't discuss your sister's pal with a girl like Pelasgie. Furthermore clearly she knew nothing about Malory and anyway, as later she let fall, she had lived in Red Brook only three years. . . . Disappointed, Gertrude talked bravely on the weather, on Pelasgie's hat *à la Princesse Eugénie* [and how that poor lady would have been glad to be in a position to discuss that libel!], on the flowers which her mother placed daily on the table these days.

"Come outa you-all's back yard," said Pelasgie blithely. "Didn't you know it? My uncle Jonathan plants 'em and spades 'em ev'y year. What he don't know about flowers ain't nuthin'. He tend to all these flowers around yere."

"Can he make a living at it?" asked Gertrude politely surprised.

"Don't hafta," Pelasgie answered with a pride which would certainly have amazed old Mr. Stede. "Seems like there ain't nuthin' he can't do when it comes to beautifyin' a place. . . . There ain't nuthin' he can't do, 'n nuthin' he don't know about things;—'n come to think of it about people, too."

"How do you mean about people?"

"I just mean about people; he knows about 'em, knows about their affairs, their secrets, their pains and troubles . . . on'y you can't get him to say nuthin' about 'em. But remember! You ain't never see nuthin' like it. Used to live down next to the Fortens years ago; he could tell you to this day ev'ything about them; when them two crazy sisters was born, how old they is,—'thout doin' no substraction; whut they used to eat for dinner Sundays. You oughta hear Matilda Gathers' father tell how ole Uncle Jonathan knowed he wus goin' to marry before he knowed, hise'f."

"My!" said Gertrude, choosing her language carefully and wondering if she gave visible evidence of the excitement simmering within her, "he sounds like a fortune teller. I'd like to see a man as remarkable as that."

"Lan' sakes Miss Gertrude, ain't you never see Uncle Johnathan? Why he out in your back yard now. He's liable to be there off'n on all this week."

. . . . . .

Of course she hunted him up. But the old man was more than a match for her. She found out about his weakness and plied him with trays heaped full of the coarse substantial food which his system so persistently craved. She praised his flower-beds, she made herself acquainted with the names of people in Red Brook of whose existence she had never dreamed. Many of them indeed she was destined never to see. The names of these people, introduced at random into her casual conversation, brought from him no response except the mention of Pelasgie whom he declared consistently in a voice absolutely unmodulated by the knowledge of her proximity in the kitchen, to be more ungrateful than a sea-serpent's tooth.

The introduction of the Eppses, the Simmonses, the Traceys, the Gatherses into their talk brought from him only the briefest of glances from his old light eyes. If she mentioned the Stranges or Melissa, if she as much as touched on the catering business in connection with the Fortens, he grew either entirely silent or talked with simply no relevancy whatever about the weather, Pentecost, a "green Christmas," and spring onions.

She was a smart girl but he had seen many smart girls and he knew that none of them bothered with an old, dirty faded man like himself unless some purpose lurked in their minds. He had known from the very first day that she wanted him to talk to her about the Fortens and he had also known that he had no intention of so doing.

Saturday came and she was leaving Sunday. In the afternoon she sought him out. He was, with his clumsy movements which so often, so amazingly produced such delicate results, gathering his tools together . . . wishing she would let him alone . . . he was an old man and weary . . . it took strength to set one's will against such a person as she. But she was a younger woman, intent on the business of life. "Mr. Stede," she told him, her eyes, as impenetrable as his own, holding his gaze, "I've got daddy's Ford down at the gate and I'm going to drive you home."

Well after all she'd be gone in a day or two; he'd soon be rid of her. "These young gals, can't nobody manage 'em at all these days," he fretted within himself. He sat, drooped down despairingly, in the car, his thin beard sweeping his chest. Almost before she had left her father's gate, she began with no pretenses left between them. "Mr. Stede, I want to ask you a question,—Mr. Stede is there any reason why a girl shouldn't marry Malory Forten?"

The suddenness of the onslaught found him unprepared, took him off his feet.

He answered, confused but cautious: "That would depend on who the gal wus, Gertrude."

It was the first breach in his wall and she was quick to see her advantage which, however, she did not immediately press.

"Would it be all right for me to marry him?"

The old quiet voice answered quickly, too quickly: "Why yes, Gertrude, why not?" She could have sworn to the note of relief in his tone. "Does he want you ter marry him, Gertrude?"

After all she had got her answer, she might have stopped there. But she must get to the bottom of all this. And suddenly without planning it she played all her best cards. Her sophistication dropped from her . . . she was like any other young girl desiring greatly an honorable young man who was already pledged to "the other woman."

"Oh," she wailed, "if he only did! No he wants to marry Melissa!" She was so sure that they met clandestinely that she voiced it as a fact. "You know they meet in secret, Mr. Stede, at night,—at her home—under that Chinaberry Tree." She had walked past there during the week and her mind had immediately created the situation.

He sat up straight, his faded eyes at last scared and miserable. "God!" he whispered and she discovered that he was talking to his Maker. "God, You know, they hadn't oughta do that."

She was as frightened as he. And yet what could it all be about? "Mr. Stede," she begged him, "tell me. You know I love Malory. I think maybe he could love me. But he saw Melissa first, she was the only girl in this town he could look at, and now she loves him too. . . I'm sure nothing could ever make him give her up."

He muttered: "He's got to give her up . . . he'd be the first one to give her up if he only knowed."

"Knew what Mr. Stede?"

He was so old; he was so tired. He didn't like this girl, who, he suspected, had all her life succeeded in getting what she wanted, who always would succeed. . . . She would probably marry Malory though what would become of Melissa in that event he could not guess. . . . On the other hand what would become of Melissa if she did marry him?

"Well," he said feebly, "they's two reasons, Gertrude, they's two reasons why he hadn't oughta marry her. One of the reasons I knows fer a fac'. The other one I don't know but I guesses. If the fust reason is true Malory won't want to marry her . . . and if they's both true. . . ."

So then he told her.

She was pale, she was frightened, she was in tears when he had finished. She knew then that in all probability some day she would marry Malory, but in her heart her triumph lay like ashes in her mouth.

.   .   .   .   .

She drove him to his house and he dismounted sad and creaking and wordless, hoping very ardently that he would never see this woman again. And yet bearing in his heart a nameless sense of freedom since he knew with no word, no promise from her that Gertrude would handle this situation; he could not leave the matter in more capable hands. But he liked her none the more for that. For all his age and weariness, for all his accumulation of his own and others' woes his reaction toward this sex remained definitely Victorian. He did not like capable women.

Gertrude drove off slowly, thoughtfully, down past Redd's Brook where the willows drooping and weeping as willows really should, made her think of Malory . . . she was an even more deliberate sentimentalist than he. . . . She would have liked to savor with him the delight of an hour passed beneath, within, their foliage. "Well," she sighed to herself, "that will probably never be, because of course he won't want to live here. . . ." And anyway one couldn't have just everything. There was the song that Jerry was lately forever singing to Kitty:

> "Got the house, got the car
> But I haven't got you . . . "

Substituting for house and car, willow-trees and the sweet romance of April, what difference did their absence make since undoubtedly,—yes with time and tact she could be sure of it,—she had her man!

Her father and mother had gone to Newark to attend a meeting of the convention which the National Association for the Advancement of Colored People was holding there. Kitty was off somewhere with Jerry Adamson flirting with him and being flirted at. She came home, rummaged about in the ice-box, bore a carefully arranged tray upstairs, ate to her delicate satisfaction, got into her lounging pajamas and so to bed where she could think. Kitty coming in about half-past ten, breathless, humming, happy, turned on the light and stared in astonishment at her recumbent sister, who lolling in her little bed returned the stare.

"Oh, hello!" Gertrude welcomed her amiably, "you thinking of living here now?"

For answer, Kitty, her eyes, very bright, went over and kissed her.

"And isn't it nice to run into a session of old home week in your own room?" the older girl murmured holding tightly none the less to her sister, and rejoicing at this tacitly implied conclusion of the great civil war. "What's on your mind, Kitten? Having a sangwidge?"

The younger girl plumped herself just any which way down on the bed. "You know, Gertrude, I wouldn't be a bit surprised if I were to marry him." She rose and walked over to the dressing table, powdering her pretty face anew, needlessly revising her mouth with a vivid lip-stick.

"Sit down and tell me all," her sister encouraged seductively. And Kitty needing nothing more than this told her of Jerry and his sudden conversion to a bigger and better life all brought about, it appeared, as the result of his becoming more and more acquainted with the fine and really womanly character of Miss Katchen Brown. "I even told him my real name," said Kitty, in proof of her newly awakened trust in him," and he liked it, and he said I was his ideal. Of course we'll have to wait, the parents would never hear to our marrying so young, but still and all it's wonderful to be engaged. . . ." She ate a sandwich, musing brightly over her changed estate.

Gertrude watched her in silence, a little enviously. Things would always work well for Kitty. Still she didn't mind a little struggle. . . . It was thrilling to breast circumstances . . . bend them to one's will.

"I've got something to tell you too, Kitty," she said quietly and something in her tone made her sister turn sharply. . . . "What would you say if I told you that I think,—no I know," she corrected herself firmly "that I'm going to marry Malory Forten?"

"I'd say," said Kitty roughly, even angrily, "that you'd have to tell me another funny story. Why I just saw Malory and Melissa a half hour ago, looking more in love than I've ever seen two people in my life. . . . Now Gertrude remember, none of your tricks."

"I'm not playing any tricks. I'm telling you," said Gertrude for once deeply excited, "only what I know. And that is that Malory Forten isn't going to marry Melissa Paul."

"Well if he doesn't, all I've got to say is he's a nasty cad. What's the reason he isn't going to marry her?"

"Because he can't marry her. He won't want to marry her."

"What are you talking about Gertrude? Not that old Colonel Halloway business?"

"Well yes and no . . . don't you suppose he knows about that already? . . . but when he comes to know something else, he'll think of that too and it will drive him away from her as far as the North is from the South pole!"

"What do you mean?" Kitty asked, frightened, whispering. "You don't mean, Gertrude, you don't mean she has some terrible disease, leprosy, or—or —something?"

"No," said Gertrude, "I don't. I almost wish I did," and suddenly and bewilderingly began to cry.

Regardless of her dainty dress, Kitty got down on her knees beside the little bed, clasped her sister about the neck. Only a disaster of cosmic import could reduce Gertrude to such misery. . . . "Darling you'll have to tell me about it."

They were only three years apart . . . they had shared all their secrets since both had been able to talk; they had disagreed and fought and respected each other. They had been each to each a confessor; they knew each other's weaknesses, generosities, limitations, but never had they known such oneness as during these moments.

.   .   .   .   .

"Oh God!" Kitty said again and again as Gertrude, using Mr. Stede's very words minus only their crudeness, told her what she had learned. "Oh God!" she murmured, hiding her face, as though in pain, in the pillow. "But Gertrude, Gertrude how could He, how could He permit it?"

"Who?" asked Gertrude in some natural bewilderment.

"God. . . ." She lifted her pallid face, ravaged with tears. "Gertrude, that poor girl! . . . You know for the first time I'm really afraid . . . I'm afraid of life, Gertrude . . . I think I'll sleep with you to-night . . . I'm scared."

"Yes," said Gertrude, "do sleep in my bed . . . I'm scared too."

It was pleasant to realize that the other was so near. In the small, eerie morning hours, Kitty spoke to her sister knowing full well that the latter was awake. "What are you going to do about it, Gertrude?"

"Me? Nothing."

"But darling, you just have to. You can't just leave it alone. Even if only the one thing is true they have to be told. . . . And if the other is so. . . ." Words failed her at that terrible thought.

"Yes of course they've got to be told. But it can't be from me. Darling I'm sorry but you'll have to see that they find out about it."

"You've gone crazy . . . why Gertrude you're stark staring mad! What have I got to do with it?"

"Nothing. That's true. But don't you see? *He* will go crazy And I must save him. . . . I honestly love him Kitten, I do want him. . . . But you don't suppose I wanted him with all this awful trouble, do you? But now that it has come on him, and because I loved him when I thought he was just like any other boy, I've got to stand by him now. . . . Well he'd never come near me if he thought I knew a word about it. . . . And he's got to come near me. . . . I'm the only one who could save him except, if things had broken differently, Melissa. And she's out of the picture. Malory can be happy only with two kinds of women, either one like Melissa whom he'll take care of, or one like me who'll make him think he's taking care of her, but who will really take care of him."

For this kind of reasoning Kitty had no answer; she saw its essential truth. "But what'll I do?" she wailed. "Will I tell Mother?"

"Not now, not yet . . . she might interfere and —Kitty, I mean to marry him. . . . I'm afraid you'll have to tell Laurentine."

"Not much I won't . . . with all the trouble she's had! I think I see myself."

In the end Kitty with a sick reluctance promised to tell Dr. Denleigh. "Everybody says they're engaged and he's a doctor. Dad says doctors have to meet up with all sorts of problems."

She fell, finally, much later than Gertrude, placid now because of shifted responsibility, into a troubled sleep.

.   .   .   .   .

On Sunday afternoon, Gertrude, serene, assured and unostentatiously triumphant, left for Boston. Within an hour, Kitty, fuming, but reliable as Horatius at the Bridge, called up Dr. Denleigh's office to receive no answer. Well she must get this thing off her chest she told herself fretfully, so, greatly daring, she called the Strange home. Aunt Sal, answering, told her mildly that Dr. Denleigh had driven Laurentine and Mrs. Ismay to New York . . . "they'll be gone for a week maybe. Did you want him very particular, Kitty?"

"No," the girl fibbed quickly, hating the lie. "I just promised Dad I'd try to find him for some old meeting. . . . Say 'hello' to Melissa for me won't you Mrs. Strange?"

"Of all the rotten breaks! What am I going to do?" she moaned. And thought of her mother. She went and found her sitting comfortably and enthralled on the little glassed in side-porch deep in her sugary novel. . . . She had been to church . . . she had seen that her husband had received a good dinner . . . she had seen one daughter off to college with less money than that daughter had demanded and yet with content. And here was her youngest daughter at her knee. . . . Kitty made no mention of Gertrude, but after all she didn't need to . . . if Gertrude was her mother's daughter, Mrs. Brown was also Gertrude's mother and knew more than her pretty, placid face implied.

"Mummy," said Kitty miserably, "I can't tell you how I know it but I know it." And told her.

Afterwards she was so glad she had. Mrs. Brown was moved and shocked and sorry but she was not worried. "We'll keep them apart," she soothed her daughter. "Nothing much can happen in three months. They're too poor to marry, and Melissa's as decent as Malory. He's going away as soon as school closes. And then we'll get word to him and he'll never come back. It's too bad for Melissa but she'll get over it. . . . Women have to get over many things," she ended with surprising sagacity.

"But Mummy how can we keep them apart?"

"That's true. . . . Well I'll have to tell Dr. Denleigh and he can speak to Laurentine . . . she's the one I'm sorry for."

"I'm sorry for all of them, Mother," Kitty said soberly. "But your way seems pretty good. That way Melissa'll never have to know about it. . . . Her cousin can manage that; she could keep her awfully busy or even she could send her away."

She was unaware of Gertrude's suspicion which the latter had forgotten to mention, that the young couple were meeting, almost nightly, under the Chinaberry Tree.

CHAPTER XXXIII

ON the morning on which Laurentine was to go to New York she awoke, yawned, stretched, lay for a few moments deliberately relaxed and sleepy. "Oh!" she groaned, "if only we were going to-morrow instead of to-day; I'm so tired! I wish, I wish I didn't have to get up!"

Denleigh had had a difficult week. Mary Ricardi had had another baby,—and had died of it. It was Denleigh's first death in Red Brook; he couldn't recover from it; he couldn't forget the trusting look in Mary's eyes. Even in the midst of all her outrageous pain she had been so sure Denleigh could pull her through. "You see me outa all this, Doc, yes?" she murmured between her terrible spasms of pain.

And then her poor strained heart rebelled and she had died after all. And the baby, the little boy who was to be named Stephen, after the doctor, had breathed a few times and he too had passed out like a slowly extinguished flame. The awful waste of it had made Denleigh deathly sick,—too sick for a doctor. It had given him a sudden depth of distaste for his calling; he wished he were a brick-layer; he wished that he too had been blotted out; he thought of the French word, *"anéanti"* with its awful suggestion of nothingness.

It was in no holiday mood therefore that he started off with Laurentine and Mrs. Ismay on the trip which both he and "his girl," as he loved to call Laurentine, had so long envisaged. "Goodness," he thought to himself, "I hope I won't keep on feeling like this!" In a way he half welcomed Laurentine's silence. Usually his expert driving made all sorts of gay badinage possible, but to-day he was driving Dr. Ismay's large car; he had not yet quite got the "feel" of it and was very glad to be able to give his task undivided attention.

The weather too which had been so promising, so divine, had definitely changed into chilliness and wind and a disheartening grayness which might have been all right by virtue of its very contrast had they been in better spirits. As it was even Mrs. Ismay, after a few forlorn attempts at cheerfulness, relapsed into thoughtfulness, though she did comment once smilingly on their fallen spirits.

"But you're both of you worn out," she said with ready understanding. "You've both tried to do too much this week. You'll be all right after a night's rest and then be that much more ready to plunge into the excitement of New York."

They were destined to run into immediate excitement for within the next hour, Denleigh, for all his careful driving, experienced a blowout,—and Dr. Ismay had forgotten to leave his "jack" in the car! It had begun to rain; they were a full mile from the nearest repair station. Maliciously enough, not a car seemed to get their signal of distress, and Denleigh had to walk half the distance back before anyone slowed down and picked him up. By the time they reached New York, worn, weary and provoked, they were only too glad, after dinner, to forego their carefully planned sortie into the gay streets and retire to their respective lodgings. Laurentine, recovering somewhat under the influence of the nourishing food and the glimpse which she had caught of her large, comfortable room, said smiling. "We'll be snapping out of all this to-morrow, Stevie. You know they sometimes say: 'A bad beginning makes a good ending.'"

Sunday turned out to be cool but beautifully clear. They went all three of them to Fosdick's Church on Riverside Drive and heard a fine sermon, scaled down to human needs. In the afternoon Denleigh took them driving along the beautiful Drive itself. Laurentine whose few previous visits to New York had been of the slightest possible duration and always for business reasons gave herself up to a girlish, almost countrified appreciation of this unexpected gorgeousness; the swift, clear river, the massive Washington bridge, the frowning Palisades across the way matched so marvelously by the towering palaces on the New York side. It made her think of what Babylon must have been and she was amazed when Denleigh reasonably pointed out that Babylon, of course, knew of no such marvels of architecture and beauty as these dwellings housing millionaires, politicians, bootleggers and other city magnates.

Then they had gone to a large colored restaurant for dinner and afterwards, Denleigh and Laurentine had gone down town to one of the immense moving picture houses with their curious combination of garishness, comfort, richness and over-ornateness. "Still," she thought, "it must be wonderful for poor people to escape to all this!"

The rest of the week sped. They went to the Lafayette Theatre where Laurentine looked at the audience more than at the stage sensing that oneness which colored people feel in a colored crowd, even though so many of its members are people whom one does not want ever to know.

She liked that and she was also intensely taken by the night-clubs, because she could not puzzle out why people should care for places such as these . . . in a Harlem cellar where a drunken black woman suddenly lurched forward and slapped a handsome yellow girl across the face and the surrounding crowd looked on as unmoved as though this were some part of the entertainment, unmindful of the tragedy destined to follow without those walls . . . where a dark, sinuous dancer, singing a song, whose words she could not catch, and making movements with her supple body, whose meanings she could not fathom, pranced and postured and gestured before a fascinated lad of twenty-one. Mechanically, he handed her, at five minute intervals, dollar bills, moistening his feverish lips, gazing unwinking into her mesmeric eyes as a bird might look at a snake.

After this she was glad to get out into the air and to ride with her lover up the mighty Concourse and through the reaches of Van Cortlandt Park where they would have liked to rest and chat a little; but vigilant policemen appearing suddenly from nowhere hurried them on since city ordinances were more important than the transports of lovers.

In the day Denleigh went to medical conferences and visited clinics and sanitariums of Harlem. And then Mrs. Ismay and Laurentine shopped and explored the huge emporiums, taking lunch in their dining-rooms, or at Schrafft's and the better class of confectioners. She loved this, for though she had, in the course of her life, run into little active prejudice, it was pleasant, aside from the convenience, not to have to stop and ponder on the wisdom or the consequences of entering this place or the likelihood of having one's feelings hurt because one was hungry and wanted his pangs relieved as soon as may be.

In Harlem too she met charming and amazing people of wealth and culture and ambition which they were satisfying according to their ability to present themselves as being just a little more advanced than anybody else; New York not caring greatly who serves it as long as it is served.

On Saturday they were to return home. By Friday, with all her enjoyment Laurentine had had sufficient. She was weary of the crowded streets, of the stares which her beauty brought her on Seventh Avenue. She would be glad to see not only Aunt Sal, yes and Melissa, she wanted to behold her comfortable home once more, to let her gaze wander over Mr. Stede's handiwork in the yard and garden, to stand beneath the Chinaberry Tree and dream dreams which were surely coming true. . . .

This last afternoon, Denleigh assured her was her very own. Originally they had planned to go to a matinée, have dinner and go back to the theatre, but the day turning unseasonably warm, they were both seized with a sudden nostalgia for the sweet openness of Red Brook and chose as a substitute a drive through the Parks. They rode, in the electric atmosphere of a New York spring afternoon, through Van Cortlandt Park, across Mosholu Parkway, out through the Bronx River Road, through an intricacy of turns and stretches to Hutchinson River Drive and across its wide perfection to the Boston Post Road. Denleigh, apologizing for its hideousness, turned as quickly as might be into Pelham Parkway. Along the road, lacy with young foliage, they drove to the Bay, stopped and looked awhile at the water, rippling and smiling in the April sun, loving every second of this precious, passing intimacy. "If ever I make any money again," Denleigh said, laughing but serious, "we'll go abroad and see London and Paris and Rome, but we'll do our actual living in the little

French towns by the side of rivers and ponds and lakes."

A little later they were on their way again toward Pelham, the lure of exploration thick upon them. A road branched off at right angles bearing a sign with the legend: "City Island." The idea of an island was too inviting. "Shall we try it?" Denleigh asked. He had already pointed the car in that direction. At first it was charming but twenty minutes of driving brought them to the familiar array of hot-dog stands, filling stations and small restaurants where one might obtain sea-food. "I'm so hungry!" Laurentine breathed mournfully.

Finally they came to the end of the long street; Denleigh took out his watch. "Quarter of six," he announced. "Suppose we got out here, darling and look at the water and get something to eat. The sea-food here should be delicious; it's bound to be fresh." A moment they loitered on the homely little fishing-dock then entered the nearest restaurant, a wide, rather low, square dwelling, very clean with the slightly festive air which belongs to places in such localities.

A colored waiter darted forward to seat them, stood for a moment aghast, then recovering himself ushered them to a table against the farthest wall, as remote as might be from the half-dozen couples sitting quietly, unobservingly at their tables in the bright, lingering light. Laurentine sensed what was to happen. She leaned toward Stephen, "Do you think we'd better try a little Italian?" They had both picked up a few phrases in "Little Italy." Denleigh indeed had become really proficient.

Being colored, the doctor knew what she meant but he shook his head. "No I hate that sort of thing. Everything will be all right, don't worry." A shadow fell athwart the table. They looked up to see, not the friendly though distressed face of the courteous Negro, but into the sallow, furious mask of a white man. A short, thin fellow he was speaking with an accent which neither recognized.

"What do you want?" he asked insolently. Denleigh, determined to see this through, quietly ordered dinner. The little fellow bustled about, making every motion, every word an insult. The menu called for soup and clam chowder. Without consulting his guests he brought them the chowder which neither of them wanted and therefore refused, ordering the soup. "The soup isn't ready," he snarled and bearing off the chowder with no word of apology returned with their order for dinner. . . . Some other guests arrived, sat down at the table next to the two colored people, regarded them negligently, and gave their order. But this the lordly white could not stand. Bending over the ladies, he whispered effusively and sibilantly and finally bore them off in triumph to a table distant the full width of the room.

One of the women looked back, her glance clearly asking: "How does it feel I wonder to be a poor colored thing . . . so different . . . to be shunned?" Laurentine feeling sorry for herself, felt sorrier for her escort and yet sorriest for the woman . . . it seemed sad to be a free agent and yet voluntarily to be a party to any action so petty and yet so cruel. . . . And suddenly while the colored waiter, keeping away from his two compatriots, passed with melancholy ostentation relishes and sauces to all the other diners, the white waiter went about, dropping a word here, accenting there his speech with a glance directly levelled at the table where the two brown Americans sat with only their courage to ease their discomfort.

People turned about and eyed them, people who would have sat beside them in the subway, theatre, drugstore and class-room without a second thought, now suddenly became overwhelmingly aware of their presence because of the machination of one little sallow-skinned foreigner whose country Denleigh, fighting in 1918, had perhaps helped to keep from dissolution.

A couple, starting to go out, engaged in a whispered conversation with the waiter . . . who talked on and on in voluble whispers. The guests nodded approvingly. The fellow grew more and more self-confident. "Yes," he announced for all to hear. "That's what I always do. Freeze 'em out."

"Quite right," announced the departing guest.

Flushed with victory the little man returned to the fray, asking Denleigh what he would have for dessert and in the same breath announcing that out of the eight items mentioned in the menu, typewritten for the day, only vanilla ice-cream and rice-pudding were to be had.

Denleigh curtly, and without consulting Laurentine, refused both.

"Suit yourself," the man said with renewed insolence and went off to get his change. Denleigh uneasy, angry, powerless, tingling to knock him down, decided to tip the colored waiter. When the white man returned he told him to ask him to step over.

"What do you want him for?"

"None of your business," Denleigh retorted, his patience snapping.

The little man raised his voice. "That'll be enough out of you." His venom, too long restrained, poured forth. "I'll have a policeman in to look after you."

"A policeman!" Denleigh almost laughed in the midst of his discomfiture. "What for?"

"Didn't you tell me to mind my business? I don't have to take that. I served you didn't I? What have you got to do with any of the other waiters? I'm in charge here."

Laurentine knew Denleigh was aching to be up and at him. She intervened. "Stephen, don't, for my sake! You know he's been talking to all these people here. You don't know what they might back him up in doing." . . .

It would have been sheer folly to do anything but go. . . .

.   .   .   .   .

All in all it would not have taken very much imagination to have pictured a more pleasant trip. Both Laurentine and Denleigh entering Red Brook the next day, a little blue a little depressed under this last unnecessary onslaught of fortune, felt themselves scarcely benefitted by their outing, almost wished they had stayed at home. Denleigh, the man, naturally felt it worse than the woman.

Laurentine tried to comfort him. "You mustn't mind Stephen, there wasn't a thing you could do without running into grave danger. They might have ganged you. It was just the fortune of war, darling!" . . . They had already left Mrs. Ismay at her house together with her husband's car. Denleigh had brought Laurentine home in one of Mr. Tracey's cabs, had carried her bags in and, resisting Aunt Sal's invitation, had gone directly to his office in North Street. . . .

    .   .   .   .

The telephone was ringing when he entered the door. With unusual irritation he thought to himself: "How can any body possibly know I'm home! I've a good mind not to answer." But the thought of Mary Ricardi was always with him . . . perhaps he might be able to save some one else in dire distress.

His irritation was not in the least mitigated on hearing Mrs. Brown's voice coming clearly over the wire. "Dr. Denleigh, my daughter just caught sight of you on the street. I'm so glad you're home. I must see you."

In natural bewilderment he asked: "Is Dr. Brown ill?" But even then he thought why in the devil didn't she call Ismay?

"No," the voice squeaked in shrill emphasis, "no indeed he's all right, but I must see you, Doctor."

His bewilderment increased. "But what about?"

"Well I just can't tell you over the phone. Could I come down?"

He didn't want her in his office just then; he didn't want any one, scarcely Laurentine. He wanted to be at peace for a few moments and go over in his mind that series of incidents in the restaurant. . . .

He should have knocked the man down. "God!" he, a man not given to profanity, exploded. "Isn't this nonsense about color ever going to stop . . . isn't a man ever going to get a chance to be a man and not an eternal compromise?" And yet he couldn't, he *couldn't* throw his life away because he preferred raspberry ice to vanilla ice-cream. . . . He wanted a bath, he wanted to get the strain of the traffic incurred between New York and Red Brook out of his weary head. . . . And now here was this woman with some problem. . . . He swore suddenly. "If it's about her daughter, she'll have to get her husband to help her out. . . . I won't be a party to anything irregular."

But she hadn't come to see him about her daughter. She had come to see him about Judy Strange's daughter. He listened to her improbable tale looking at her, speechless. She was a short, plumpish woman, very beautifully dressed to disguise her size. She had a round face that was not only still pretty and far from vapid but which was moreover, quite strong. He had never noticed it before because she had one or two fascinating, if rather foolish, tricks —one of closing her eyes, for instance, for quite a long time and then opening them and looking at you clearly, disconcertingly. The last time she closed them he thought: "Isn't she ever going to open them again?"

But he said: "My God! Mrs. Brown, are you sure this is true? You know the people around here are awfully hard on the Stranges. Jealousy I suppose. They like to think the wages of sin is death. . . ."

"Well," she said, unclosing her eyes and giving him her long, unwavering scrutiny, "it is, isn't it? In the case of Laurentine's mother it meant the death of her own and the colonel's good standing in the community didn't it? And in the case of this poor child, if she's told, it means the death of hers and Malory's love. And if she isn't told, if somehow we manage to tell just him, and spirit him away without letting her know, which, I own, is my choice, —it means the death of illusion for both of them."

He thought to himself quite frankly: "Now who would have supposed you'd have the sense to work that out?"

Aloud he asked her why she had come to him.

"Well I thought you might want to consult Laurentine." . . . But of course he knew that she wanted to get rid of the terrible responsibility.

"You're sure that part, anyway, of this matter is true, Mrs. Brown? Even part of it is enough to separate them."

Mrs. Brown assured him. Kitty had acknowledged that the original information came from Mr. Ștede. Every one knew the old man's devotion to the Stranges.

"Well," he said sighing heavily and wishing he'd never been born, "I'll look into it. Of course this rests here?"

She hadn't, she assured him, closing her eyes in her intensity, informed even her husband of what she had heard. And, although, at the time he thought this queer, he was constrained to believe her.

By the time she left he was so numb with fatigue, dismay and distaste of life that there was nothing left for him but to go to bed. He fell into an immediate stupor.

. . . .

As soon as he woke up it all came rushing back on him . . . the death of Mary Ricardi, the incident in the restaurant and last of all Melissa. "Poor little girl," he thought, "poor little innocent kid. And poor Laurentine too."

He called on all his patients. He went and smoked a pipe with Dr. Ismay, sitting in his office and reading the huge edition of a Sunday paper from cover to cover. But at last he could put it off no longer. He must go to see Laurentine. He found her alone, expecting him. Melissa had gone with Aunt Sal to a gospel meeting, one of a series being conducted by the Reverend Mary Lewis in Madison. . . . He simply did not know how to begin. In a moment she was aware of his confusion; his strange aloofness.

"Why Stephen, what's the matter?"

His manner was so strange and his hands, when they tried to catch at her own, were so icy, that she was frightened, and then poor girl, since she had never been able quite to forget Phil Hackett, she was suspicious.

"Stephen!" she said again, but made no movement toward him. He remained where he was.

"Laurentine," he began, "if you'd only let me

know at the beginning about Melissa,"—and knew immediately that this was the wrong approach.

"Don't you think if you'd let me know about her mother? . . ."

She interrupted him furiously, "Why, what difference could it have made to you?"

"Well of course, actually, it couldn't make any difference to me. But it would have been fairer,"—he was going to say, "to Melissa," but she wouldn't let him, so obsessed she was with her great fear of seeing her house of life tumble into nothingness because of Melissa.

"Listen, Stephen! Melissa and her mother have nothing to do with me. I have nothing to do with them."

"Oh, Laurentine, you can hardly say that. Well I feel I have something to do with them."

"You mean that they affect our relationship?"

He said in amazement: "You know I couldn't mean that. On the other hand this is a really serious matter and you and I have just got to face it."

"Face what?"

"Well here she is going about with young Malory . . . why I've seen them together on the streets myself . . . she's clearly in love with him . . . well Great Scott don't you think she ought to be told? A girl with—with that blood in her veins—why there's no telling what might happen. And then you'd never be able to forgive yourself. . . ."

She said icily. "She has the same sort of blood in her veins that I have. I suppose it will affect her as it has affected me. . . . But anyway I'll attend to Melissa and the case of this boy. . . ."

Not quite satisfied he said: "It's all so distasteful." In her blind misunderstanding, she could have screamed at him. But she said mildly: "I guess we Stranges are a difficult morsel for anyone who is a bit squeamish."

"Squeamish? Why Laurentine you couldn't call my concern over a case like this 'squeamish,' could you? Why considering her antecedents, . . . well it's enough to drive one almost crazy." He really wondered if it hadn't affected her somewhat.

She said in a low voice: "Crazy! Drive one crazy! You're right Stephen, I should have told you this from the very beginning . . . then it wouldn't have affected you so. I'm afraid it's too upsetting for you. I think I'd better attend to my own and my family's affairs entirely by myself now and hereafter. . . . Don't bother coming round to discuss them with me ever anymore."

He said roughly: "What are you driving at Laurentine? What's happening to us?"

"Nothing except that I don't want to hear any more about our blood and our antecedents even from you . . . it's all over."

He asked her one more question. "Do you understand what I've been talking about?"

"I certainly do . . . about Melissa and her mother and this horrible boy whom she shouldn't have known. . . . Did his family send you over here to me?"

"No," he said, "but naturally they would if they knew anything about it,—me or some one else."

"Well I'll 'tend to it for them and for you too. Now Stephen there's the door. Please go. I've no

more to say and I'm going up to my room." Resolutely she mounted the stairs and left him.

· · · · ·

She could have cursed Melissa. Melissa so smug,
so sure of herself, so pitiful of "poor Laurentine,"
and yet doing her best to pull down that reputation
which Laurentine had so hardly built up. . . .
What, she wondered, could the child have been
doing? . . . It was not like her thus to fling proprie-
ties to the winds; like Gertrude Brown she, too,
recognized in her cousin that strong leaning toward
sheer respectability. And this Malory boy, who
could he be? Why had she never seen him? Of
course it must have been the lad whom she had seen
kissing Melissa that night under the Chinaberry
Tree. . . . In a sense she blamed herself for that,
—but in her heart she had always trusted Melissa. . . .

Evidently this boy's parents had found out about
the affair,—it couldn't actually be an "affair" she
said to herself aghast,—and they had also made
some inquiries. New people, as they evidently were,
naturally they had misjudged her poor mother and
if they had heard the old gossip revived of Judy and
her amorous poachings it had not tended to allay
their natural anxiety. . . . Well she'd promised
Stephen to keep them apart . . . she could easily
do that by loading Melissa down with work and by
seeing that she no longer got out of the house at
night. And as soon as school was over the child
should go away . . . she could go to Chicago to her
mother. . . . There was no reason why she should
bother her own mother about it.

And later on in the summer she'd go away herself, to New York, maybe. . . . She had no especial fitness for the theatre except her looks but those together with her rather fair singing voice were a considerable asset. She'd forget Stephen; there'd be plenty of men, she realized, with a new icy assurance, who would care nothing for a woman's "blood and antecedents" provided only she had beauty and youth.

CHAPTER XXXIV

NOW it was May. Thanks to Laurentine's precautions Melissa and Malory rarely saw each other; indeed their only time together was their brief walk to and from school. But this they did quite openly; as a matter of fact they had never seriously attempted to conceal their interest in each other from any one save Laurentine. . . . Why should they? And yet it was being born in on the sensitive natures of the two of them that their little romance was causing undue notice. Malory, the least self-conscious of young men could not help observing the attention paid them on the street by citizens of colored Red Brook whom he had never known, indeed, had scarcely noticed.

Both he and Melissa were becoming uneasily aware of the curious hush which seemed to rise around them if ever they were part of any assembly, —in Sunday School say, or in any of their small community clubs. It was rarely that they were part of any other gathering. From time to time Kitty

Brown still asked Melissa to her house but on such occasions there was only a group of other girls there. Malory, dropping into the Brown homestead, never happened to run into Melissa; in some curious, silent, inexplicable manner they were being kept apart.

There really was something behind it. Laurentine, going about the house, pale and quiet, completely composed, no longer stayed up late entertaining Denleigh, for the simple reason that he no longer came. But she paid for this by remaining up till all hours of her own accord and for her own reasons. . . . The weather being very warm she sat frequently, these nights, on the side porch, sometimes she trailed langorously out on the tender grass and sat for hours under the Chinaberry Tree.

Occasionally she had a visitor from New York, a slender swarthy man, finely almost dude-ishly dressed, with a manner too completely at ease, too sophisticated. Evidently a man of the world, he was, for all that, clearly excited about Laurentine who looked at him with negligent invitation in her eyes. . . . Aunt Sal watching them without ostentation, but grimly, severely.

"I don't know what she's up to," Melissa laughed uneasily to Malory, telling him about Laurentine, "but she's completely changed. And I know that whatever she means or doesn't mean she's found out about us and means to keep us apart."

This would always infuriate Malory. "The nerve of her," he used to mutter. "I wish you'd let me go to her, Melissa, and talk to her. What business has she to take such a dislike to me, when she's never even seen me?"

But Melissa begged him to wait. "We have so little time left now. My but I'd like to see her face when she knows we're married!"

.   .   .   .   .

On the second Saturday in June the Sunday School was to hold its picnic. Melissa was to attend with Malory. Laurentine forgetting church, rarely, these days, going to see even Mrs. Ismay, knew nothing of all this. As usual she had arranged to utilize the girl's Saturday, by sending her as she often did to deliver her creations. Melissa proffered no objections.

"Hey! Hey! and also Hey!" she whispered jazzily to Charles, a small black kitten, who had come up to her room to help her with the business of going out. The day was sunny, bright and propitious; she donned a sleeveless white crêpe dress, a little nonsensical cherry jacket and a cherry colored beret. Laurentine did not give her a second thought as she passed through the sewing-room and picked up her box. . . . All of them in that house were careful of their dress. . . . Two blocks down the street Melissa was joined by Giovanni Ricardi; the box, a piece of money, a paper with directions thereon changed hands. . . . Near the Post Office she met Malory and the two proceeded to Redd's Woods to the picnic.

That was a strange experience. The two arrived a little after noon. Most of the picnickers were gathered in the open pavilion where Mrs. Simmons, Mrs. Brown and a few trusty church pillars were dispensing lunch. Everything was noise, gayety, happy confusion. . . . The two young people, serene in their enjoyment of having outwitted Laurentine and in their prospect of a pleasant afternoon, walked leisurely, laughing, assured, across the clearing.

"Look," Harry Robbins said suddenly, "here comes the bride!"

And suddenly the noise and gayety died away; the whole group stood petrified, immobile with the immanence of some grave, some unspeakable awfulness closing in upon them. Speechless they waited.

The silence was palpable. Malory could feel it even before he was close enough to realize that it actually was silence. . . . Just before they reached the pavilion Melissa glancing at his face saw the change there, looked up, saw the group of icy statues.

And then in a moment the queerness was dissipated. Mrs. Brown came rushing down the steps; she seized the young girl's hand. "Oh Melissa," she cried, "you're just the one we want to help with the sandwiches." Kitty annexed Malory and Herbert Tucker and drove back to town for some needless article without which the luncheon could not proceed. With a determination none the less palpable because it was so invisible the pair were kept apart all afternoon.

Toward evening Mrs. Brown, still keeping Melissa by her side, contrived to wound her arm slightly with a small knife. It frightened her beyond words she said; she and Kitty would take her home to Dr. Brown and have the cut washed and sterilized.

She could not tell Malory how sorry she was that there was no room in the car for him, but they had so many things besides themselves "to carry home and all. . . ." Malory, his face set and pale, managed to whisper to the bewildered patient. . . . "Don't worry darling. I'll straighten all this out. Be sure to wait for me after school on Monday."

Both of them found Sunday a nightmare.

. . . . .

On Monday he met her, his face as pale and set as when he had left her Saturday. He made no pretense about the anxiety and blind fury which for two days had been raging within him. Melissa, already frightened, felt her own fear growing, so greatly did his attitude emphasize the strangeness of this curious, puzzling mystery which so enveloped them.

Slowly they walked down side-streets, hardly speaking, until the girl, realizing that they had come to a part of the town with which she was barely familiar, asked him where they were going.

"To my home," he told her proudly. "After all my mother is a woman and she *is* my mother . . . she'll take care of you . . . she's lived here such a long time I know she'll understand these hateful busybodies and their ugly ways. She'll know how to handle them. It's been a long time since I've asked her to do anything for me. . . . And to-morrow Melissa we'll get her to go to Morristown with us and we'll be married. Then let's see what they'll say!"

Speechless, she looked at him, admiring his pluck, his courage, her heart strangely lightened.

Presently they were walking down his street, a

rather narrow one, small, thick maples growing on either side. The houses belonged to another date; they were of a greenish brown wood, with ugly, jutting bay windows and small stoops. He stopped before one so like its neighbors that the wonder was he could pick it out. Opening the gate, he stood back to let her precede him and perceived that she was greatly trembling. She raised her pale face to him.

"Oh, Malory!" she whispered pitifully, "must I really go in? C-c-couldn't we wait a few days longer?"

But he was determined to scotch this snake *now*. "Darling, you'll just have to be brave; we must get through with this. . . . My mother will be very kind."

His hand under her elbow he helped her up the steep steps. But when he stretched out that hand to open the much discussed screen door, he perceived his sister Reba on the other side of it . . . barring his way. Melissa, her eyes still dazzled by the sun and by her grief saw at first only a bodiless head topped, half way above it, by another one, older, more sunken, deathly with an ancient sorrow. . . .

The first head spoke: "Malory, she can't come in here. . . ."

He was so frantic, he swore, the oath coming strangely from his prim, boyish lips. "Damn you! Has the whole world gone crazy? Open this door! Open it, I say, and let us in!"

The other head speaking in a slow and measured tone uttered its confirmation: "No, Malory, she can never come into this house."

Melissa cried out: "I don't want to go into that house!" . . . She was halfway down the steps before Malory could stop her.

"Go home, Melissa, Angel," he told her gently, sternly. "Go home now and remember I'll see you to-morrow."

Running back up the steps like a mad man, he dashed into the house slamming the screen door and turning on those two subdued, lifeless figures like a tiger. "Now damn it, I say, damn it!" he cried, "tell me what you mean, tell me what it's all about!"

Very gently, then, they got him up to his room and slowly, quietly, inexorably they told him . . . told him what he had to know . . . told him why they were always so sad . . . told him how much they had hoped to save him from sadness.

. . . . . .

Melissa ran all the way home. When she got up to her room she was half fainting, but she dashed to her mirror, pulled all her clothes off, examined minutely her delicate, yellow body. "Could I have the leprosy, I wonder? Oh God what is it?" She fell into an agony of weeping.

It was better, she knew, to go down to dinner since her absence would mean a visit from Aunt Sal and she did not think she could hold out against that tenderness. . . . When she was doing the dishes Mr. Stede wandered in, in hope of largess, but even more in hope of helping her. His old eyes traced the marks of anguish in her face.

From afar off he began to approach his subject by speaking of Asshur. "Hope he's as peart as ever."

Languidly she answered that he seemed to be all right. "Said in his last letter that he had a horse and was riding all over the place."

The old voice chuckled. "Like to see Asshur ridin' a hoss; bet he cert'ny makes some pitcher. . . . . I remember I usta ride a hoss when I was a lad, cert'ny could go . . . many's the fall I've had off that old gayly hoss. . . ." With a jerk he returned to the real subject in his mind. . . . Riding with Mr. Gathers in his little truck, to-day, he had caught sight of the young lovers, had noted with a sinking heart their pitiful absorption. "See much of that young Forten feller these days, Melissa?"

And suddenly she knew the meaning of his presence, his rambling words about Asshur and the "gayly hoss" whatever that might mean. He was like all the rest of Red Brook, prying into her affairs, picking at her because she was Sal Strange's niece. Well then she'd give him some information for his pains. . . . "No," she said clearly, "I've been seeing very little of him . . . but I expect it'll be different after to-morrow."

He was very silent then. If she had looked at him, she would have seen a strange, ashen pallor spreading over his face. But barely murmuring "Good-night," she passed out of the kitchen, leaving him. . . . She had a lot to do between now and to-morrow.

The old man, apostrophizing as on a former occasion, groaned: "God, You know, that hadn't oughta happen. . . ." Well he had trusted Gertrude Brown; her mother had come to see him to confirm his statements. And they had both failed him. He couldn't tell Sal Strange. . . . And suddenly he thought of Dr. Denleigh.

.   .   .   .   .

Melissa, awakening, said to herself unhappily: "I'm going to be married. To-day I'm going to be married." And couldn't believe it.

She did not see Malory before school nor during lunch period but she did not greatly mind. . . . Undoubtedly she would see him after school. And meanwhile she had this new thought to occupy her.

But she did not see him after school either.

At first she had stood at the corner where she could see the stream of pupils issuing from the two exits. But he was not there. Never doubting she walked to a store two blocks off where they sometimes met though always by appointment. It was so easy for the boys eluding complaisant monitors to slip out ahead. . . . But he was not there. Confused and worried she waited a long time; she needed her thought now to sustain her. . . .

At the end of an hour she said to herself suddenly: "The Romany Road! . . ." Of course the Romany Road! Something had happened; he'd been delayed, detained. But he'd trust to her common sense . . . it was true they had never been on it together since that day Harry Robbins had discovered them. . . . Doubtless he had meant to tell her about it yesterday; it would be so like Malory's foolishness to want them to begin their last adventure on the Road which had brought them such joy.

But, as she plodded on through the dusty streets under the blazing June sun, she did not smile over Malory's foolishness. . . . And the instant she set foot on the Road she knew that it was the road of her dream. She said to herself sadly: "Now, now it's going to happen!"

Far, far up the clearing she spied the bowed figure, plodding on like herself with footsteps, slow, unwilling and shuffling, stirring up little clouds of blinding, acrid, dust. . . . She knew, child though she was, that to accost him would be the death of love, of all, all happiness. She knew that the face he would turn on her would be the face of the Comic Mask and that she would see it for the rest of her life, perhaps after life. . . . She caught up with him, she put her hand on his sleeve.

"Malory!" she said timidly.

So suddenly he whirled that he nearly knocked her down. His recognition was instant. And sure enough, the face which he turned on her,—oh terrible!—was laughing,—with a horrible, insane laughter.

"You!" he said, still laughing, his mouth set in that unspeakably awful rictus . . . "and to think you were to be my wife!"

She said to him gently: "Malory what is it? Of course I'm to be your wife. Why shouldn't I?"

His burning eyes scorched her. As she stretched bare, pleading arms toward him his burning hands corroded her skin.

"Why shouldn't you? I'll tell you why. . . . Because you're my sister! Isn't it funny? God! Why don't you laugh? My sister! Isn't it the grandest joke?"

She knew then that he had gone insane. Pleadingly she tried to put her arms about him, tried to

calm him, actually put up one small bronze hand and
tried to close those awful, gaping lips. "Malory,
you don't know what you're talking about." . . .

"I do know what I'm talking about. . . . Your
mother . . . with that rotten Strange blood in her
. ·. . she was never married to any man named Paul;
she—she was my father's mistress, his woman . . .
and you're his child and my—my sister!" He raised
his tortured eyes, he strained frantic arms toward
the blazing, pitiless sky. "Oh God, how could You
do it? You knew I loved her . . . You knew I
wanted her . . . and she's my sister!"

Even yet she couldn't believe him. "But tell me
Malory,——"

"Your mother was my mother's best friend—and
she betrayed her. She ate my mother's bread . . .
and slept with my father; my father went off with
her and came home to die and told my mother. . . .
You're bad, bad, all of you!"

He was crying now, full of pity for his own lost
love and of loathing for her who had so inadvert-
ently caused the loss.

"You bastard!" he spat at her and thrusting her
roughly aside he plunged down the clearing and into
the road leaving her lying stricken in the black,
black abyss into which she had fallen.

It was there that Laurentine and Denleigh found
her.

    •   •   •   •   •

Denleigh had spent the night in Newark, as he
had often done since his rift with Laurentine. There
were several of his class-mates down there with
whom one could play a little poker, drink a little

whiskey. In the morning he drove back leisurely. It was two o'clock when the old man located him. . . .

For six weeks he had not seen Laurentine; for three weeks, infuriated by her mad stubbornness, he had not even tried to talk to her over the telephone. . . . Well he'd have to see her now and he cursed himself for being such a stubborn fool. She saw him coming up to the porch, saw his face and, mindful of the sewing girls, dashed down the steps to meet him. Breathless and fearful they stood for a moment under the Chinaberry Tree.

"Laurentine," he asked, "where's Melissa?"

"In school."

It was then quarter of three. "Get in the car, Laurentine, we may be able to save her yet. They're planning to get married."

In palpable relief she hung back a moment. "But Stephen, tell me, what's the matter with that? Why shouldn't she marry this Malory boy?"

"You don't mean you're willing for her to marry Malory Forten! Why Mr. Stede says,——"

But then she had caught it. . . . "Forten, Forten! Why I thought his name was Malory! Oh why didn't I know! Oh Mother, Mother!" She was like a maenad. . . . She ran into the house, the doctor at her heels. Her mother was up in her own room, putting away the winter clothes. For a long time no one of the three could smell camphor without remembering that scene.

"Oh Mother, Mother, he says, Stephen says that Melissa is planning to marry young Malory Forten!

You know, you remember that man,—you remember
Aunt Judy. . . ."

She turned to Denleigh. "I should have told you
before Stephen, but I was so afraid. It's God's
curse! Before she married, Melissa's mother used
to—to run with this Forten boy's father; he actually
went off and lived with her for a time. . . . Why
it would be horrible for him to marry her. . . ."

Aunt Sal's eyes met his puzzled, questioning ones.
She sighed. "It's worse than that, daughter. Melissa herself is Forten's child. . . . I should never
have let her come here. . . ."

Denleigh thought the younger woman would
faint. But she rallied. "Come, Stephen," she said
calmly. "We've got to find her. But remember if
anything has happened, it's all my fault and,—and
Stephen, for her own sake, I shall have to kill her."

.   .   .   .   .

Sometimes the thick darkness that lay upon her
like a blanket would lift and rays of light would
steal in. At such times Melissa lifting languid lids
ever so slightly, would descry Laurentine, strangely
pale and altered sitting, apparently doing nothing,
somewhere quite near her. . . . She wanted to
speak to her but it took all her strength to reason
out the cause of that pallor and that idleness and
before she could do that the darkness had descended
on her again. . . .

But once her eyes must have opened quite wide and
very plainly she saw Laurentine coming quickly toward her, bending over her and saying very loud,
very pitifully: "Melissa, Melissa darling, do you

know me?" . . . She couldn't remember ever having heard Laurentine call her "darling" before . . . but it seemed very pleasant, she hoped she'd do it again.

Often thereafter she'd glance at her cousin through barely opened lids, but the older girl said nothing, just sat there idle; pale, distracted and lovely.

Then there was the time when her lids quite of their own accord remained wide open and she said to Laurentine faintly: "You know you called me 'darling.' Do you mean you don't hate me any more?" . . . She didn't remember ever having seen Laurentine cry before, either.

Then there was Aunt Sal, standing erect and quiet beside her bed and slipping something stiff and squarish into her hand. She couldn't tell what the object was, for, oddly, her hands refused to lift anything into her line of vision. . . . Sometimes she lost the object on the bedspread . . . she hated that; it made her feel lost herself. And then Aunt Sal would slide it back into her hand and she felt infinitely relieved and very, very safe.

One day her grasp became suddenly normal and lifting the square of paste-board she realized that it was a letter and the writing on it was from a boy whom she knew very well, a boy named Asshur. She did not ask any one to read the letter to her. . . . She knew very well what it would contain. It would tell her to be very good. . . . She never doubted but that Asshur would be glad to know that she had followed his advice and that she had always been very, very good.

Another face too came and went. At first she couldn't place it . . . but after awhile she knew it was the face of Stephen Denleigh. Then for a long, long time it disappeared. . . . And one day the face with the tall figure which belonged to it came back. And with it came another figure, younger and very slightly taller; another face, also younger, and darker, and looking,—"Oh, so slick!" . . . And it was Asshur!

Over night she reflected on Malory. . . she was so sorry for him, sorrier for him than for herself. . . . He wasn't very—solid—she thought. Imagine, imagine any one becoming so cruelly so revealingly bitter over a thing that neither he nor she could help . . . he really wasn't very strong—all nerves and ideals—he would need a girl like Gertrude Brown, her mind amended clearly. . . .

In the morning Asshur came in and finding her eyes wide open, slid all his marvelous length of brawn and limb down beside the bed and looked at her. . . . She rested her pale brown hand on his curly head that made her heart throb, and loved him dearly.

But her voice was very steady when she spoke. "Asshur," she said, "you know I'm nobody. Not Melissa Paul, nor just any one. My mother,—you know, my mother,—Asshur. . . ."

He interrupted her. He said: "After we marry you'll be Melissa Lane; but until then, and after, you are Melissa the Queen." . . .

CHAPTER XXXV

IT was Asshur who restored them. He it was, who with his nice, keen sense of values unperturbed by the world's standards of weights and measures, brought them healing. He had a fine, sweet, sanity, a strength, and above all, a comprehension which made it possible for him to guess and anticipate this stricken household's needs. For himself he had no false pride; Life, Death and Essential Honor were the only matters which greatly concerned him in his simple code. Life was for enjoyment; Death was to be met,—with great dignity,—only when it could be no longer avoided; Honor consisted in downing no man and in refusing to consider oneself downed, "especially by these Acts of God," he told Denleigh flashing his wonderful smile. The doctor admired him greatly, found him completely fascinating.

His simple good sense was astounding. He it was, who sleuthing quietly and persistently with the aid of his Uncle Ceylon, and of his own trusty cohorts scattered here and there throughout the town, brought back the soothing report that no one dreamed of the awfulness of the thing which had almost happened. Only Mr. Stede and the Browns suspected that Melissa was really Forten's child. The rest of the oldest inhabitants had merely guessed, merely pieced out that Judy and Malory's father had been on too intense terms of intimacy.

Some deep-lying natural sense of decency within

them reared up to consider itself outraged at the thought of young Malory's marrying the daughter of the woman who had caused his mother such an agony of wounded pride and humiliation. . . . Such a matter, they felt, called for a direct visitation from God and they were rather waiting, half hopeful, half fearful, to see in what shape the Wrath would come. . . . If they had known the actual truth! Imagination could not picture their reaction.

It was Asshur too who said to Denleigh quite simply: "Don't you think we ought to find out from Aunt Sal if there's anything else that could happen to these girls? . . . They've had so much trouble."

But there was nothing more, Aunt Sal said. She blamed herself terribly for not having told Laurentine, for not having refused to take Judy's child in. . . . "But who'd ever have guessed of such happenings?" she said trembling, half crying.

Asshur put his strong young arms about her, bent his splendid head and kissed her tenderly, respectfully. "You mustn't feel like that. I'll bet it wasn't Judy's fault. . . . I've often heard Uncle C. mirate on what a rake Forten senior was."

"And it's the God's truth," Sal asseverated piously. "Judy never meant to carry on with him; she really liked Mrs. Forten. She used to say she was a fool but she felt sorry for her. . . . Only Sylvester Forten wouldn't leave Judy alone. She ran away from him to Philadelphia and he followed her; she couldn't get rid of him. . . . But he was frightened when the child came. . . . He really died of the shame of it. . . . Judy now, she wasn't that way; she'd say 'there's no use givin' in to trouble, that's just an invitation for trouble to step in and hand you another punch.' "

. . . . .

Melissa could not bear to let Asshur out of her sight. If he could have been spoiled he would have succumbed that summer. But he was too essentially sound for that. He had no notion of his own power. . . . It was, only he didn't know it, with an almost absurd timidity that he approached Melissa on the question of an immediate marriage.

"You know Melissa I've still got another year at Tuskegee. . . . Do you think you could stand living in the South? My father's got a big house over in Rising Sun, that's a settlement just about as big as your hand. But you could get well and strong there . . . and afterwards we could come back here to Uncle Ceylon's farm. . . ."

Melissa looked at him radiantly. "Rising Sun! Oh, Asshur, I'd love to live in a place called that. How soon do you think we could go? Asshur you're sure you want me? No foolin'?"

"No foolin'!" the boy rejoined happily.

. . . . .

Denleigh and Laurentine said almost nothing, the fewest words. She hoped, she said gently, that he could forgive her mad stupidity, her instant leap to such a stubborn misunderstanding. "It was because I thought I had lost you darling, and I didn't see how I could stand it . . ."

He understood. "People only fall out like that

with some one they love very dearly," he told her, happy, satisfied.

    .   .   .   .

On Melissa's first day downstairs Aunt Sal said they would picnic under the Chinaberry Tree. . . . They piled a table high with strawberries, salad, upside down cake, a bowl of punch, sandwiches, a deep dish of iced cantalopes and watermelon scooped out in little balls. . . . Charles, the small, black kitten, who, without changing size, ate as though his were the strength of ten, patted Melissa's hand every time she lifted the spoon containing one of these balls, and made her drop it . . . his eyes followed it negligently, he seemed to smile through his whiskers which were really too profuse for such a little cat.

Mr. Stede appearing from the tool-house offered to bear him away but Pentecost choosing to rain showers of blessing on him at this moment he walked off with his calculated booty and forgot all about Charles.

There they sat the five of them,—Aunt Sal, Asshur, Dr. Denleigh, Laurentine and Melissa, under the Chinaberry Tree, all happy, all talking, all enjoying a brief span of peace in the tragic disorder of their lives. And underneath that peace ran differing currents of thought.

Aunt Sal was thinking: "Now, my child is safe, and Melissa too. These are such splendid men. . . . Dear Asshur did any one in this world ever look as happy as he? Frank and I were like that once." And suddenly she felt free to think of her dead lover,—with ease and gratefulness and the complete acceptance which always made their lack of conformity of absolutely no moment. She had always been willing to pay the Piper. Now, with Laurentine safe and satisfied, she was at liberty to recall the Piper's tune.

Denleigh felt himself recovering . . . he had really been badly frightened. He mused: "There actually is such a thing as Greek Tragedy even in these days. . . . We were almost swamped with it. But the wave missed us. . . . I ought to get Laurentine out of all this. . . . Lovely thing! But I don't believe she'll really ever want to go away. . ."

Asshur looked at Melissa. In his veins his blood ran hot and thick. His thoughts were inchoate; he was the triumphant male. Boyishly, crudely, he pictured the rapture of his marriage. . . . There would be Melissa, home, children . . . he would order their well-being. He would work for them, protect them, love them, *have* them . . . he stretched strong, sinewy arms well above his head. . . . He could have broken into a dance all rhythm and joy.

.   .   .   .   .

But Laurentine and Melissa, so widely different, were thinking on none of these things. Caught up in an immense tide of feeling, they were unable to focus their minds on home, children, their men. . . . Rather like spent swimmers, who had given up the hope of rescue and then had suddenly met with it, they were sensing with all their being, the feel of the solid ground beneath their feet, the grateful monotony of the skies above their heads, . . . and everywhere about them the immanence of God. . . . The Chinaberry Tree became a Temple.

FINIS